The Bookshops of London

Martha Redding Pease

FOURTH ESTATE   LONDON

Publisher's Note

Every effort has been made to ensure the accuracy of information listed in *The Bookshops of London*. Details were correct at the time of going to press, but the publisher can not be held responsible for any subsequent changes.

© 1981 Martha Redding Pease

First published in Great Britain
Revised edition 1984
Fourth Estate Ltd
100 Westbourne Grove
London W2 5RU

Pease, Martha Redding
   The bookshops of London.—2nd ed.
   1 Booksellers and bookselling—England—London—Directories
   I. Title
   381'.45002'025421   Z330.6.L6

ISBN 0–947795–10–3

Typeset by Photo-graphics, Yarcombe, Devon, England
Printed and bound in Great Britain by Biddles of Guildford

Table of Contents

Acknowledgements   vi
Introduction   vii
How to Use the Guide   x

London WC   General Bookshops   1
London WC   Speciality Bookshops   12
London WC   Second-hand Bookshops   65
London WC   Antiquarian Bookshops   71

London EC   General Bookshops   76
London EC   Speciality Bookshops   82
London EC   Second-hand Bookshops   89
London EC   Antiquarian Bookshops   91

East London   General Bookshops   91
East London   Speciality Bookshops   98
East London   Second-hand Bookshops   102

North London   General Bookshops   103
North London   Speciality Bookshops   110
North London   Second-hand Bookshops   122
North London   Antiquarian Bookshops   125

North West London   General Bookshops   125
North West London   Speciality Bookshops   135
North West London   Second-hand Bookshops   147
North West London   Antiquarian Bookshops   155

West London   General Bookshops   156
West London   Speciality Bookshops   173
West London   Second-hand Bookshops   206
West London   Antiquarian Bookshops   211

South West London   General Bookshops   220
South West London   Speciality Bookshops   240
South West London   Second-hand Bookshops   268
South West London   Antiquarian Bookshops   271

South East London   General Bookshops   274
South East London   Speciality Bookshops   284
South East London   Second-hand Bookshops   293
South East London   Antiquarian Bookshops   297

Index: Bookshops by Speciality   299
Index: Alphabetical   315

To David with love and thanks

Acknowledgements

My sincere thanks go to all the London booksellers who tolerated my incessant questioning. I am grateful, also, to my publishers for their confidence in the book, and for the work of my in-house editor. Most of all, I want to thank my parents without whom I would have never ventured this far.

Introduction

'If a book is worth reading,' said Ruskin, 'it is worth buying', but first it must be found. For the busy professionals in the City who can't locate that hard-to-find reference book, for students who need a source for second-hand textbooks, for the sci-fi fanatics who have looked all over for issue number 34 of *Weird Fantasy*, for visitors who want to explore part of London's rich literary heritage, indeed, for anyone who wants to find a particular book, or merely wants to browse looking for nothing in particular — this book is for you. This is a guide to London's bookshops, the first comprehensive account of one of London's greatest resources.

When William Caxton set up his printing press in Westminster in 1476, he also became London's first retail bookseller and heralded an age and tradition of English pre-eminence in bookselling which we still enjoy to this day. Now there are over 500 bookshops in London, each of which, in its very existence, testifies to the continuing English delight in the written word. And though a book from the press of Caxton is virtually priceless, a wealth of affordable and fascinating literature can be found in the bookshops of today, from paperback reprints of Caxton's titles to books on technologies never dreamed of even a hundred years ago.

Within the last century booksellers have benefited incalculably from sophisticated distribution and supply networks, modern methods of printing which have increased the available range and number of books, and a growing book-buying public. Shops have sprung up all over London, from the northernmost suburbs of Southgate and Mill Hill to the southern reaches of Wimbledon, Dulwich and Crystal Palace.

The face of London bookselling today is a far cry, literally, from the booksellers of Caxton's era when all but Caxton were huddled in the churchyard of St Paul's. In fact, the ravages of fire, war and progress have all but destroyed the traces of one of the world's most active book centres. From the fifteenth through the eighteenth centuries, hundreds of English and Continental printers and booksellers teemed in the areas of Little Britain around Smithfield market, Cornhill and Lombard Streets, Paternoster Row, Chancery Lane, St Paul's and even on the old London Bridge. Until the late eighteenth century, the

City harboured the combination printers, publishers and booksellers from the dictatorial control of the nobility and the dominion of university presses. Sadly, only two antiquarian booksellers are left within the square mile of the City, along with a handful of general bookshops and a few speciality shops.

In the last century Charing Cross Road became the locus of quality London bookselling and today, still lining the road from Trafalgar Square to Oxford Street, are some of London's leading bookshops: Foyles, Zwemmer, Collet's and Waterstone's - a major new force in London bookselling, with five branches throughout the centre. Along the narrow side streets of Charing Cross Road are newer specialized bookshops in fields like science fiction, photography and Greek studies. Kensington, Chelsea, Mayfair, Marylebone and Bloomsbury, too, have their booksellers dating back many decades, like Maggs Bros, Sotheran and Andrew Block. But many of London's newest shops have avoided the sky-rocketing rents and rates of Central London and set up shop in established residential and small business areas all over town.

New energy and direction have been given to modern bookselling in London with these recently established, often smaller and sometimes specialized shops outside Central London where the personalities of the neighbourhoods are reflected in the make-up of a bookshop's stock. The Kilburn Bookshop, for example, has special sections of books on Ireland, the Caribbean, Africa and radical politics which give an immediate sense of the special racial and political mix in the neighbourhood. Islington has a women's cooperative running Sisterwrite, a complete feminist bookshop where working-class, professional and home-bound women from all over North London can come to find the best in recent feminist fiction and non-fiction. In East London two shops — the Tower Hamlets Arts Project and Centerprise — not only sell books, but publish local authors, organize discussion groups and make a continual effort to improve the quality of life for people in their neighbourhoods, while South London is seeing the slow, but encouraging, rise in the number of quality second-hand booksellers such as Stone Trough in Camberwell and Chener Books in Grove Vale, as well as their own community bookshops such as the Bookplace in Peckham and Sabarr Books in Brixton.

The myriad specialities of the shops in London have been long in developing, linked directly to the cessation of censorship and the ever-expanding range of subjects in which the public demands books. In the first 200 years of bookselling, titles rarely deviated from religious and classical subjects; indeed, in 1520, the bestselling authors were Erasmus and Luther. Caxton sowed the seeds of popular literature in the fifteenth century by printing and selling books in English (rather than Latin), books that might delight the literate nobility rather than instruct the grave divines. Jacob Tonson, a printer and bookseller in eighteenth-century London, finished opening the doors of the literary world to the general public when he published Rowe's edition of Shakespeare in 1709. Today we have access to all the corners of human knowledge, from the life cycle of red ants to previously heretical political philosophies.

Not only do we have choice in the books we buy, but we also have convenience. Our word 'book' derives from the German 'buch' meaning beech, as in beech wood. Early handwritten manuscripts (the precursors of our Penguins) were protected with beech wood covers, which were cumbersome to say the least. Wisecracking Erasmus said of the bound manuscript of Thomas Aquinas's *Secunda Secundae*, 'No man could carry it about, much less get it into his head'. The advent of paperbacks have made bookselling and book-buying easy, high-speed and high-volume activities, as books can be produced quickly, in large numbers and not take the place of furniture in our homes.

So between the old and the new worlds of book production sit hundreds of bookshops in London. This book brings them together in an easy-to-use format with descriptive, rather than judgemental, information about each shop. Here are all of London's bookshops, from the shop selling 10p second-hand thrillers to the shop with priceless incunabula. 'Where is human nature so weak,' asked Henry Ward Beecher, 'as in a bookshop?' At least one of the shops listed in the pages below should prove his point.

How to Use the Guide

As the form and content of books have evolved through eight centuries, so have the language and structure of the business of bookselling. With specialized publishing and retailing, specialized terminology is used in the trade, and this often filters down to the consumer. I have used many 'bookseller's' terms in this book, so a few definitions are appropriate here.

In-print versus out-of-print books
A book is 'in-print' if it is currently available from the publisher's stock. Out-of-print books are no longer printed by the publisher, nor are they usually available through normal channels of stock ordering. Titles which have recently gone out-of-print can sometimes still be found on the shelves of a shop which carries in-print books.

New or current titles
Any book which is in print is a 'new' or 'current' book. Current titles include books being published for the first time, new editions of previously published works and 'back list' titles such as classics of English literature and reference books which are continually published over the course of many years and are always kept in stock.

Remaindered and end-of-run books
When a publisher declares a title out-of-print a sizeable stock of the end of the printer's run of a book may still be sitting in a warehouse. The publisher makes these unsold, soon to be out-of-print books available to booksellers and the public at significantly reduced prices, as 'remainders'. Remaindered books are usually restricted to hardcover titles, as it is cheaper to shred out-of-print paperbacks than go to the expense of distributing them.

Second-hand books
Out-of-print and remaindered titles, books which have been sold and resold, antiquarian and rare books, and 'review copies' of newly published titles (see below), all of these kinds of books are classed as second-hand. Within this classification fall valuable modern first editions, the rarest of incunabula and the tattiest of used paperbacks.

Antiquarian and rare books

It seems that no one in the book trade can agree on a definition of antiquarian books. For my purposes I have clasified 'antiquarian' books as those which were published before 1850. The further distinction of 'rare' books denotes antiquarian and second-hand books which are particularly valuable because of their scarcity, condition, associations and/or content. An antiquarian book does not necessarily have to be rare, and a 'rare' book could just as easily be a modern first edition as a finely bound volume of the King James Bible.

First editions

The term 'first edition' describes the first print run of a particular title. Throughout this book I have referred, also, to first editions of sought-after writers' works in the twentieth century as 'modern first editions'. To most bibliophiles, these are valuable and collectable books, be they paperback Penguins or hardcover titles.

Review copies

With the publication of a new title, publishers send copies of the book to newspaper, magazine and TV reviewers and to people working in the book trade. Many second-hand book dealers have access to these review copies and sell them as 'brand new' at bargain prices.

Reprints

Theoretically any book that is re-issued in either paperback or hardcover is a reprint. In reality, reprints usually refer to scholarly works which are in great enough demand by academics, librarians and researchers to warrant a small print run by the publisher.

Mail order

Many shops will post books to customers provided the client pays postage fees. Mail order does not always mean that a shop produces a mail order list or catalogue from which books can be ordered.

Special order

Usually on a basis which is limited to the range of publishers from which the shop orders, individual books which are not on the shelves can be specially ordered by the shop. A deposit is most often required before the shop orders the books.

Search service

Antiquarian and second-hand bookshops often provide an active search service for customers looking for hard-to-find books. The shop will place advertisements in a variety of trade and professional magazines to locate one or several volumes. Depending on the shop, there may or may not be a fee.

Wants list

Several antiquarian and second-hand bookshops are willing to accept customers' 'wants lists' for out-of-print, antiquarian and valuable books which the client has not been able to locate. Wants lists differ from a search service in that the bookseller simply keeps an eye out, so to speak, for titles on wants lists he or she has received. No guarantees are given that the particular book will be found (through either a search service or a wants list), but it is not unusual for a bookseller to contact a client many years after a wants list has been received with news of the desired title.

Book exchanges

In recent years second-hand paperback 'book exchanges' have cropped up all over the city. These shops give a 50 per cent credit on books bought at the shop and returned for exchange toward more books from the same shop. Most of these shops carry low-price paperback science fiction, fantasy, romance, war and western novels as well as second-hand magazines and comics (which are not sold on the basis of 50 per cent return and exchange).

In this book you will find general, second-hand, antiquarian and speciality bookshops which have a retail outlet in a numbered postal code in London. Every shop is in these pages with the exception of the railway station and hotel kiosks and the Popular Book Centre's chain of book exchange shops. Also excluded from these pages are the combination newsagents and booksellers, unless the book portion of the business is in some way specialized (as in the case of Witherby & Co.). Students of the history of bookselling may groan at this omission arguing that the patent medicines, sewing machines and sundries which Victorian bookshops often sold to augment their incomes did not exclude them from the bona fide ranks of their contemporary booksellers. Indeed, today almost every high street newsagent has a limited selection of the newest paperback fiction, and chain shops like Menzies and Lavells often have extensive ranges of paperback and hardback fiction and non-fiction. Their numbers, however, are almost endless, though their contribution to making books accessible is not to be discounted.

This guide is divided geographically according to London's postal codes. Within each postal code are subdivisions listing (1) general bookshops (2) speciality bokshops (3) second-hand bookshops and (4) antiquarian bookshops. Shops considered as 'speciality bookshops' do not always deal exclusively with books in their speciality.

Often they will have a general stock of titles but the strength and distinction of their stock is in a particular subject area which determines its listing. Shops which sell both second-hand and antiquarian books have been listed under the heading in which the larger portion of their stock falls. For example, Sotheran is considered an antiquarian bookshop though they sell new books as well.

The first index provides an overview of London's bookshops. Bookshops are grouped here by speciality. Thus, all the general bookshops will be listed together, as well as all the religious bookshops and all the shops specializing in children's books. Shops, of course, may well fit under several headings, so Sotheran will be indexed under the categories of 'Antiquarian', 'Second-hand', and 'New', and in certain speciality areas such as 'Bibles', 'Literature', 'Illustrated Books' and 'Natural History'.

A complete alphabetical listing of all of the shops in this book can be found in the second index, with their postal codes noted as well as the page on which they can be found in the text.

Note

It is inevitable in a guide of this sort that in the period between final preparation of copy and the appearance of the finished book that changes will have occurred; some shops will have moved, others closed down altogether; more cheerfully, others will have opened. Especially in the second-hand areas, shops so often depending on the cheaper end-of-lease properties, it is difficult to keep track of these shiftings. The publishers will be glad to receive details of any such moves and new appearances, both from proprietors and customers, so that the guide can be made as useful as possible in each printing. An increasing number of booksellers are working from home with the regular issue of catalogues, such is the difficulty of meeting the rate bills of a shop (the present state of the once-splendid Charing Cross Road is evidence enough of this); where the proprietor is willing to meet customers at fairly regular times it might prove worthwhile to be listed in a guide essentially devoted to bookshops – again the publishers would be happy to hear from such bookdealers.

It is clear, meanwhile, that there is sufficient enthusiasm among both dealers and customers to combat those planners and developers who would be happier with a bookless capital.

LONDON WC
General Bookshops

Book Inn
(Leicester Square)

17 Charing Cross Road WC2
839-2712

M–Sun 9:00–11:00pm

art biography children's books cookery crafts fiction military history natural science science fiction travel guides

This is a general bookshop selling new and remaindered titles, with a particularly large selection of science fiction books.

Non-book material: cards, London and UK maps, stationery, video tapes.
Services: mail order special order

Books Etc.
(Tottenham Court Road)

120 Charing Cross Road WC2
379-6838

M-Sat 9:30–8:00

antiques art biography children's books classics crafts crime DIY fiction film gardening health history humour literary criticism literature music natural history philosophy photography plays poetry politics psychology reference religion science fiction sports thrillers travel guides

The redecoration of **Books Etc.** has opened up the basement, thereby doubling the selling space. There are more paperbacks than hardbacks but, especially in this larger branch, recent new books are given a fair amount of space. New paperbacks are often to be found on sale before they are in other shops at this chain.

Non-book material: cards wrapping-paper
Services: special order

1

The Booksmith

(Tottenham Court Road)

148 Charing Cross Road WC2
836-3032

M–Sat 9:30–8:00

Just next to Centre Point is **The Booksmith** which carries bargain priced hardcover and paperback books in a range of subjects (the stock changes frequently). Full price paperback fiction and non-fiction are also available.

Catalogue: regular book lists available through Bibliophile Book Club

The Booksmith

(Charing Cross)

33 Maiden Lane WC2
836-3341

M–F 9:30–5:30

Hardcover and paperback books at bargain prices can be found at this small **Booksmith**. As with all the **Booksmith** shops, the stock varies from week to week, but always good quality, and low-priced, books can be found.

Services: mail order
Catalogue: regular lists are produced and available through their book club, Bibliophile.

Claude Gill Books

(Holborn/Temple)

140 Strand WC2
240-3042

M–F 9:30–6:00   Sat 9:30–4:00

biography   children's books   cookery   fiction   illustrated books
literature   music   natural history   non-fiction   Penguin   plays
poetry   reference   travel guides

One of four bookshops owned by the American bookseller Brentano, this is a general bookshop selling current hardcover and paperback fiction and non-fiction.

Non-book material: cards   maps   posters
Services: mail order   special order

Dillons Bookshop

(Goodge Street
or Euston Square)

Gower Street WC1
636-1577

M W–F 9:00–5:30   T 10:00–5:30   Sat 9:30–5:30

basement:
agriculture astronomy biochemistry biology botany chemistry computers education engineering environmental planning geography geology history and philosophy of science maps and atlases mathematics medicine metallurgy natural history physics psychology science technology zoology

ground floor:

Anglo-Saxon and medieval texts and criticism   bargain books children's books classic fiction cookery drama English literature gardening guides and travel literary criticism new fiction Penguin department poetry science fiction sport and indoor games study aids

balcony:

classical records and cassettes   music books

first floor:

archaeology art and architecture crafts dictionaries English language and English language teaching film foreign languages Graeco-Roman studies history linguistics philosophy religious studies

second floor:

accountancy Africa anthropology Asia commerce and secretarial skills economics Latin-America law management Middle-East politics second-hand and antiquarian sociology Third World literature *separate Malet Street entrance:*

Athena prints and cards and stationery shop

With much of the University of London on its doorstep, **Dillons** naturally caters to a student and academic clientele, though it now wishes to drop the 'University' from its title. **Dillons** has had a rather chequered history: it was once generally held to be the best bet for anything beyond the most recent bestseller, but then financial difficulties resulted in a lack of stock. There are, however, indications that **Dillons** is returning to its old self. The staff are knowledgeable about what is on their shelves, but queues can develop because only certain desks are equipped with tills, the others being merely 'information posts'.

Dillons occupies a building with a remarkable ornamental exterior. Their floorspace has recently been expanded to the second floor, in the form of a pleasingly decorated area chiefly housing politics and social sciences. The second-hand and antiquarian department, also on the second floor, is quite large in itself and provides most of the services of an antiquarian shop, although its stock, too, has been changing less frequently than it used to. Prices here, assiduously geared to the current list-price, are not always cheap but do often make for a good saving on expensive academic texts. The bargain department, on the ground floor provides the most comprehensive academic remainder department in London, with a frequent change of stock (regular customers can watch prices of certain books being reduced still further as the weeks go by).

It remains a pity that London University cannot support a single bookshop to match Blackwells in Oxford.

Non-book material: Audio-visual language teaching aids   cassettes   records   computers and software   art materials   stationery and card shop
Services: special order

Essex Hall Bookshop (Aldwych)

Essex Street WC2
836-0525

M–F 9:30–5:30

antiques   biography   children's books   classics   cookery   crafts   DIY   fiction   gardening   health   humour   illustrated books   literature   natural history   philosophy   photography   reference   religion   romance   science fiction   travel guides   war

Essex Hall Bookshop is a general bookseller of new books carrying a few remaindered books as well. Approximately 10% of the stock is devoted to books on the Unitarian church and religion in general.

Non-book material: cards   stationery   wrapping paper
Services: mail order   special order
Catalogue: Unitarian titles
Publications: Essex Hall are agents for the Lindsey Press

Foyles   (Leicester Square/Tottenham Court Road)

119 Charing Cross Road WC1
437-5660

M–W 9:00–6:00   Th 9:00–7:00   F–Sat 9:00–6:00

basement:

bargains   dentistry   medicine   nursing   veterinary sciences

ground floor:

autobiography   B.B.C.   beauty   biography   catering   children's books   cookery   dictionaries   English literature   fiction   humour language teaching   linguistics   literary criticism   literature   Penguin   poetry

first floor:

commerce   economics   education   geography   history   law   management   mathematics   politics   physics   sociology   technology

second floor:

anthropology   antiques   archaeology   architecture   art   classics crafts   drama   foreign literature   music   military history   natural history   rare books   sports   topography and travel guides   zoology

third floor:

ballet   cinema   drama   music   occult   philosophy   plays   psychology   records   religion   scores   sheet music   theatre history   theology   video-tapes

Foyles has recently sold one of its buildings to Waterstones. In its new arrangement it continues to stock an exceptionally broad range of titles in each of the subject areas outlined above, some of which have become shelved by publisher rather than the more conventional, useful way by alphabet or subject.

5

Unfortunately **Foyles** is one of the most disorganized bookshops in London with books bursting from the shelves, piled on the floor and haphazardly ordered. (Its English literature section, for example, contains more than Dillons.) Because the staff does not seem to cull the shelves regularly, recently out-of-print titles are often mingling next to new books which are often at less than the list-price. If you are willing to hunt you may well find the book you want – somewhere. Should you be lucky enough to locate what you want, the next obstacle is paying for the book. **Foyles** has an absurd system, redolent of a Moscow department-store, of wrapping your book and giving you a receipt for the merchandise which you then take across the floor to the usually long queue in front of the cage-like cashier's box. There you finally get to pay before returning to the wrapping desk to claim your purchase.

My experience with **Foyles** suggests the staff are as baffled and frustrated by the chaos of the shelves as most of the customers. The sales people are distinctly unhelpful and ill-informed, but part of this is possibly a result of the lack of training at the start of their tenure at the shop. Or, perhaps, they get this attitude from their management, who, when I stopped by to chat, were extremely uncooperative towards 'someone wandering in off the street'.

There must be many customers who now turn to Waterstones for efficiency and enthusiasm.

Non-book material: records   stationery   video-tapes   art gallery
Services: mail order   special order

Hammicks   (Covent Garden)

1 Covent Garden Market WC2
379-6465

M–Sat 10:00–8:00

The first floor is devoted to children's books – one of the most comprehensive of such sections in London – with fiction and non-fiction for infants to early teens. On the ground floor and in the basement are new hardcover and paperback books on a variety of topics such as art, literature, fiction, cookery, sport. It is also an Open University Foundation Course stockist.

Non-book material: postcards   maps   posters   greeting-cards
  wrapping-paper
Services: mail order   special order

Kings Bookshop

(Russell Square)

17a Rugby Street WC1
405-4551

M–F 9:30–6:00

autobiography biography children's books cookery fiction natural history   UK/London guidebooks

This is a very small general neighbourhood bookshop, with a selective stock of mainly UK publishers' titles. Because of the nearby children's hospital the shop stocks books for children under age 10.

Services: special order (any subject)

St Martin's Lane Bookshop

(Leicester Square)

36 St Martin's Lane WC2
836-5110

M–F 9:30–8:00   Sat 11:30–8:00

There are two floors of bargain books in a variety of subject areas at this shop which is part of Booksmith's mail order section. Indeed its stock is almost the same as that to be found at the Booksmith chain. It, too, has a basic range of full-price paperbacks.

Catalogue: regular lists are available through Bibliophile Book Club

W. H. Smith – A General Note

The branches of this chain-store are listed in each area's section of general bookshops.

W. H. Smith's slogan that it stocks books and a great deal more has often been castigated: its ever-increasing expansion in to such fields as computers and video-games has been regarded as diverting funds and attention from the books with which the firm began at the time of the spread of the railway-network; while the book departments still exist, nobody goes to them for markedly specialized needs.

7

W. H. Smith do, however, manage to keep a surprisingly wide range of books, with some branches such as Sloane Square, Holborn and Notting Hill Gate keeping more hardbacks than others do. That they are often the only outlet for books in an area is a pity (especially outside London), but books can be ordered (and, just as a publisher is free to publish almost anything, so a bookseller is not compelled to stock it); for this it is advisable to locate somebody more directly attached to the books section than to assail an assistant replenishing the Mars Bar rack.

Its enthusiastic promotion of the Book Marketing Council's Best of Young British Novelists campaign and the one for older writers is some evidence that it realizes customers continue to want books as well as other things.

Remaindered books as well as damaged stock from its Book Club Associates division are often on sale; the most interesting of these are frequently to be found at the railway bookstalls.

W. H. Smith   (Holborn)

7 Kingsway, WC2
836-5951

M–F 9:00–5:30

Souvenir Press Ltd   (Tottenham Court Road)

43 Great Russell Street WC1
580–9307

M–F 9:30–5:30

children's books   cookery   crafts   fiction   guides and maps   hobbies   non-fiction   reference

This is a small shop with a few new titles on display in what is basically the **Souvenir Press** publishing office.

Non-book material: maps
Catalogue: publisher's catalogue bi-annually
Publications: Souvenir Press is a general book publisher

Templar Books   (Chancery Lane)

75 Chancery Lane WC2
405-3189

M–F 9:00–5:30

art biography classics fiction law literature natural history
non-fiction reference travel guides

Current hardcover and paperback titles are stocked in this general
bookshop, including paperback series of Pan, Penguin, Pelican, and
Fontana.

Non-book material: cards   posters
Services: mail order   special order

Templar Books   (Chancery Lane)

87 High Holborn WC2
242–5454

M–F 9:00–6:00

ground floor: new books

art cookery crossword fiction home decoration literature natural history science fiction teach yourself travel guides

basement: bargain books

art children's books cookery crafts fiction home decoration
literature M&E handbooks natural history science fiction teach
yourself travel guides

New books, both fiction and non-fiction, can be found on the ground
floor of this general bookshop, while downstairs are damaged and
remaindered books. The stock of bargain books changes frequently so
the above list is only an approximation of what is available.

Non-book material: cards   games   wrapping paper
Services: mail order   special order

9

Vermillion Books   (Holborn)

57 Red Lion Street WC1
242-5822

M–F 10:00–6:00

architecture   applied art   biography   children's books   cinema
collecting   criminology   dance   drama   education   games   gastronomy   history   law   literature   military history and affairs   music
occult   ornithology   poetry   politics   sculpture   sport   theatre
transport   travel

This is a general bookshop selling new books at reduced prices and
some second-hand titles, with an emphasis on the subjects of
literature, ornithology, military history, cinema and theatre. Despite
the moderate sized display space, the shop has an excellent range of
titles and is well worth a visit. Almost any recent paperback can be
found here at a third off normal price.

Services: wants lists accepted

Waterstone and Davies   (Holborn/Russell Square)

62–64 Southampton Row WC1
831–9019

M–F 8:30–6:30

ground floor:

bestsellers   children's books   classics   cookery and food   fiction
London   travel

basement:

art   atlases   bargains   biography   Bloomsbury   crafts   current
events   DIY   drama   economics   Faber   gardening   history   military and naval   performing arts   philosophy   poetry   politics
psychology   reference   religion   sociology   sports and games

Keeping hours suited to the local business customers, this, the
smallest of the **Waterstone's** group, maintains an excellent stock with
sections also useful for the local student population. An earlier
population, continuing to grow in print, is well represented by a

section devoted to the Bloomsbury Group. The shop is close to Faber and Faber's offices in Queen's Square and has developed a section containing almost all the firm's books (and it can obtain anything from the Harlow warehouse within twenty-four hours); the back-list contains numerous fascinating titles some of which one might have thought to be long out-of-print.

Non-book material: cards   maps   magazines
Services: mail order   special order   school supply   a **Waterstone's** credit card which can be used in the shop and by telephone

Waterstone's   (Tottenham Court Road)

121–125 Charing Cross Road WC2
434-4291

M–Sat 9:30–7:30

basement:

classics   literary criticism   poetry

ground floor:

atlases   best-sellers   biography   children's   travel

first floor:

antiques   art   architecture   bridge   chess   cookery and food   drama   English language   games   gardening   natural history   performing arts   reference   sports

second floor:

astrology   astronomy   business   computer science   current affairs   economics   feminism   foreign languages   health   history   military   occult   philosophy   psychology   religion   social sciences   transport

This, the largest branch of the excellent new **Waterstone's** group, also concentrates on the humanities but has a substantial section about computer science as well. With some irony it bought one of Foyle's buildings and has rapidly shown that it can provide a far more rapid, knowledgeable and enthusiastic service – the staff gives the impression of really working in a bookshop rather than their neighbours' one of listlessly filling in time. The emphasis is more on academic topics than at the other branches but a wide general stock is maintained, religion, philosophy and new fiction being especially

11

strong areas. Notable, too, is the expanding section of second-hand art books – out-of-print and rare – for which a search service is also provided.

While the second-hand shops in the Charing Cross Road have declined and the remainder shops have remained much the same, the arrival of this efficient, lively shop is a highly encouraging sign.

Non-book material: cards   posters   maps   magazines such as the *Fiction Magazine*, the *Literary Review*, the *London Review of Books* and the *Times Literary Supplement*. A record department, specializing in classical and spoken-word titles, has been opened on the first floor.

Services: mail order   prompt special order   a **Waterstone's** credit card which can be used in all branches and by telephone

LONDON WC
Speciality Bookshops

ACADEMIC

The Golden Cockerel Bookshop   (Holborn)

25 Sicilian Avenue WC2
405-7979

M–F 9:30–5:30 (sometimes to 6:30)

Africana   architecture   art   biography   drama   film   history   literature and criticism   music   natural history   philosophy   politics   sociology   theology

As another addition to Sicilian Avenue **The Golden Cockerel Bookshop** has opened, selling books published by the Associated University Presses, whose members include such publishers as the Folger Shakespeare Library, University of Delaware Press, the Philadelphia Art Alliance Press, Fairleigh Dickinson U.P. and Cornwall Books. All their books, whose emphasis is on the humanities, are kept in stock. Although currently available books include such unlikely titles as *Lapsing Out: Embodiments of Death and Rebirth in the Last Writings of D.H. Lawrence* and *The Moon's Dominion: Narrative Dichotomy on Female Dominance in the first five Novels of D.H. Lawrence*, there are certainly enough interesting books here, many of which do not get sufficient prominence in other shops, to make a visit to **The Golden Cockerel Bookshop** well worthwhile.

Services: mail order   special order
Catalogue: currently available titles

AFRICA

Africa Book Centre   (Covent Garden)

38 King Street WC2
240-2666

M–F 9:30–5:30

architecture art bibliography economics education fiction history politics

This is a bookroom on the ground floor of the Africa Centre, which functions as an exhibition space for a variety of new titles about Africa, the Carribean and the Third World. Some of the books, but not all, are for sale, being part of publishers' exhibitions.

ALBANIA

The Albanian Shop   (Covent Garden)

3 Betterton Street WC2
836-0976

M–F 12:00–6:00   Sat 12:30–5:00

Situated in a large basement beneath a barber's shop, this shop has an almost complete stock of English-language publications from the foreign-lanugage press in Tirana, as well as some titles in Albanian. The books in English, of which there are a surprising number, cover current affairs in Albania and abroad, history, archaeology, art, literature, music and travel. Some recent Albanian illustrated periodicals in English are kept in stock.

Non-book material: cards map posters records handicrafts
Services: mail order.

ARCHAEOLOGY

The Museum Bookshop

36 Great Russell Street WC1
580-4086

M–F 10:00–6:00   Sat 12:00–5:30

Africa   America   applied art   archaeology   civilisation   Egyptology   European history and literature   fine art   Greece   India   Italy   Islamic studies   Israel   literary criticism   literature   London   Middle East   philosophy   pre-history   Roman classics   Russia   theology

With a speciality in archaeology (including British) and classical studies, this lovely shop sells both new and antiquarian books in the general area of the humanities. Current and back issues of archaeological journals are also available.

Non-book material: cards   maps of the classical world   prints
Services: mail order   special order   search service in speciality
Catalogue: selected book lists four times yearly

ARCHITECTURE

Triangle Bookshop

36 Bedford Square WC1
631-1381

M 12:00–6:00   T–F 10:00–6:00

architectural biography   architectural history   art history   contemporary essays   crafts   photography   theatre and stage

Triangle is a lovely shop tucked away downstairs in the Architectural Association building (though run independently of it), selling primarily new books on architecture and those subjects that 'stimulate architects' (e.g., other visual arts and aesthetics). Quality remaindered books can often be found here, and there are a few small shelves of out-of-print and antiquarian titles, as well as a range of the leading architectural journals.

Services: mail order   special order   wants lists accepted
Catalogue: annual selected list

ARTS

The Art Book Co.   (Covent Garden)

18 Endell Street WC2
836-7907

M–F 9:30–5:30

advertising   airbrush   architecture   art education   ceramics   cinema   crafts   design   fashion   fine art   furniture   graphic design(ers)   graphic design annuals   museum collections   photography: technical and illustrated   photography annuals: UK and foreign

This relatively small shop, now incorporating the old Bloomsbury branch, on Endell Street focuses on design and graphics. Most of the books are illustrated and their stock of graphic design annuals is particularly large. Periodicals on design and graphics are also available, with monographs and *catalogues raisonnées*.

Services: mail order   special order   microfilm service for periodicals
Catalogues: lists on a variety of topics (e.g., architectural history)
Publications: under the imprint of **The Art Book Company**, a few titles have been published, e.g. *Tubular Steel Furniture*

Arts Bibliographic-Modern Arts   (Tottenham Court Road)
Bookshop

37 Great Russell Street WC1
636-5320

M–Sat 10:00–6:00

architecture   art criticism, history and theory   contemporary art movements   dance   decorative arts   design   drama   exhibition catalogues   film   illustration   modern classic literature   modern masters   music   photography   poetry   private collections   theatre

Here is an unusual cross-section of new books on all aspects of the visual arts, titles on the performing arts. Leading UK, US and Continental art magazines and journals are also sold, with (mainly new) exhibition catalogues.

Non-book material: calendars   diaries   tapes
Services: mail order   special order
Catalogue: catalogue and supplements

Arts Council Bookshop   (Covent Garden)

8 Long Acre WC2
836-1359

M–Sat 10:00–7:45

Visual Arts

architecture   drawing   exhibition catalogues   general fiction   literary criticism   painting   poetry   photography

Performing Arts

ballet   cinema   drama   music: popular/classical   opera   play texts theatrical techniques

The Arts Council Bookshop is divided into two sections: one housing books on the visual arts and the other (in the rear and with an extra entrance in Garrick Street) concentrating on the performing arts. In addition, the shop is the principal source for publications by the Arts Council of Great Britain: catalogues of exhibitions supported by the Arts Council; and literature about arts projects all over the world. The shop keeps a wide range of art journals and magazines, and some overseas publications with foreign-language texts, primarily Continental.

Non-book material: Posters   jewellery   museum replicas   bone china   chess sets   paperweights   still photographs from films and theatrical postcards are just a few of the additional gift items in the shop. It has an excellent range of magazines and journals, including some from abroad.
Services: mail order   special order
Catalogues: The Arts Council produces a listing of their own exhibition catalogues with some poetry and literature titles included.
Publications: Under the imprints of various commercial publishers

(depending upon the subject) the Arts Council does co-publish reports, poetry, literature and art books.

M. Ayres Rare Books

(Tottenham Court Road)

31 Museum Street WC1
636-2844

M–Sat 10:00–6:00

art   children's Victorian books   illustrated books   individual illustrators   literature   philosophy   private presses

This antiquarian shop specializes in art and illustrated books from the 15th century onward, though most of their visible stock appears to fall into the eighteenth, nineteenth and twentieth centuries.

Non-book material: antiquities   engravings   English and Continental prints   postcards
Services: mail order   wants lists accepted for collections of individual illustrators

Bernard Shaw Bookshop

(Holborn, Russell Square,
or Tottenham Court Road)

British Museum
Great Russell Street WC1
636-1555

M–Sat 10:00–4:45   Sun 2:30–6:00

art   British Museum guides   coins and medals   Egyptian antiquities   general history   Greek and Roman antiquities   Romano–British antiquities   Oriental antiquities   pre-history   Western Asiatic art

All the books in the BM shop are related to collections in the museum. Many of the titles are BM publications, but there are also books from other UK publishers and the US. Normally the shop does not keep out-of-print titles, nor are there any remaindered books.

Non-book material: cards drawings medallions prints reproductions slides
Services: mail order
Catalogue: complete list of BM publications
Publications: British Museum Publications produces books related to the museum's collections

National Portrait Gallery Bookshop (Leicester Square)

2 St Martin's Place WC2
930-1552   ext. 23

M–F 10:00–4:50   Sat 10:00–6:00   Sun 2:00–5:50

art history   biography: artists and their subjects   children's books crafts   history: UK and London   Penguin   photography   royal family   classics

This is a rather large shop, as museum bookshops go, in which most of the books have some relationship to the artists, and their subjects, in the adjacent gallery. Remaindered books are often on sale on the bargain tables in the shop.

Non-book material: Badges   bags   calendars   cards   diaries medallions   miniatures   posters   prints and slides
Services: mail order   special order in field of British art
Catalogue: National Portrait Gallery publications list   slide collection catalogue
Publications: The **National Portrait Gallery** publishes books about 'arts with a British face'

Paperchase (Goodge Street)

213 Tottenham Court Road WC1
580-8496

M–W 9:00–6:00   Th 10:00–7:00   F–Sat 9:00–6:00

African art   American art   applied art   architecture   art   British art   children's illustrated story and craft books   crafts   DIY   fine art   Italian art   London art and architecture   modern art   natural history   photography   primitive art   reference

The first floor of this large and wonderfully frivolous shop has a book department with a particularly good selection of colourfully illustrated children's books. There are also books on the fine and applied arts.

Non-book material: stationery   paper gift items
Services: mail order   special order

Ian Shipley (Books) Ltd   (Covent Garden)

70 Charing Cross Road WC2
836-4872

M–Sat 10:00–6:00

This shop specializing in the visual arts has become one of the better art bookshops in London. Their wide stock of new and out-of-print titles includes books in English and foreign languages, from India to China to Holland, as well as exhibition catalogues and art periodicals from the UK, US and the Continent. The shop regards art in a wide sense, to include fashion, photography, architecture and landscape gardening. It does not cover theatre, dance or cinema. In addition to their extensive holdings, **Ian Shipley** pride themselves on being able to obtain books from any part of the world.

Services: mail order   special order   search service
Catalogue: new title lists two to three times annually, together with a wide range of publishers' catalogues

A. Zwemmer   (Leicester Square)

24 Litchfield St & 80 Charing Cross Road WC2
836-4710

M–F 9:30–6:00   Sat 9:30–5:30

ancient art   architecture   art history   biography   carpets   ceramics design   film   furniture   glass   graphics   modern art   porcelain

As part of the retreat of bookshops from the Charing Cross Road, **Zwemmer** has recently moved most of its stock a few yards round the corner to Litchfield Street. Subjects such as film, photography, theatre, media studies (e.g. advertising, typography) remain in the Charing Cross Road while the new shop continues to offer new books on virtually all aspects of the visual arts. (There are also some second-hand, antiquarian and remaindered books.) The shop carries a selection of major art and design periodicals, as well as local arts reviews.

Services: mail order   special order
Catalogue: selected list of new titles
Publications: A. Zwemmer Ltd publishes books about specialized areas of fine arts

AUSTRALIA

Australian Gift Shop   (Charing Cross)

Western Australia House
115 Strand WC2
836-2292

M–F 9:00–5:30   Sat 9:00–1:00

aborigines   children's books   culture and lifestyle   fiction   history illustrated books   poetry   travel guides   wildlife

This is a complete gift shop, with the sunny atmosphere of Australia surrounding both the staff and their stock. The books in the shop are imported from Australia, all are current titles, and cover all aspects of Australian society.

Non-book material: gifts, including their top-selling item – Vegemite (a form of Marmite)
Services: mail order   special order

BUILDING AND CONSTRUCTION

Building Bookshop Ltd   (Goodge Street)

26 Store Street WC1
637-3151

M–F 9:30–5:15   Sat 10:00–1:00 (except Bank Holidays)

right of the foyer:

alternative energy at home   antiques   carpeting   DIY   energy home building   home maintenance and repair   wood craft *left of foyer:*

accountancy   acoustics   architecture   building technology   earthworks   engineering (civil and structural)   land and property   law   maintenance   management   mathematics   municipal engineering   plant   roads   site organisation   surveying (land, quantity, structural)   technical drawing   town planning

This shop in the front of the Building Centre is split into two rooms: one with books for adventurous do-it-yourselfers and one with titles useful to building trade people and professionals. A variety of trade, professional and consumer magazines and journals in the field are also available.

Non-book material: cards   prints   surveyors tapes
Services: mail order   special order in field
Catalogue: annual complete list   new titles list three times yearly

BUSINESS

British Institute of Management   (Holborn)

Parker Street WC2
405-3456

M–F 9:30–5:00

This is a very small shop next to the BIM library specializing in books and booklets on subjects of interest to top level managers in the UK. It sells only its own publications. Employee financial participation, recruiting, report writing, problems in the workplace and international business are a few of the areas covered, and the shop does a yearly list of new titles of particular interest to managers.

Non-book material: check-lists for managers, pamphlets, reports
Services: mail order
Catalogue: annual list of **BIM** publications
Publications: **BIM** publishes the quarterly *BIM Review and Digest*

Chapman's Professional Bookshop   (Covent Garden)

20 Endell Street WC2
240-5011

M–F 9:00–5:30

accounting business business law commerce management office
administration statistics taxation

The field of accounting is the speciality of this business bookshop
where current titles from the UK and US are stocked. Students and
professionals will find that most of the titles are relevant to business in
the UK, although there are some that deal with commerce within the
EEC. The *Accountant* journal is also stocked, as are all of the Gee &
Co. publications.

Non-book material: see above
Services: mail order   special order
Catalogue: Gee and Co. Publishers' list with books in accounting
and management

Economists Bookshop   (Holborn/Temple)

Portugal Street/Clare Market WC2
405-5531

M–T 9:30–6:00   W 10:00–6:30   Th–F 9:30–6:00   Sat 10:00–1:30
(closed Sat in summer and out of term)

anthropology development studies economic history economics
labour and management law left-wing publications philosophy
politics psychology socialism sociology statistics

Run by *The Economist* and the London School of Economics, this
bookshop not only has an excellent range of economics titles, but new
books in all areas of social sciences. The publishers are UK and US,
texts are in English and all the paperback series are stocked (e.g.,
Granada, Pan, Fontana, Penguin and Pelican). Social science and
political journals are carried, as are specialized pamphlet publications. The neighbouring second-hand shop also carries out-of-print
and remaindered books (see separate entry).

Services: mail order   special order
Catalogue: annual list updated monthly

Economists' Second-hand

(Holborn)

Portugal Street/Clare Market WC2
405-8643

M–T 9:30–6:00   W 10:30–6:00   Th–F 9:30–6:00

accounting anthropology applied economics banking development studies economic history economic theory foreign policy history international economics international politics labour law management philosophy politics sexual politics social history social policy sociology

This shop, whose entrance is off the foyer of St Clement's Building at the London School of Economics, is the second-hand branch of **The Economist Bookshop** and is an especially good source of affordable books for students from the LSE. Remaindered, out-of-print and an occasional antiquarian title on economics and the other social sciences are stocked in the shop. A wide range of current journals and periodicals in the social sciences is also available.

Services: mail order   out-of-print search service
Catalogue: annual list of titles

Parks Bookshop

(Holborn)

244 High Holborn WC1
831-9501/9502

M–F 9:00–6:00   Sat 9:00–1:00

accountancy banking computers economics law management reference tax: VAT

This new, bright, neat shop has been opened close to Holborn station to meet the needs of those professions that do not find themselves dealt with sufficiently quickly by more general shops, the owners feeling that such shops 'tend to have a somewhat antiquated image'. **Parks**, with books in both hardback and paperback, certainly is vigorous in its stock of books for the accountant, businessman, banker and lawyer – both practitioner and student – and expert in its staff. It has up-to-date stock from such bodies as the Institute of Chartered Accountants, Institute of Bankers, Institute of Personnel Management and HMSO as well as home-study material from such publishers as Holborn Law Tutors, Brierley Price Prior and Emile Woolf.

For relief from totting up the columns there is also a small range of paperback fiction and a few hardback bestsellers, as well as standard dictionaries.

Services: special order   prompt mail order
Catalogue: specialized lists

CHILDREN'S BOOKS

Peter Stockham at Images   (Leicester Square)

16 Cecil Court WC2
836-8661

T–F   11:00–6:00 First Sat of each month 11:00–2:00

Images specializes in children's, illustrated and art books, as well as children's and decorative ephemera. The stock consists of new, out-of-print and antiquarian titles. The shop also carries facsimile reprints of rare books, reference books and scholarly monographs on collecting, art and illustration.

Non-book material: Ephemera new and antiquarian games and toys
Services: mail order   special order   search service
Catalogue: many lists, e.g. children's literature, toys and games, antiquarian books
Publications: Peter Stockham publishes chap-books and facsimile reprints of children's illustrated books

Pleasures of Past Times   (Leicester Square)

11 Cecil Court WC2
836-1142

M–F 11:00–2:30, 3:30–5:45   first Sat of each month 11:00–2:30 (other Sats by appointment)

This is a wonderfully colourful bookshop feasting second-hand children's literature along one wall, and books on entertainment and the performing arts on another. Books are brought into the shop according to the owner's taste, resulting in rows of bright bindings and familiar titles from the Edwardian and late Victorian eras. Out-of-print (and some new) plays and collections of individual authors are stocked, and there are unusual sections on conjuring and the circus. Remainders, when relevant, are sold as well. The owner is always willing to help serious researchers.

Non-book material: another feature of the shop is the large collection of Victorian greeting-cards and Edwardian postcards, which are boxed according to country, subject or person. Also on hand are theatre playbills, posters and decorative ephemera.
Services: mail order picture research and supply in children's literature and entertainment

CHINA

Collet's Chinese Gallery and Bookshop
(Tottenham Court Road)

40 Great Russell Street WC1
580-7538

M–Sat 9:45–5:45

ground floor:

acupuncture and medicine Buddhism Chinese pottery civilization cookery dictionaries Japan language teaching literary criticism literature philosophy politics post-revolutionary history pre-revolutionary history travel guides Zen

first floor:

applied Chinese art techniques archaeology art (China & Japan) ceramics Percival David Foundation press specialized collecting

Amid a variety of gifts (ground floor) and oriental art (first floor) are books on all aspects of China and, to a lesser extent, Japan. Most of the books are in English, although titles are imported from China, the US and the Continent. There are a few remaindered books, as well as a selection of magazines and journals about China. The shop has a special section of publications from the Percival David Foundation of Chinese Art.

Non-book material: artists materials for Chinese brush painting gifts original art and sculpture

Services: mail order   special order
Catalogue: specialized lists (e.g. acupuncture, Chinese art)
Publications: Collet's publishes books on Chinese language
teaching

Guanghua   (Leicester Square)

7–9 Newport Place WC2
437-3737

M–Sat. 10:30–7:00   Sun 11:00–7:00

acupuncture art biography children's books cookery cultural
history Eastern healing arts Engels fiction health history
language teaching Lenin lifestyle Marx medicine poetry politics sciences shipping tales and legends war and revolution

In the heart of Chinatown, this is a large gift and book shop
specializing in China. Most of the titles are imported from China and
Hong Kong, in Chinese, but there are an increasing number of
English language books especially in the area of language teaching.
The level of the books starts at titles for children and reaches up to
scholarly and academic texts on specialized subjects. A wide range of
literary, cultural, sports and science magazines is also available at the
shop.

Non-book material: gifts imported from China   prints
Services: mail order   special order
Catalogue: regular lists of new and specialized titles

CINEMA

The Cinema Bookshop   (Tottenham Court Road)

13 Great Russell Street WC1
637-0206

M–Sat 10:30–5:30

avant garde film biography censorship cinema annuals criticism
film guides gangsters genres history music musicals pre-
cinema reference technical theory TV

This is, to my knowledge, one of only two bookshops in London specializing in the literature of film. Selling mostly new but also a large number of out-of-print titles, **The Cinema Bookshop** has a large stock of books about films and the people who make them. I was a bit disappointed to find that books of biography and history far outnumber those of criticism and film theory but it does none the less keep all that are in print and for those interested in the world of film, the shop is a delight. The shop also boasts a large stock of still photos from films of the past, comprising an archive which is a fine resource for students, writers and others wishing to hold a bit of the glamour.

Non-book material: film ephemera   magazines   posters
Services: mail order   special order

DANCE

Dance Books Ltd   (Leicester Square)

9 Cecil Court WC2
836-2314

M–Sat 11:00–7:00
With new, and some antiquarian, books on all aspects of ballet modern dance, **Dance Books Ltd** has a particularly strong section of titles on dance education. They also carry books on choreography, technique, dance history and biography, as well as the major UK and US dance and arts journals.

Non-book material: calendars   posters   records   still photographs of dancers and dance scenes
Services: mail order   special order   search service in field
Catalogue: selected annual list and list of new books
Publications: Dance Books Ltd, with fifty books in print, is the largest publisher of dance books in the country. It has books on all areas of dance including criticism, education and scene painting.

EASTERN EUROPE AND SOVIET UNION

Central Books (Chancery Lane)

37 Gray's Inn Road WC1
242-6166

M–F 9:30–5:30   Sat 10:00–2:00

Africa art biography British Labour movement children's books
civil rights cookery drama economics education feminism
fiction film Ireland literary criticism London Marxist classics
Middle East minorities and race relations peace movement poetry politics Russian fiction socialism sociology Soviet Union
Third World

The ideological slant of most titles is progressive and leftist, even in
the general areas of fiction, literary criticism, art, etc., as well as in the
imported Eastern European books in translation.

The British labour movement and related socialist subjects are the
specialities of the shop, and a second-hand section in the field is now
flourishing. Also interesting is the selection of Soviet children's books
and the wide range of Eastern European, Continental and Third
World political newspapers and pamphlets.

Non-book material: badges posters postcards
Services: mail order   special order
Catalogue: general list of Soviet titles   Soviet children's books
Journeyman publications   Lawrence and Wishart publications list
three to four times yearly
Publications: Central Books is the UK distributor for English-
language books and magazines from the national Soviet publisher
Progress Books (Collet's International distribute foreign language
books and magazines for Progress Books).

Collet's International Bookshop (Leicester Square)

129 Charing Cross Road WC2
734-0782

M–W 9:30–6:30   Th 9:30–7:30   F 9:30–7:00   Sat 9:30–6:00

art Black studies cookery education & E.F.L. feminism fiction
history literary criticism literature music philosophy photogra-

phy politics psychology reference Russian and Eastern European
literature Russian language teaching sociology Soviet and Eastern
studies travel and travel-guides

Russian, Slavonic and Eastern European subjects are the focus of
most of the books in this shop. As distributor for the national Soviet
publisher, Progress Publishing, **Collet's** maintains an extensive stock
of Russian language texts (including fiction, politics, classics), as well
as Russian and Soviet works in translation. Another speciality of the
shop is language teaching aids for learning Eastern European languages.

Otherwise **Collet's** can be called a general bookshop, where there
is a solid section of feminist literature and a selection of art books,
enhanced by imported titles from the Soviet Union. **Collet's** staff, for
the most part, are very well trained booksellers and can be most
helpful in tracking down titles from behind the Iron Curtain.

Non-book material: folk art from Eastern Europe language
teaching cassettes and records Melodia (Soviet label) records
posters badges
Services: mail order special order catalogues
Publications: The **Collet's** imprint appears on selected Eastern
European titles

FEMINIST

Silver Moon (Leicester Square)

68 Charing Cross Road WC2
836-7906

T–Sat 10:30–6:30

arts black women children's books cookery crime education
fiction (men's & women's) health lesbian reference religion &
philosophy science fiction social organisation travelling women
women's lives: history & biography

Silver Moon has an assertive stock, courteously managed. The shop
has access to the disabled; but the cafe, open from 10:45–4:30, is
closed to adult males.

Non-book material: jewellery postcards posters records of
women's music T-shirts
Services: search service special order

GOLFING

Golfiana Miscellanea Ltd (David White) (Holborn)

Hampden House, 84 Kingsway WC2
405-5323

By appointment during office hours

David White is the only London bookdealer to specialize in all matters relating to golf, from planning and designing a course to P.G. Wodehouse's fictional representations of the game. His stock, all of which is second-hand, covers such topics as architecture, biography, histories of players and clubs, instruction manuals and upkeep of a course.

Non-book material: antiques ephemera magazines paintings prints
Services: mail order
Catalogue: lists issued
Publications: The Ellesborough Press Ltd publishes specialized limited edition reproductions of long-out-of-print books on historic golfers.

GREECE

The Hellenic Book Service (Leicester Square or Tottenham Court Road)

122 Charing Cross Road WC2
836-7071

M–Sat 9:00–6:00

archaeology architecture art Byzantium cookery costumes Crete Cyprus dictionaries fiction history (modern & ancient) language teaching literature magic medicine mythology natural history poetry (modern & ancient) philosophy politics theatre theology travel accounts & guides Turkey

Said to have one of the world's largest ranges of new, second-hand and antiquarian books in Greek and about Greece, this shop is certainly a rich source for students, academics, travellers, writers and anyone interested in Greece. The mother and daughter who own and run the shop are extremely knowledgable about their books and the people who write them, and are energetic in locating new and out-of-print titles in Greek and English. Books in both modern and ancient Greek are stocked in subjects ranging from children's stories to the academic texts in archaeology and mythology. Also available is a selection of Greek newspapers, magazines and journals.

Non-book material: antiquarian prints   icons   language teaching cassettes and records   old and modern maps   postcards
Services: mail order   special order (in any field)   search service

Zeno   (Tottenham Court Road)

6 Denmark Street WC2
836-2522

M–F 9:30–6:00   Sat 9:30–5:00

archaeology   architecture   art   biography   Byzantium   children's books   classics   Cyprus   diction   drama   Egypt   fiction   history language teaching   literature   music   natural history   poetry   politics   religion   travel guides and maps   Turkey

Zeno is a long established Greek bookshop selling new, second-hand and antiquarian books, in a variety of languages, on ancient and modern Greece. The shop carries popular Greek magazines and newspapers and, as well as being an active bookshop, **Zeno** prides itself on being a meeting place for Greek scholars, students and writers.

Non-book material: cards   engravings   maps   prints
Services: mail order   special order   search service
Catalogue: general catalogue annually; individual specialized lists throughout the year
Publications: **Zeno** publishes reprints of Greek history and travel

HEALTH AND NUTRITION

Robert Chris Bookseller (Leicester Square)

8 Cecil Court WC2
836-6700

M–F 10:45–5:30

acupressure acupuncture allergies childcare and pregnancy first aid healing herbalism massage and relaxation nutrition osteopathy radionics recipe-books Shiatsu special diets women's health yoga

Since Robert Chris's death in 1982 the shop has continued to be run by his family. Now, however, it concentrates on complementary medicine. The original stock, much of which is still being stored, is none the less being retained (together with the well-known armchair) in the basement. The 15,000 volumes, especially good for fiction, literature, history and reference, should last for some while to come.

The ground floor contains a comprehensive number of books about the idea of positive health and non-suppressive therapies. The emphasis is on diet, nutrition and health. The staff is friendly and knowledgeable, happy to explain the various subjects displayed. The section on women's health is especially good, as are those on specific conditions such as heart disease and arthritis. The shop is devoted to the idea of taking responsibility for one's health, a condition not often heeded by many booksellers used to wheezing in the dust.

Services: mail order library supply specialized book lists available
Non-book material: photographs pictures pressed-flowers pendulums posters yoga and meditation cassettes. The shop also acts as an agent for bio-feedback and Kirlian photography-machines.

HOLISTIC AND RELATED SUBJECTS

Watkins Books Ltd (Leicester Square)

19/21 Cecil Court WC2
836-2182

T–Sat 10:00–6:00

alchemy astrology Buddhism China Christianity and related traditions consciousness diet dreams Egypt esoteric religion healing and holistic medicine   India   Japan   Judaism   Jungian psychology   Kabalah   meditation   new age   new sciences   parapsychology   prophecy   psychic communication   radiesthesia   related fiction   reincarnation   spiritualism   sufi   symbolism   theosophy   Tibet   yoga   Zen

For books on esoteric and holistic subjects **Watkins**'s large, elegant and friendly shop is one of the oldest and best-known in London. As well as Eastern religions and philosophies there are sections on new developments in holistic sciences and inner development, on related literature, as well as a number of related magazines and journals. Towards the back of the shop there is also a substantial second-hand section.

Non-book material: astrological charts   pendulums   biorhythm kits   magazines   tapes   posters
Services: mail order   special order
Catalogue: subject book-lists
Publications: Robinson and Watkins publish 'books for the inner and outer worlds'

HORTICULTURE

Grower Books   (Russell Square)

50 Doughty Street WC1
405-7135

M–F 9:00–4:30

amateur growing and horticulture   commercial growing   crop information   environment   glasshouse   harvesting   husbandry marketing   open air growing   preparation   vegetables

While the premises on Doughty Street are not really those of a bookshop, individuals looking for new books about commercial growing and horticulture can stop by **Grower Books** for a browse. The titles are from the UK and US, including Ministry of Agriculture and Royal Horticultural Society publications, and provide a comprehensive source of information to the commercial grower, and amateur.

Services: mail order   special order
Catalogue: complete list continually updated
Publications: Grower Books publishes titles on horticulture

HOUSING

Housing Centre Trust Bookshop (Leicester Square)

33 Alfred Place WC1
637-4202

M–F 10:00–5:00

This is a very small but compact space in the Housing Centre Trust building. The shop deals with publications on social and legal aspects of housing and urban planning as well as finance, management and administration. Though its holdings are not large, it can get any British housing publication and has access to many overseas publications in the field; its emphasis is on those aspects rather than design or planning.

Services: mail order   special order
Catalogue: selected list of new housing publications, updated frequently
Publications: The Housing Centre Trust publish a bi-monthly magazine, *Housing Review*, as well as books on housing issues.

INDIA

Books from India (UK) Ltd/ (Holborn) Hindi Book Centre

145 Museum Street WC1
405-7226

M–F 10:00–5:30   Sat 10:00–5:00

art biography classics cookery crafts dictionaries education fiction health administration history homeopathy language teaching law lifestyle literature medicine philosophy politics religion sociology

The owner of this shop is a journalist and BBC commentator whose vision of 'India' is shaped by social, cultural and political realities, rather than geographically defined borders. There are books on all aspects of Afghanistan, Bangladesh, Nepal, Ceylon, Bokara, Burma and more, in English, Hindi, Urdu, Punjabi, Gujarati and Bengali. The Centre also is engaged in publishing books, information sheets, catalogues and pamphlets on India. Out-of-print books are kept in stock, as are scholarly journals, and occasionally they have remainders.

Non-book material: cards cassettes paper posters prints records
Services: mail order special order search service
Catalogue: various lists (forty, at present) in specialized areas
Publications: Books from India (UK) Ltd publishes books on all
aspects of India and has recently begun a series of books (in English)
on the rest of the world in collaboration with a French publisher

JUDAICA

Jewish Memorial Council Bookshop   (Euston)

Woburn House
Upper Woburn Place WC1
388-0851

M–Th 10:00–5:30 F 10:00–2:00 winter 10:00–4:00 summer
Sun 10:30–12:45

bible and Talmud biography comparative religion culture and
civilization fiction history holidays literature music philosophy scholarly texts

Judaism is, of course, the focus of the **Jewish Memorial Council
Bookshop.** Most of the books here are in English; there are, however,
some Hebrew texts imported from Israel, including recent literature,
and all the books are new. A few related journals and newspapers are
kept as well. Once a year a book fair is held, at which publishers from
around the UK speak about new titles from the UK, US and Israel.

Non-book material: religious requisites
Services: mail order special order
Catalogue: general catalogue

LANGUAGE TEACHING

European Bookshop (Goodge Street)

19 Store Street WC1
637-9491

M–F 9:30–5:30

ground floor:

children's books classics dictionaries drama fiction language
teaching literature reference travel guides

basement:

reduced-price books

This shop, formerly known as Hans Priess in Bury Street, continues
to function as a showroom for the audio-visual language-teaching
courses in which European Schoolbooks Ltd specializes. The firm,
which is based in Cheltenham, specializes in supplying libraries with
titles in all languages and on all subjects, but is willing to do the same
for individual customers; librarians are welcome to visit this large
London outlet, where the manager will arrange for orders to be
despatched from the Cheltenham headquarters.

Non-book material: cassettes film strips language teaching
overhead transparencies games slides
Services: mail order special order specialized search for collections of individual authors
Catalogue: library lists of new titles in four languages available to
public

Grant & Cutler Ltd (Charing Cross)

11 Buckingham Street WC2
839-3136

M–F 9:00–5:30 Sat April–August 9:00–12:30 Sept–March 9:00–1:00

Grant & Cutler is a major source in London for foreign language
texts, especially in French, German, Spanish, Portuguese and Italian.
The range of subject areas is varied, including contemporary literature, classics, history, linguistics, the social sciences and the sciences.

New and second-hand titles are sold, and because most of the shop's stock is on the premises mail orders are quickly filled.

Services: mail order   special order

Catalogue: for each language, new title lists are produced two to three times annually   school-texts with relevant critical works   lists of technical dictionaries

Publications: Grant & Cutler publishes literature, primarily in Spanish and French

Tutor Tape Co. Ltd   (Tottenham Court Road)

100 Great Russell Street WC1
580-7552

M–F 10:00–6:00   Sat 10:00–2:00

This company specializes in language teaching courses and aids for English as a foreign language, and all other languages for which there is a demand. The course subjects range from technical, sciences, maths and business shorthand dictation to drama, poetry and music. The books are sold in conjunction with cassettes, study tapes and video-tapes as part of E.L.T. courses.

Non-book material: cassettes   records   slides   video-tapes

Services: mail order   special order   demonstration room for audio visual materials   language lab.

Catalogue: English/foreign languages annually

Publications: Tutor Tape Co. Ltd publishes books on foreign language teaching and English as a foreign language

LAW

Butterworth's Legal Bookshop   (Temple/Chancery Lane)

9–12 Bell Yard WC2
405-6900

M–F 9:00–5:30

This modern, quiet, well-organized shop is one of London's leading legal booksellers and publishers. **Butterworth's** stock covers all aspects of law in the UK, as well as some international legal subjects.

Their customers are primarily members of the legal profession or students of law. All books are new, with **Butterworth's** titles comprising approximately 50% of the stock.

Services: mail order special order LEXIS service for transferring books to computer programs
Catalogue: available by subscription annually with monthly updates in the form of *The Butterworth's Bulletin*
Publications: Butterworth's publishes books in the fields of law, medicine, science and technology

Frognal Rare Books (Leicester Square)

18 Cecil Court WC2
240-2815

M–F 10:00–6:00 Sat – by appointment

Early law, economics (especially banking) and history are the specialities of this elegant-looking shop. Two floors house books dating back to the 16th century, from all over the world and in a variety of languages.

Services: mail order
Catalogue: antiquarian law books economics special lists – four times annually

Hammick Sweet & Maxwell (Chancery Lane)

116 Chancery Lane WC2
405-5711

M–F 9:30–6:00

This shop is the main retail outlet for Sweet & Maxwell legal publishers, and now the shop's stock is approximately two-thirds law books and one-third general titles (e.g., poetry, drama, classics, fiction, cookery and travel guides). The law books cover all areas of the legal profession in the UK, including titles on unions, socio-political topics, the workplace, individual rights and student text books. Foreign legal texts can be ordered and the major legal journals are stocked.

Non-book material: cards 'legal' prints of personalities bills and legislation wrapping-paper
Services: mail order special order
Catalogue: list of law books
Publications: law books are published by Sweet & Maxwell and Stevens

Law Notes Lending Library   (Chancery Lane)

25–26 Chancery Lane WC2
405-0780

M–F 9:30–5:00

Both new and second-hand books on all aspects of British law, together with some international and EEC law, are sold at this combined bookshop and lending library. Major law journals are available here, as are the book series produced by the leading legal publishers.

Services: mail order special order
Catalogue: selected list produced annually
Publications: *Law Notes* is a monthly publication from the **Law Notes Lending Library Ltd**

Wildy & Sons Ltd   (Holborn)

Lincoln's Inn Archway
Carey Street WC2
242-5778

M–F 8:45–5:15

This is the oldest and grandest of London's law bookshops, tucked away behind the Law Courts in the archway into Lincoln's Inn. With possibly the widest selection of new, second-hand and antiquarian law books in the world, **Wildy** can cater to the student, practitioner, theoretician, legal philosopher, book collector and even the computer law specialist. Their stock is international in subject and language, and though **Wildy** does not provide a search service for out-of-print titles, they do keep requests on file indefinitely. Very few law journals are kept in the shop, but they do specialize in supplying sets of law periodicals (and individual back issues can be ordered).

Non-book material: modern and antiquarian engravings and prints, from serious to silly
Services: mail order   special order   wants lists accepted   book binding
Publications: Wildy & Sons Ltd publishes new law titles, while facsimile reproductions and reprints are published under the imprint of Carey

LESBIAN AND GAY ISSUES

Gay's The Word   (Russell Square)

66 Marchmont Street WC1
278-7654

M–Sat 11:00–7:00   Sun 12:00–6:00

art   biography   black studies   feminism   fiction   gay/lesbian plays   poetry   politics   US imports

Gay's The Word are happily building their stock to include new, out-of-print and second-hand books on gay and feminist issues. New books cover the range of political, social and economic issues, as well as classic gay and feminist literature, while the second-hand section holds rare, hard to find gay and feminist classics. The shop also has a good section of new titles from the US and a selection of gay and feminist journals from the UK and abroad. Sadly, however, it has a sexist policy of some books being for sale only to women.

In addition to book selling, the shop is kept busy hosting various discussion groups – lesbian, gay, black and men's groups are those currently running – and there is a coffee bar at the shop as well. The staff are cordial, accessible and knowledgeable.

Non-book material: badges   posters
Services: mail order   special order
Catalogue: complete list of new books with some second-hand titles included
Publications: a two-monthly newsletter, *Gay's the Word Newsletter*

MAPS AND GUIDES

McCarta Ltd
(King's Cross)

122 King's Cross Road WC1
278-8278

M–Sat 9:30–5:30

This shop specializes in maps and guides to Europe, from large-scale walking maps and town-plans to more general maps of countries.

Coverage of France is particularly extensive, the shop being agents for the Institut Géographique National, the Bureau de Recherche Géologique et Minières, Editions Cartographiques Maritimes, as well as for Vagnon, the publishers of bilingual guides to the French waterways. The bibulous will be grateful for the various wine-maps of the country.

Non-book material: see above
Services: mail order   special order
Publications: *French Farm and Village Holiday Guide*, to the gites, chambres d'hote and loisirs acceuil services of France, is issued annually

MARTIAL ARTS

Atoz Martial Arts Centre
(Leicester Square)

3 Macclesfield Street WC2
734-4142

M–Sat 10:00–6:00

This is a relatively small shop which, none the less, carries a complete range of new books (in English and Chinese) on all aspects and forms of martial arts for beginner and black belt.

Non-book material: martial arts equipment
Services: mail order   special order
Catalogue: annual comprehensive list

MEDICAL HISTORY

Jenner Medical History Bookshop (Russell Square)

19 Great Ormond Street WC1
404-4415

M–F 10:00–6:00 (occasionally Sat lunchtimes – ring first)

bibliography   biography   clinical medicine   ear, nose, throat
medical history   neurology   orthopaedics   paediatrics   physiology
sciences   surgery

Close to the National Hospital for Nervous Diseases and to the
Hospital for Sick Children, Dr Nicholas Dewey's small, somewhat
Dickensian shop contains a large number of old, second-hand and
new books on all aspects of medical history. A former academic and
lecturer, he runs his friendly, surprisingly busy shop with great
enthusiasm and knowledge; its wide-ranging, efficient mail order
frequently brings customers from America, Australia and the continent to see this storehouse of past medical practice for themselves.
Reunions and meetings have been known to occur amid the scattered
chairs and peering skulls (on one occasion two enthusiasts, previously
unacquainted, astonished other customers by breaking out into an
1830s song about Morrison's Pills). Whether doctors were wrong or
right in the past, this shop has comprehensive, fascinating record of
their work and lives.

Non-book material: instruments and medical artefacts   medical
prints such as hospitals, anatomical and surgical prints   medical
portraits   paper skulls   some London prints
Services: mail order
Catalogue: regular, specialized, entertaining lists issued world-wide

MEDICINE

H.K. Lewis & Co. Ltd (Warren Street/Euston Square)

136 Gower Street WC1
387-4282

M–F 9:00–5:30   Sat 9:00–1:00

ground floor: medical books

anaesthesia   anatomy   bacteriology   biochemistry   biography   cardiology dentistry diabetes diagnosis dictionaries endocrinology first aid & home nursing forensic medicine haematology hospitals immunology industrial medicine infectious diseases medical history medical statistics medicine memoirs midwifery neurology nursing obstetrics/gynaecology ophthalmology orthopaedics paediatrics pharmacology pharmacy physiology physiotherapy psychiatry psychoanalysis psychology sex surgery therapeutics toxicology

first floor: natural sciences

aeronautics agriculture animal behaviour applied mechanics aquatic biology astronomy biology botany building construction computer science ecology electrical engineering electronic engineering entomology forestry fuel technology general & inorganic chemistry genetics geology heat engineering hydraulics industrial chemistry industrial management materials science mathematics metallurgy microscopy organic chemistry ornithology physical chemistry physics plant pathology refrigeration sanitary engineering statistics surveying veterinary science zoology

Located across the street from University College Hospital, **H.K. Lewis** is one of London's largest medical and scientific booksellers. New books, periodicals and journals are stocked and the shop also houses a rather large second-hand book department.

Services: mail order special order wants lists accepted
Catalogue: weekly new book lists regular specialized catalogues
Publications: H.K. Lewis publishes medical books

West End Books   (Russell Square)

82 Lamb's Conduit Street WC1
405-3029

M–F 9:30–6:00

anaesthesia anatomy biochemistry cancer cardiology community medicine dentistry dermatology diagnosis dictionaries embryology endocrinology gastroenterology immunology infectious diseases medicine microbiology neurology nursing obstetrics/gynaecology ophthalmology orthopaedics otolaryngology paediatrics pharmacology physiology psychology and psychiatry radiology surgery tropical diseases urology

West End Books is a new medical bookshop hoping to serve the doctors and nurses of the area's hospitals with a full range of books on medical and nursing subjects and specialities.

Non-book material: stethoscopes
Services: mail order   special order
Catalogue: in preparation – annual

MIDDLE AND FAR EAST

Al Hoda   (Leicester Square)

76-78 Charing Cross Road WC2
240-8381

M–Sat   9:30–6:00

art & culture   biography   children's books   cookery   economics dictionaries   Farsi   Hadith   history   jurisprudence   literature   mysticism   philosophy & ethics   Quran   reference   science   theology

Al Hoda is given over entirely to the broad concerns of Islam and the Middle East. It is planned soon to have all the Arabic literature philosophy and theology in the basement. The children's books are in both English and Arabic. This is a small, new, but most friendly and enterprising bookshop.

Non-book material: Arab, Middle Eastern and Third World periodicals   children's educational games and jigsaws
Services: catalogue (six-monthly)   mail order (in preparation) special order

Arthur Probsthain   (Tottenham Court Road)

41 Great Russell Street WC1
636-1096

M–F 10:00–6:00   Sat 10:00–3:30

Arabic   art   China   civilization   history   India   Islam   Japan language teaching   literature   Middle East   religion   South-East Asia

The **Arthur Probsthain** bookshop is a long-established shop specializing in books on all aspects of the Middle and Far East. Most of the books are new, although there is a large second-hand stock and there are also a few remainders on sale. The shop's clientele tends to have academic or specialized interests as well, so that 'students' of the Orient will be well served here. A range of journals, in a variety of languages, is available.

Non-book material: cards   posters
Services: mail order   special order – all fields
Catalogue: specialized lists on a number of subjects   occasional second-hand list
Publications: Arthur Probsthain Oriental Series has published scholarly translations of Oriental writing

Knightsbridge Books   (Goodge Street)

32 Store Street WC1
636-1252

M–F 9:00–5:30

Africa   anthropology   art   crafts   culture and lifestyle   Far East   fiction   history   Indian subcontinent   literature   Middle East   poetry   politics   religion

New books about the Far and Middle East, Africa and India are the specialities of this shop. Most of the titles are scholarly and specialized, many are lavishly illustrated and a few are imported from the Continent and beyond.

Stock is kept of Routledge and Kegan Paul books, which specialize in literature, history and social science.

Services: mail order   special order
Catalogue: lists on Africa, Far East, Near and Middle East

Luzac & Co. Ltd ('Tottenham Court Road')

46 Great Russell Street WC1
636-1462

M–F 9:00–6:00 Sat 9:00–5:00

Arabic literature art: Chinese, Islamic, Japanese Buddhism business central Asia complementary medicine crafts dance drama Far East health history India Islam language teaching literature magic Middle East Mughal Empire mythology occult photography Quran religion spiritualism Sufism textiles theatre Turkey

Established in 1740, **Luzac** specializes in current titles on the Middle and Far East, with texts and studies of Buddhism a particular strength in its stock. Literature in translation, illustrated art books and titles on comparative religion are also good sections, and the extremely helpful staff are able to assist scholars, students and business people in locating new and out-of-print titles on the Middle and Far East.

Non-book material: cassettes cards badges
Services: mail order special order
Catalogue: specialized list for the Buddhist Society quarterly selected lists
Publications: Luzac & Co. Ltd publishes books about the Middle and Far East, especially in the field of art

MILITARIA

Solosy (Leicester Square)

50 Charing Cross Road WC2
836-6313

M–F 10:00–6:00 Sat 10:00–6:00

aviation and Air Force history Army and Navy history military history and uniforms, weapons, equipment

This general newsagents and specialized bookshop deals with new titles in the subject areas listed above. Predictably enough it stocks a wide range of magazines in the fields of aviation, military and naval history.

Non-book material: see above
Services: special order

MODERN FIRST EDITIONS

Bell, Book & Radmall Ltd   (Leicester Square)

4 Cecil Court WC2
240-2161   836-5888

M–F 10:00–5:30

anthologies   autographs and manuscripts   fantasy and detective
fiction   literary criticism   literature   modern first editions

For any student of modern literature (with a few quid to spare) the
two floors of this shop are heaven. **Bell, Book & Radmall** claim to
have Europe's largest stock of modern first editions (1880 to the
present) of English and American literature. The shelves are lined
with first editions, alphabetical by author, but the most valuable titles
are kept in cases. In addition to the subjects listed above, the shop
carries classics in translation, back issues of literary magazines such
as *Horizon* and *Criterion* and a few illustrated books. The shop's prices,
though, are often as exclusive as their stock. (They have a distinct
edge over their competitors in that many of their books have the
original dust-jackets.)

Non-book material: literary prints and paintings
Services: mail order   search service in field of modern first editions
Catalogue: selected lists produced four to five times yearly

MUSIC

Collet's Record Shop   (Covent Garden)

180 Shaftesbury Avenue WC2
240-3969

M–F 10:00–6:00   Sat 10:00–4:00

Collet's Record Shop is distinguished as being one of London's first
folk and jazz record shops. There is, however, a limited (though not
meagre) selection of books on music. The jazz department carries

titles about musicians, composers, instruments and the history of jazz, while books on musical styles and learning to play instruments are in the folk department. All the titles are new, although the shop is willing to buy second-hand books in the field of jazz, folk and blues.

Non-book material: cassettes   records   songbooks
Services: mail order   special order
Publications: The parent company, **Collet's**, publishes books about Eastern Europe.

J. B. Cramer & Co. Ltd. (Leicester Square)

99 St Martin's Lane WC2
240-1612

M–F 9:30–6:00   Sat 10:00–5:00

biography   conducting   history   humour   jazz   libretti   madrigals musical education   musical instruments   musicals   opera and operetta   teaching   vocal methods

Cramer specializes in new books on all aspects of music, from classical (a particularly strong section) to contemporary composers and works. Sheet music comprises a large portion of the stock and major music periodicals are available.

Non-book material: sheet music   song books
Services: mail order   special order
Catalogue: occasional list of available sheet music
Publications: J. B. Cramer & Co. Ltd publishes a large list of sheet music and has recently acquired two other firms' lists.

The Gramophone Exchange (Covent Garden)

3 Betterton Street WC2
836-0976

M–F 12:00–6:00   Sat 12–30–5:00

A large section of second-hand books about the gramophone and records, as well as numerous titles on other aspects of music, can be found here.

Non-book material: second-hand records (including rare 78s)
Services: mail order

Travis & Emery   (Leicester Square)

17 Cecil Court WC2
240-2129

M–F 10:00–6:00 Sat 10:00–1:00

Antiquarian and second-hand books and musical scores grouped according to country, composer and instrument are the speciality of **Travis & Emery**. Books are both new and used.

Non-book material: musical ephemera prints
Services: mail order special order search service
Catalogue: selected lists three times yearly

OCCULT

Atlantis   (Tottenham Court Road)

49a Museum Street WC1
405-2120

M–F 11:00–5:30 Sat 11:00–5:00

alchemy astrology divining dream interpretation folk lore healing magic occult palmistry practical magic and witchcraft psychic worlds spiritualism symbolism witchcraft

Atlantis sells new and second-hand books on witchcraft, magic, the occult and related fields, and most of the titles focus on these phenomena in the Western world. For the would-be practitioner, **Atlantis** has a large section of 'how to' books on witchcraft, divining and dowsing, among other subjects.

Non-book material: crystal balls tarot cards
Services: mail order special order wants lists accepted
Publications: Neptune Press publishes books on magic and witchcraft

The Theosophical Bookshop   (Holborn)
& Publishing House

68 Great Russell Street WC1
405-2309

M–Sat 9:30–5:00

astrology Buddhism diet meditation mythology occult philosophy psychology reincarnation Sufism Taoism theosophy Western mysticism

This firm has been established since 1881 and the shop has been in operation since 1926. In the relatively small shop space is a selective, high-quality stock of primarily scholarly books on theosophy and philosophy. Most of the titles are by Western writers, from UK publishers, and all of the books are new.

Services: mail order   special order in field
Catalogue: Theosophical Publishing House Ltd publications catalogue
Publications: Theosophical Publishing House Ltd publishes books in the fields of theosophy and philosophy

ORIENTAL

Fine Books Oriental Limited   (Holborn/Chancery Lane)

·Empire House,
34/35 High Holborn WC1
405-0650

M–F 9:00–5:30

Central Asia   China   Indian sub-continent   Japan   Middle East South-East Asia

This well-known Oriental specialist shop, the largest of its kind in Europe, is to be found several floors up a somewhat ironically-named building. Books on all aspects of these countries – from architecture and crime to religion and travel – are stocked here and all, including the antiquarian works which form about a quarter of the shop, are at reasonable prices. (A card inside each book contains full bibliographical details.) Some are in the original languages, and Japan is the largest section. From government reports of 19th-century sanitary conditions to religious studies, this excellent, friendly shop contains a wide range of fascinating books.

Non-book material: early photographs   learned periodicals and journals
Services: mail order   special order   24-hour answering machine
Catalogue: specialized catalogues regularly issued

PHILATELIC HISTORY AND COLLECTING

Harris Publications Ltd   (Leicester Square or Charing Cross)

42 Maiden Lane WC2
240-2286

M–F 8:30–5:15   Sat 9:00–2:00

Although **Harris Publications** is primarily a mail order house providing books and accessories for stamp collectors, their Maiden Lane premises do serve, as well, as a retail outlet. New, second-hand and a few antiquarian books are available from UK and foreign publishers, in English and other languages. Reference works, general collecting literature and philatelic history books form most of the stock.

Non-book material: stamp collecting accessories
Services: mail order   special order
Publications: Stamp Collecting Ltd publishes two philatelic magazines, monthly and weekly

Stanley Gibbons   (Covent Garden)

37 Southampton Street WC2
836-8444   ext. 223

M–F 9:00–5:30   Sat 9:30–12:30

Although **Stanley Gibbons** primarily sells stamps and stamp albums, the shop does carry some new books of interest to the philatelist, mainly published by Gibbons.

Non-book material: stamps   stamp collecting accessories
Services: mail order   special order
Catalogue: general catalogue is available which includes books
Publications: stamp and other collecting books are published by
Stanley Gibbons

PHOTOGRAPHY

The Bookroom – Creative Camera   (Russell Square)

19 Doughty Street WC1
242-0565

M–F 9:00–5:30

annuals   catalogues of photography collections   collections of individual photographers' works (US, UK, France, Japan, Russia,
China, Middle East)   history   period albums   yearbooks

It is rather a pity that this shop in a listed Queen Anne house is
tucked out of the way because, although the display space is small,
there are lovely new (and a few remaindered) books on photography,
particularly from the Far East and the US. The emphasis is on the
artistic, cultural and historical aspects of photography, as well as the
technical elements. A selection of major international photography
magazines is sold. There are many photographic studios in the area
and so the shop is able to meet speedily both professional and
amateur needs.

Non-book material: sets of postcards   portfolios of reproductions
Services: mail order   special order   library and college supply
Catalogue: complete list annually
Publications: the affiliated firm Coo Press Ltd publishes *Creative
Camera International Yearbook* and *Creative Camera Magazine*

The Photographer's Gallery   (Leicester Square)

8 Great Newport Street WC2
240-1969

T–Sat 11:00–7:00

history of photography   individual photographers   international
photography   monographs   technical aspects

This combination gallery and bookshop stocks a few out-of-print and remaindered books about photography, but the majority of the books are current titles on photography and related visual and performing arts. Also available is a selection of international photography magazines, yearbooks and journals.

Non-book material: cards   film   gallery exhibitions   postcards   posters
Services: mail order   10% discount to museums and colleges
Catalogue: complete title list

POETRY

Bernard Stone/Turret Bookshop   (Russell Square)

42 Lamb's Conduit Street WC1
405-6058

M–Sat 10:00–7:00

Bernard Stone's remains London's leading modern poetry bookshop. Many writers and illustrators congregate here and Ralph Steadman's books, illustrations and some original work are prominently featured.

Hours can easily be spent browsing through new and second-hand books (as well as a few remainders) of poetry and selected literature, looking at their candid photos of notable literary figures or chatting with the staff about the latest work and gossip in the world of modern poetry. Children's poetry and literature, books on music, biography and the performing arts are also stocked, and they carry a wide range of UK and US theatre, literary and poetry journals (back issues are also available).

Non-book material: cards   contemporary book illustrators' works   prints of local scenes
Services: mail order   special order
Catalogue: specialized lists, e.g., poetry, children's books
Publications: Turret Books publishes modern poetry

POLITICAL

The Alternative Bookshop (Covent Garden)

3 Langley Court WC2
240-1804

M 11:30–6:00   T–Sat 10:30–6:00

anarchism   civil liberties   class   defence   economics   energy   environment   fiction   foreign affairs   history   liberalism   philosophy   psychology   race relations   religion   sociology   Third World politics   USSR

The Alternative Bookshop is concerned with individual liberties, libertarian ideals, a free market economy and an open society. Books and periodicals on subjects within this political and economic context form the majority of the shop's stock, with most of the titles relating to British society, although there are a few foreign language titles. It also carries some second-hand books on general topics.

Non-book material: badges   posters
Services: mail order   special order in field
Catalogue: selected lists   second-hand catalogues

Collet's London Bookshop (Leicester Square)

66 Charing Cross Road WC2
836-6306

M–W 10:00–6:30   Th 10:00–7:00   F 10:30–7:00   Sat 10:00–6:00

Africa   the Americas   Asia   British industry   China   disarmament   drama   economics   European affairs   fiction   literary criticism   literature   Marxism   Marxist classics   philosophy   poetry   politics   psychology   race & class   rights & benefits   sexual politics   sociology   Soviet Union   trade unions

Collet's London Bookshop is one of London's largest left-wing bookshops and its range of social, political and economic books on world regions is particularly broad. Their basement houses second-hand and remaindered books, and at the rear of the ground floor is a small periodical room packed with left-wing political magazines, papers and pamphlets from all over the world.

Non-book material: badges   diary   postcards   posters
Services: mail order   special order
Catalogue: list of books about trade unions
Publications: Collet's publishes books about Eastern European affairs

The Corner House Bookshop   (Covent Garden)

14 Endell Street WC2
836-7909

M–Sat 10:00–7:00 (winter: closes at 6:00)

anti-nuclear   culture and communication   family   feminism   minorities and race   political studies   rights   self-help   sexual politics sociology   Third World   women writers

The Corner House Bookshop is a radical bookshop. Women's issues, race relations, individual rights and sex-role awareness are some of the shop's interests. Much of it, clearly, is meant for adults but there is also a section of children's books. Magazines and journals on education, politics, community affairs, and feminism are available.

Non-book material: badges   posters
Services: mail order

PSYCHIC WORLDS

Psychic News Bookshop   (Holborn)

23 Great Queen Street WC2
405-2914

M–F 9:00–5:00

astrology   psychic worlds   religion   spiritual healing   spiritual nature   supernatural

This is London's only bookshop dealing solely with literature about the psychic and supernatural worlds. Most of the books are new, though there are a few second-hand titles and an occasional remaindered book. The speciality of the shop is quite narrowly defined and does not include books on the occult, mysticism, magic and witch-craft.

Non-book material: cards   records
Services: mail order   special order
Catalogue: quarterly list of selected titles
Publications: The **Psychic Press** publishes the newspaper, *Psychic News* and a few books on psychic worlds

PUBLISHER'S BOOKSHOPS

Collet's Penguin Bookshop   (Leicester Square)

52 Charing Cross Road WC2
836-2315

M–Sat 10:00–6:00

buildings of England   classics   crime   economics   education   English Library   fiction   linguistics   new titles   Pelican   plays   poetry   reference   sociology

This branch of **Collet's** sells only new (and a good range of second-hand) Penguins and Pelicans.

Services: mail order   special order (Penguin and Pelican only)

Penguin Bookshop   (Covent Garden)

10 Covent Garden Market WC2
379-7650

M–Sat 10:00–8:00

art   biography   business and economics   children's books   classics   cooking   crime   drama   education   feminism   fiction   film/TV   games/sports   history   humour   language   literary criticism   literature   music   natural history   poetry   politics   psychology   reference   science/mathematics   science fiction   sociology   travel guides   'world of the mind'

This is a general bookshop in the new Market, which despite the shop's name is not devoted exclusively to Penguin books, although all

Penguin titles in print are here. One room downstairs is devoted to children's books. Certain hardbacks are stocked as well.

Services: mail order   Penguin monthly stocklist

Zwemmer's Oxford University Press Bookshop (Leicester Square)

72 Charing Cross Road WC2
240-1559

M–Sat 9:30–5:30

architecture art bibles biology carol books children's educational books classics economics education English as a foreign language fiction folk tales geography historical monographs history law legends linguistics mathematics medicine Oxford companions philosophy physics political science prayer books sciences

Zwemmer's OUP Bookshop stocks only OUP titles and has computerized inventory and stock ordering systems for quick delivery of whatever is not on the shelves. The OUP specializes in world classics, but the shop also has an excellent section of books on English language teaching.

Non-book material: Oxford diaries
Services: mail order   special order
Catalogue: OUP publisher's catalogue is available for a fee   selected specialized lists produced frequently

RAILWAYS AND TRANSPORT

Hambling (Models) Ltd (Leicester Square)

29 Cecil Court WC2
836-4704

M–F 9:00–5:30   Sat (Oct–March) 10:00–4:00

This is a model railway shop which also sells books on Great Britain's railways, engines and tracks for the enthusiast. Illustrated and railway history books are stocked, as well as track layout diagrams, and British monthly and quarterly railway publications.

Non-book material: model railway equipment and trains
Services: special order

Motor Books (Leicester Square)

33 St Martin's Court WC2
36 St Martin's Court WC2
836-5376

M–F 9:30–5:30   Sat 10:30–5:00

At number 33 St Martin's Court **Motor Books** specializes in new books on motoring, railways and steam powered vehicles (including manufacturers' repair manuals) while at number 36 books on military, naval and aviation subjects are featured. Both shops import titles from abroad, so a few of the books are in languages other than English. The bias in these shops is towards material which is technical and informative (e.g., a history of aviation with detailed specifications of aircraft) and there is a wide range of DIY material, from books on boat building to assembling explosives. Both shops stock a number of current magazines in their respective areas of speciality.

Services: mail order   special order
Catalogue: annual, specialized catalogues

RUDOLF STEINER

Rudolf Steiner Bookshop (Tottenham Court Road)

38 Museum Street WC1
242-4249

M–F 10:00–5:30

This shop stocks a complete range of Rudolf Steiner's works, and other new books which are related to Steiner's interests (e.g. religion, philosophy and social commentary). A small selection of children's books is also available.

Services: mail order
Catalogue: annual selected listing
Publications: Rudolf Steiner Press imprint on works by and about Rudolf Steiner

SCIENCE FICTION

Forbidden Planet   (Tottenham Court Road)

23 Denmark Street WC2
836-4179   mail orders: 240-3017

M–W 10:00–6:00   Th 10:00–7:00   F–Sat 10:00–6:00

anthologies   collections   fantasy   fiction   film and TV   illustrated books   science fiction   sorcery

Forbidden Planet is making it in the competitive world of science fiction bookshops, with current sci fi and fantasy books from the US and UK, and a large selection of new and second-hand (many are collectors' items) comics and sci fi magazines. The shop is owned by a major UK distributor of sci fi books, so they do have quick access to recently published titles. Sci fi artists' portfolios and illustrated books on fantasy and sci fi are also featured.

Non-book material: artists' portfolios   film & TV stills   posters
Services: mail order   special order
Publications: Forbidden Planet produces posters and artists' port-folios
Note: There is a **Forbidden Planet II** at 52 St Giles High Street W1, 379-6042

SPORTS AND OUTDOOR ACTIVITIES

Anglebooks Ltd   (Leicester Square)

2 Cecil Court WC2
836-2922

M–F 10:30–6:00

This shop specializes both in second-hand and antiquarian books on the sport of angling, and books on British local history. The books on fishing range from instructions on fly-tying to Walton's *Compleat*

Angler and Brautigan's *Trout Fishing in America*. Personal accounts of village life, from as far back as the 17th century, characterize their books on local history.

Non-book material: downstairs is a gallery with 19th and 20th century watercolours, prints and drawings, many of which are original works
Services: mail order   search service
Catalogue: occasional ones on local history and angling

Edward Stanford Ltd
(Covent Garden)

12–14 Long Acre WC2
836-1321

M–F 9:00–5:30   Sat 10:00–2:00

atlases   camping manuals and maps   cartography   English country guides   geology   guide & travel books worldwide   historical reprints of maps   mountaineering   nautical books and charts   topography walking guides

As the world's largest retail mapseller since 1852, **Stanford**'s has only recently gone into bookselling, and their book stock reflects the kinds of title their traditional clientele wants, i.e., guides, outdoor activities, nautical and maritime subjects. Most of the shop is taken up by maps and charts; downstairs is a specialized department of military, overseas and aeronautical maps.

Non-book material: compasses   map measures   thematic maps world area maps   the best selection of globes in London
Services: mail order   special order   map mounting referral
Publications: Stanford's is part of the George Philip & Son group which publishes marine and country maps and charts. **Stanford**'s produces a sales promotion map for England and Wales.

YHA Bookshop   (Covent Garden)

14 Southampton Street WC2
836-8541

M–Sat 9:30–5:30

budget travel guides (international)   canoeing   caving   London
guides   mountaineering/climbing guides   outdoor activities   phrase
books   UK guides/illustrated   US sectional guides (Dollarwise)
Sierra Club publications   Ski guides (international)   treasure hunting   Wainwright guides

YHA (Youth Hostel Association) is a complete outdoor sports shop,
with a terrific travel and outdoor sport bookshop catering to both the
low-budget traveller and the serious sportsperson. **YHA** pride themselves on their range of international mountaineering and climbing
guides from all the major mountaineering clubs. They have excellent
worldwide travel guides, including European guides and some general interest/hobby titles. Journals include *Hosteling News*, *Descent* and
Crags.

Non-book material: ordinance survey maps   UK, US and Euro-
pean maps   occasional posters
Services: mail order   special order
Publications: YHA publishes a *Guide to Europe* and the *YHA
European Guide* to individual countries

TECHNOLOGY

Intermediate Technology   (Leicester Square/Covent Garden)
Bookshop

9 King Street WC2
836-9434

M–F 9:30–5:30

agriculture   alternative energy   building   disseminating information   education and teaching guides   health   sanitation   small
industries   suitable technologies   Third World development

This very small shop (which is part of a consulting and research
group) specializes in, as its name suggests, books and booklets on
intermediate technology. Particularly interesting is the literature on

61

getting information about alternative energy sources, sanitation systems or building techniques to large groups of people, say a village population in India.

Non-book material: various leaflets, pamphlets and journals on projects and studies in intermediate technology throughout the world
Services: mail order
Catalogue: general list annually, updated regularly
Publications: a list of courses in the UK about intermediate technology is published by the **Intermediate Technology Group**, as well as a quarterly journal, *Appropriate Technology*

THEATRE

RSC Bookshop (Holborn)

47 Aldwych WC2
240-0494

M–F 11:30–7:30   Sat 12:15–8:15

literary criticism   literature   non-Shakespearean play texts performed by the RSC   Shakespeare play texts and sonnets   Shakespeareana   stage history   texts of selected West End plays   theatre annuals

In addition to new books about the theatre, the **RSC Bookshop** sells theatre programmes from current Stratford-Upon-Avon productions and past Aldwych productions. A wide range of stage and literary magazines are available. The Penguin Shakespeare texts carry the RSC stamp for a bit of distinction. The bookshop also sells tickets for productions at the RSC's Barbican auditoria.

Non-book material: calendars   cassettes   diaries   gifts   key fobs   prints   slides   T-shirts   yearbooks
Services: mail order   special order
Publications: The **RSC** has co-published a few books about its own productions, as well as an RSC annual and an edition of the sonnets.

TOPOGRAPHY

Alan Brett (Leicester Square)

24 Cecil Court WC2
836-8222

M–Sat 9:00–6:00

Alan Brett specializes in antiquarian and second-hand books, maps and prints on topography. Also available are antiquarian fiction, gothic novels, antiquarian magazines and some theatre ephemera

Non-book material: boxes of prints grouped according to country and topic, e.g., fruits, caricatures, military, etc.

TRAVEL

Remington (Leicester Square)

14 Cecil Court WC2
836-9771

M–F 10:00–5:00

Remington specializes in books dealing with voyages and travel, generally antiquarian and second-hand, from Hakluyt and earlier to the Kon-Tiki expedition and beyond. Such discursive writing, rather than guides, is the shop's interest; and it is the more adventurous who fill the reasonably-priced shelves – Africa, China and the Americas rather than Europe. (The more expensive antiquarian titles are kept upstairs in the shop's suite at 26 Charing Cross Road.) Runs of periodicals, such as *The Alpine Journal*, are kept, and there is a useful stock of more general, miscellaneous titles as well as natural history.

Non-book material: maps   prints
Services: mail order

UK GOVERNMENT PUBLICATIONS

HMSO Bookshop

(Holborn or Chancery Lane)

49 High Holborn WC2
928-6977

M–F 8:30–5:00

Acts of Parliament agriculture art building design and construction careers computers ecology economics education energy environment finance Hansard parliamentary debate health and medicine historical monuments history housing and planning industrial training/relations/society law management metrification natural history ordinance survey maps reference road and traffic social services statistics trade and commerce

HMSO is the source for government publications in the UK, most of their titles originating in some governmental department. Legislation and regulations which are out of print are kept on film, and HMSO is the international agent for the UN, EEC and OECD publications.

Non-book material: Imperial War Museum/National Portrait Gallery posters, maps and prints
Services: mail order special order
Catalogue: complete annual catalogue with publications from the year 1235 (in facsimile or reprinted) selected listing in specialized areas
Publications: HMSO publishes prints, e.g., National Portrait Gallery

UNIVERSITY BOOKSHOPS AND TEXT BOOKS

City Lit Bookshop

(Holborn)

22 Stukeley Street WC2
242-9872 ext. 22

M–F 11:30–7:45

art biography classics drama economics feminism fiction film Greek classics history languages literary criticism literature mathematics music Penguin philosophy poetry politics psychology reference religion – East & West sociology UK travel guides

This small shop in the foyer of the City Lit caters to the students of the college, but the shop also keeps solid stock of recent titles in areas other than college course subjects, including contemporary fiction, feminism and travel guides.

Non-book material: stationery
Services: special order

LONDON WC
Second-hand Bookshops

The Bloomsbury Bookplace   (Russell Square)

11 Grenville Street WC1
278-8496

M–Sat 11:00–7:00   Sun 1:0–5:00

ground floor:
anthropology antiques archaeology architecture comparative religions criminology economics environment fiction handicaps history linguistics literature occult performing arts philosophy pocket editions politics psychology race sex & gender social & welfare sociology theology visual arts women's studies

basement:
business studies cookery & domestic crafts foreign fiction & non-fiction languages law mathematics medicine naval & military sciences sports & games technology transport travel

The Bloomsbury Bookplace, only newly-opened, is already a formidiable addition to the neighbourhood book trade. Its stock is vast (about 30,000 titles) and gratifyingly cheap. The proprietor, who has extended his activities from the Greenwich Book Place, has the healthiest attitude to books I have ever come across in a second-hand dealer: he thinks of them not as objects, but as vehicles of information. His special interests in philosophy, politics and the social sciences are reflected in the stock, which is serious, academic, and meticulously classified. But one has a sense too, especially in the organized chaos of

65

the basement, of looking through shelves (or piles) of books that just might have been overlooked — and underpriced! Well worth a visit.

Non-book material: 78s singles classical records sheet music postcards old periodicals *London Review of Books*
Services: special order
Catalogue: in preparation

Chancery Lane Bookshop   (Chancery Lane)

6 Chichester Rents WC2
405-0635

M–F 9:00–5:30

art astrology history Ireland literary criticism literature medicine modern first editions music occult pastimes poetry religion sports travel guides

This general second-hand and antiquarian shop is tucked away off the noisy streets and run by an Irishman whose mates are usually smoking and chatting at the front of the shop while customers browse around. The atmosphere is just fine for an easy hour of looking despite (or perhaps because of) the rather dishevelled, slightly grubby look of the place. The owner specializes in books on Ireland and Irish writers, and 18th to 19th-century illustrated books.

Non-book material: engravings prints
Services: mail order search service in certain field
Catalogue: general and specialized lists twice yearly

Holborn Books   (Leicester Square/Charing Cross)

14 Charing Cross Road WC2
240-2337

M–Sat 10:00–7:00 Sun 11:00–4:00

'No Book Over £2' proclaims a poster in the window of this second-hand shop. Such a policy, while meaning that rare books are unlikely to be found here (and if they are one could make a quick profit by nipping round to Bertram Rota with them), is welcome in central London. The stock is of a general nature – from crime fiction to history and especially notable for its art books – which makes a visit when passing likely to prove worthwhile. An interesting range of new and old Penguins is kept in several places around the shop.

Non-book material: old magazines, chiefly about the theatre and cinema

James Smith   (Chancery Lane)

94 Gray's Inn Road WC1
405-5697

M–F 9:00–6:00

antiques art atlases cars clocks collecting cookery dictionaries gardening London poetry railways

While there is not much space in which to browse, **James Smith** has a good selection of remainders and end-of-run books in 'practical' subject areas (e.g., collecting antique watches or refinishing furniture). The staff are very diligent about looking for recently out-of-print titles, or ordering the last of an end-of-run book.

Services: mail order   search service

The Marchmont Bookshop   (Euston)

39 Burton Street WC1
45 Burton Street WC1
387-7989

39 – M–F 11:00–6:00 (hours may vary)
45 – M–F 1:00–5:00

architecture art children's books drama history literature modern first editions natural history philosophy poetry topography

Between them the **Marchmont** shops, both rather jumbled, have a fairly wide range of lower priced second-hand books, as well as a few remaindered titles and review copies. There is also a more specialized and more expensive range of better quality second-hand and antiquarian titles.

Services: mail order   search service
Catalogue: modern first edition list occasionally

Henry Pordes   (Leicester Square)

58-60 Charing Cross Road, London WC2
836-9031

M–Sat 9:30–7:00

art   Israel and Judaica   literature   philosophy   poetry   theology   travel

Henry Pordes, a recent addition to the Charing Cross Road, stocks second-hand and remaindered books. Perhaps it is because they cater for the very general tourist market that their second-hand department is not that interesting, or maybe they are still building up their stock.

Provincial Booksellers Fairs Association (Russell Square)

Royal National Hotel
Woburn Place WC1

Sun 5:00–8:00   M 10:00–8:00

also:
Imperial Hotel
Russell Square WC1
M   12:00–8:00   T 10:00–3:30

For three days each month, always beginning on the second Sunday, the **Provincial Booksellers Fair Association** (PBFA) holds book fairs at the hotels listed above. Antiquarian and second-hand booksellers from all over England come to London to trade and buy books, and the general public is just as welcome as those in the book business. This is one of Londoners' unique opportunities to browse through a country bookseller's stock without having to leave the city.

Reads

48a Charing Cross Road/13 Gt Newport Street WC2
Reads 379-7669   **Francis Edwards** 379-7692

M–Sat 10:00–10:00   Sun 12:00–8:00

anthropology art Australasia and Pacific autobiography British
history children's books cinema classics crime dance Eastern
Europe Eastern religion economics education elocution exploration and travel fantasy Far East French, German, Spanish
literature gastronomy Gilbert & Sullivan history humour journalism Judaica literary criticism literature medicine Middle
East military history modern first editions music mythology
North America occult peace studies Penguin performing arts
philosophy plays politics South America theology theosophy
topography

Reads, formerly trading as Read Judd, has recently been bought by
the Pharos Group and undergone some changes. The opening hours
are longer, including Sunday (**Reads** is one of the few general
second-hand shops to work on Sunday), there is new shelving and in
the basement three bargain rooms have been opened where very
reasonable prices can be found. The back room now houses the
famous **Francis Edwards**, formerly of Marylebone High Street and
owned by the same group, which specialises in naval, military and
aviation books. The range of stock at **Reads** means that not all
subjects are comprehensively covered, but there is generally much of
interest and the staff remain knowledgeable and helpful.

Non-book material: magazines (ballet, cinema, records) sheet-
music of old popular songs modern maps theatre programmes
Services: mail order vigorous search service
Catalogue: miscellany specialist subjects

Skoob Books Ltd

15 Sicilian Avenue
Southampton Row WC1
404-3063

M–Sat 10:30–6:30

antiques architecture art chemistry cookery crafts education
engineering esoterica Everyman Library Folio Society language

linguistics   literary criticism   literature   local history   medicine
modern prose   Oxford World Classics   Penguins   philosophy   physics   poetry   reference   theatre   theology   topography

Now permanently housed in this elegant Sicilian-Avenue shop **Skoob**
has established itself as the largest and best second-hand shop in
central London where its interesting stock, with some emphasis on
English and American literature, is frequently augmented. Its other
sections, such as foreign literature and the sciences, are large, and all
the prices are reasonable. Sets of authors, such as the *Waverley* novels,
can be found here, together with runs of magazines (and individual
copies) ranging from *Penguin New Writing* to *Scientific American*. The
Penguin section is extensive; there is a good chance of finding any title
that has been published there. More recently the shop has developed
a section of modern first editions and antiquarian titles. Any visitor to
London or inhabitant who does not visit **Skoob** will miss one of the
capital's best assets.

Non-book material: a few second-hand records
Services: mail order   search service   10% discount for NUS mem-
bers
Catalogue: selected list in preparation

Templar Books (Chancery Lane)

76 Chancery Lane WC2
242-8669

M–F 9:00–6:00

art   cookery   crafts   fiction   history   literature   military history
music   poetry   politics   transport   travel guides

Next door to a Templar bookshop selling new books, this shop sells
both remaindered and damaged books at bargain prices. As most of
their books are publishers' remainders, it is difficult to predict exactly
what their stock will be from week to week, though books in the
categories listed above are usually available.

Non-book material: records
Services: mail order   special order

LONDON WC
Antiquarian Bookshops

Andrew Block   (Holborn)
20 Barter Street WC1
405-9660

M–F 10:00–5:00 (opening hours can vary)

architecture   art   botany   children's books   conjuring   drama
film   incunabula   literature   medicine   modern first editions   private press publications   reference   theatre   topography   typography

The four jumbled rooms of this antiquarian bookshop are presided
over by London's oldest bookseller. Mr Block is still running his
famous business from Barter Street. There are a great many good
books in this shop, but don't stop by expecting to browse as the
quarters are tight with titles and only Mr Block knows exactly where
things can be found, although a list of books in stock can be consulted.
A rummage can reveal a bargain.

Non-book material: prints   theatre posters   postcards

Arthur Page Books   (Tottenham Court Road)
29 Museum Street WC1
636-8206

M–Sat 10:30–6:30   Sun 12:00–6:30

antiquarian   English literature   history of science   music

Arthur Page and his partner Anthony Rhys Jones have now moved
round the corner from their well-known shop in Coptic Street to
rather larger premises, where the emphasis has been given to
antiquarian books, especially medicine, history of science and English
literature. These, remarkably, are available to browsers on the open
shelves; the prices are as reasonable as the stock is varied and
interesting. Often pleasant reading-copies of early editions of such
books as Stow's *Survey* are to be found at low prices. There is also a

71

distinct antiquarian music department, selling both books about music, composers and musicians as well as scores.

The general second-hand section has not been neglected in the move, continuing to range from academic texts at knock-down prices to a good supply of early Penguins and Pelicans (and some original King Penguins). Runs of magazines, such as *The Strand*, can often be found here; so, too, can good sets of novelists and poets, such as Meredith, Conrad and the *Waverley* novels.

Services: mail order   wants lists
Catalogue: specialized lists bi-annually   antiquarian list   general list

Bertram Rota Ltd (Covent Garden)

30 Long Acre WC2
831-0723

M–F 9:30–5:30   Sat by appointment

American literature   autographs   English literature   history   poetry   private presses   sciences   topography   travel accounts

With an international reputation to recommend it, this elegant shop is well worth a visit if you are looking for (expensive) antiquarian books or modern first editions of English and American literature. (A few of these have the original dust-jackets.) Many of the choicest books are not on the shelves upstairs but may be lurking in the storage area below, so ask if you don't find what you want. There are some new titles as well, on topics which relate directly to modern literature.

Services: mail order   search service in certain areas
Catalogue: numerous – produced six to eight times annually (e.g., poetry, rare boks, fine printing)
Publications: the shop publishes limited editions of poetry and a few bibliographies

Bondy Books

16 Little Russell Street WC1
405-2733

M–F 10:30–6:30   Sat 10:00–5:00

architectural history   ballet   bibliography   British history   British
topography   caricature   children's books   English literature   fine
art   French literature and history   miniature books   music   poetry
theatre

The owner of this antiquarian and second-hand bookshop is one of
the few people in the world who specializes in miniature books, and
he has published widely on the subject. In addition to miniatures, the
shop's stock ranges from very rare, early printed books to 20th-
century second-hand titles. Of particular interest in the shop are
illustrated children's books, and books on art, architectue and
caricature.

Non-book material: caricatures   ephemera   prints
Services: mail order
Catalogue: an irregular one of recent purchases   miniature & early
printed books, four or five times a year

H. M. Fletcher

27 Cecil Court WC2
836-2865

M–F 10:00–5:30

Despite the rather disorderly and slightly grubby appearance of this
general antiquarian and second-hand bookshop, there is said to be a
wealth of interesting stock out of sight. Second-hand paperbacks at
50p, modern private press offerings and 16th century are all available
and give an idea of the range of books, and prices, to be found.

Services: mail order

Green Knight Bookshop

34 St Martin's Court WC2
836-3800

Hours are variable – ring first

This is a lovely, Dickensian looking antiquarian shop specializing in late 19th-century English literature, illustrated books, fine bindings, art and travel books.

Services: mail order
Catalogue: irregular specialized lists

Harold Storey

3 Cecil Court WC2
836-3777

M–F 10:30–6:00

This is a general antiquarian shop with a bias toward travel, exploration, voyages and illustrated books. It also carries a few second-hand books on aviation and naval history and has a good stock of sets of English literature (Dickens, *Waverley* novels etc.) in fine bindings.

Services: mail order

Quevedo

25 Cecil Court WC2
836-9132

M–F 10:00–1:00 2:00–5:30

Quevedo is a general antiquarian bookshop specializing in travel and English literature, mostly of the 16th–18th centuries, together with a large number of foreign languages and some illustrated books.

Services: mail order
Catalogue: irregular lists

Stanley Crowe
(Tottenham Court Road)

5 Bloomsbury Street WC1
(entrance on Streatham Street)
580-3976

M–F 11:00–4:30   may vary, advisable to ring

Mr Crowe's small, crowded antiquarian shop gives me the feeling of
what Bloomsbury must have been at the beginning of the century.
Indeed, the books here are about British topography and local
history, and many of the faces and places of old Bloomsbury can be
found in their pages. Don't go looking for a 50p paperback here, but
books about old and obscure aspects of Britain might be in stock.

Non-book material: prints
Services: mail order
Catalogue: annual selected listing

The Woburn Bookshop
(Russell Square or Euston)

10 Woburn Walk WC1
387-7340

M–F 10:00–6:00

Africa biography children's books China development studies
economics history India Japan Jewish history Latin and Greek
classics Latin America literary criticism literature medicine
Middle East natural history philosophy poetry politics population Russia science sociology theology travel US

An antiquarian and second-hand bookshop with primary holdings in
the humanities, **The Woburn Bookshop** was started by a man who
has gone on to become a publisher but still keeps the shop as an active
business concern.

Services: mail order   search service
Catalogue: by subject, bi-yearly
Publications: Frank Cass Publishers publish reprints and mono-
graphs

LONDON EC
General Bookshops

Barbican Bookshop (Barbican)

Barbican Centre EC1
628-4190

M–Sun 12:00–9:00

This is perhaps the most difficult bookshop to find in London, situated on 'Level 4' of a windswept building that may well come into its own during the nuclear war but for the moment remains an impersonal, concrete labyrinth. Now that, sadly, the building also houses the RSC's London theatres this small shop, which caters for the building as a whole, contains a number of playtexts, biographies and fiction titles among a stock ranging from records and sweets to Alka Seltzer and key-rings. The RSC has plans to open a rather more comprehensive shop in the building; perhaps it will be signposted.

Non-book material: see above

The Bookcase (St Paul's)

26 Ludgate Hill EC4
236-5982

M–F 9:00–6:00   Sun (summer) 12:00–4:00

academic texts art biography business classics collecting cookery crafts economics fiction gardening history literary criticism literature natural history Penguin performing arts poetry politics reference royal family science fiction sociology sports technical travel guides

The Bookcase sells new, but mainly remaindered books (prices start at 50p) in general subject areas, as well as the fields of business, academic texts and technical books. An odd second-hand title may turn up occasionally, as well as review copies, and the general subject areas vary weekly. Recently the dull job-lots of remaindered paperbacks have been replaced by new ones at full price.

Services: mail order   special order (with publishers in stock)

Books Etc.
174 Fleet Street EC4
353-5939

M–F 9:00–6:30

antiques   art   biography   children's books   classics   cookery
crafts   crime   fiction   film   gardening   health   history   literature
music   natural history   plays   poetry   politics   reference   science
fiction   thrillers   transport   travel guides

As with much of the area this branch of **Books Etc.** does not operate
on a Saturday, but otherwise it provides a service similar to the others
in the chain.

Non-book material: cards   wrapping-paper
Services: special order

The Booksmith
7 Byward Street EC3
626-3346

M–F 9:00–5:30

ground floor

antiques and collecting   art   biography   classics   cookery   fiction
gardening   history   language teaching   literature   music   natural
history   poetry   reference   sport

downstairs

astronomy   business   children's books   crime   fiction   health   Open
University   philosophy   photography   psychology   romance   science fiction   technology

This branch of **Booksmith** carries bargain hardbacks and full-price
current hardcover and paperback books, all in a variety of subjects.

In an age when the staff of chain stores are apparently expected to present no personality at all, it is a pleasure to encounter the friendly, personable, almost jolly group of booksellers working at the shop.

Services: mail order through Bibliophile   special order
Catalogue: Bibliophile is the mail order arm of **The Booksmith** shops and produces frequent lists of bargain books available by post

Chain Libraries Ltd (Moorgate)

151 Moorgate EC2
606-5061

M–F 10:00–5:45

adventure   classics   cookery   crime   history   horror   non-fiction Penguins   romance   science fiction

A general bookshop selling primarily paperback fiction.

Non-book material: cards   wrapping-paper   postcards
Services: special order

City Booksellers Ltd (St Paul's)

80 Cheapside EC2
248-2768

M–F 8:30–5:30

children's books   classics   cookery   cosmology   crime & adventure dictionaries   fiction   games   gardening   history   horror   humour literature   natural history   reference   romance   science fiction sports   travel guides   war   westerns

City Booksellers is a general bookshop primarily catering to the business people of the City with particularly strong sections of cookery and gardening books, dictionaries and paperback fiction.

Non-book material: cards   stationery   toys
Services: special order

City Booksellers Ltd   (Monument)
64 Leadenhall Market EC3
626-5811

M–F 8:30–5:30

basement:

children's books   classics   cookery   cosmology   crime & adventure
dictionaries   fiction   games   gardening   history   horror   humour
literature   natural history   reference   romance   science fiction
sports   travel guides   war   westerns

On the ground floor of this spacious shop in Leadenhall Market are
toys, stationery, records and even luggage. Downstairs are new books
in a variety of general subject areas.

Non-book material: calculators   cards   gifts   luggage   records
stationery   toys
Services: special order

Dennys Booksellers Ltd   (Barbican)
2 Carthusian Street EC1
253-5421

M–F 9:00–6:00

general:
art   car manuals   children's books   cookery   crafts   economics
fiction   food   gardening   literature   management   natural history
Penguin   reference   travel guides

medical:
anaesthetics   anatomy   biochemistry   diagnosis   genetics   haemo-
tology   histology   immunology   lecture notes   nursing   obstetrics/
gynaecology   ophthalmology   surgery

Half of **Dennys** is a general retail bookshop with hardcover and
paperback fiction and non-fiction. The other half of the shop features
medical, technical and scientific books in a variety of specialized
subject areas.

Non-book material: cards   posters   wrapping-paper   own greetings-cards

Services: mail order   special order
Publications: Dennys Publications publishes medical, technical and scientific books

Harvid Bookstore   (Blackfriars)

68 Fleet Street EC4
353-3929

M–F 9:30–6:00   Sat 11:00–5:00   Sun 1:30–5:00

Opposite the Cheshire Cheese, this branch of **Harvid** contains a stock similar to the King's Road branch with rather more space given to film and theatre books. It is one of the few shops to be open on a Sunday in this area.

Non-book material: cassettes   maps   postcards   wrapping-paper
Services: special order

Harvid Bookstore   (Tower Hill)

10 Tower Place EC3
623-1081

M–F 10:00–6:00   Sat 11:00–6:00   Sun 10:30–6:00

The largest of the three **Harvid** shops, this one, in addition to a stock similar to the King's Road branch, is aimed at the local tourist market: as well as maps and guides, many of the books are illustrated histories of London and the country.

Non-book material: cards   cassettes   maps   postcards   wrapping-paper
Services: special order

L. Simmonds

(Temple)

16 Fleet Street EC4
353-3907

M–F 9:30–5:30

The small front of **L. Simmonds** shop conceals an excellent general bookshop with an academic section which has a good range of new titles, both in paperback and hardback, as well as established works. There is also a section of recent books at knock-down prices which often contains interesting titles.

Services: mail order   special order   library supply

W. H. Smith

(Chancery Lane)

124 Holborn EC1
242-0535

M–F 9:00–5:30

W. H. Smith

(Moorgate)

115 London Wall EC2
638-8499

M–Sat 9:00–5:30

W. H. Smith

(St Pauls)

145 Cheapside EC2
606-2301

M–F 9:00–5:30

LONDON EC
Speciality Bookshops

BUSINESS

Barbican Business Book Centre   (Moorgate)

9 Moorfields EC2
628-7479

M–F 9:00–5:00

accounting   banking and investment   business studies   commercial
practice   economics   finance   industrial relations   law   M & E
handbooks   management   marketing   shipping   statistics   taxation

Specializing in business, management and finance books for students
and professionals, this shop is well organized, clearly labelled and has
a good range of UK and US publishers in each subject area.

Services: mail order   special order
Catalogue: complete catalogue annually, bimonthly updates issued

Jones & Evans Bookshop Ltd   (Mansion House)

70 Queen Victoria Street EC4
248-6516

M–F 9:30–5:15

art   biography   business   economics   finance   history   law   literature   management   natural history   politics   royal family   sciences

With a speciality in current business and finance titles, **Jones &
Evans** reflects the interests of the working population in the City,
although they also stock recent fiction and non-fiction.

Services: mail order   special order

Witherby & Co. Ltd   (Monument)

147 Cannon Street EC4
626-1912

M–F 7:00–5:30

art banking business management children's books cookery
economics export fiction insurance language texts law M & E
handbooks marine and shipping marketing reference travel
guides

Witherby & Co. specializes in new books on insurance, shipping and
business. A few general fiction and non-fiction titles are stocked
alongside the business titles. This Cannon Street shop is also a
newsagent and stationer which opens at 4.30 a.m. and if such books
are needed at that time they can be sold.

Non-book material: see above
Services: mail order   special order
Catalogue: Witherby Publications catalogue   book list on insur-
ance and related subjects
Publications: Witherby Publications publishes books on insur-
ance, marine business and insurance, and general business subjects
Note: Books from **Witherby & Co.** can also be obtained from their
order department: 32 Aylesbury St, EC1, 251-5341

HEALTH AND SPIRITUALITY

Genesis Books   (Old Street)

East West Centre
188 Old Street EC1
250-1868

M–F 11:30–7:00   Sat 11:00–3:00

acupuncture astrology child care and pregnancy classics cookery diet Eastern religions and philosophies healing health
herbs history macrobiotic nutrition magic massage and shiatsu
medicine mysticism psychology society women and sexual politics yoga

Although run independently from the East West Centre in which it is
located, this shop is, none the less, closely associated with the purpose

of the centre. The shop specializes in new books on alternatives in health, medicine and spirituality, and carries titles on a range of subjects from diet to iridology to acupuncture to sexual politics. Also available are journals and magazines in these fields, especially in the areas of herbal and holistic medicine, psychology and nutrition. The owner is an acupuncturist and can give advice on literature in the field.

Non-book material: vegetarian candles   gifts   herb teas   bags   badges   massage slippers   charts
Services: mail order   special order
Catalogue: selected list
Publications: The centre publishes booklets on health and nutrition

JUDAICA AND HEBRAICA

Jewish Chronicle Bookshop   (Chancery Lane)

25 Furnival Street EC4
405-9252

M–F 9:30–5:00

books for the younger reader   culture   ethics   history   holidays   Israel   Jewish legends   lifestyle   music   mysticism   reference   Talmudic studies   Torah

This bookroom, off the foyer of the *Jewish Chronicle* building, carries a well-chosen range of new books (mostly in English) on Judaism and Israel.

Services: mail order for books they distribute or publish
Catalogue: monthly updated book lists
Publications: Jewish Chronicle Publications publishes books about Jewish faith, culture, lifestyle, etc. They are distributors for: Behrman House (US); Jewish Publication Society of America; Jonathan David (US); Keter Publishing House (Israel); Ktav (US); SBS Publishing (US); Schochem Books

LONDON

The Museum of London Bookshop (Barbican)

150 London Wall EC2
600-3699

T–Sat 10:00–6:00 Sun 12:00–4:00

This is a gift shop with a small selection of books on London history, architecture and monuments.

Non-book material: cards gifts posters
Services: mail order special order

MENTAL HANDICAP

MENCAP Bookshop (Barbican)

Royal Society for Mentally Handicapped Children and Adults
123 Golden Lane EC1
253-9433

M–F 9:00–5:30

This bookshop provides a source of specialist literature on all aspects of mental handicap to parents and professional workers such as teachers, nurses and therapists. The shop is the sole UK distributor of SEFA (Social Education First Aid) Assessment and Teaching Materials and of Nicholls and Mott Individual Learning Programmes.

An RSMHC Library Reference Set, which has been developed by the shop, is a useful foundation on which to build a library in this field and the staff are very willing to advise in this area.

Also welcome are comments and suggestions from parents and teachers about books they have read which might be added to the RSMHC lists.

Non-book material: individual learning programmes
Services: mail order (cheques payable to RSMHC Ltd) special order
Catalogue: complete list of titles in stock SEFA catalogue Individual Learning Programmes Information Sheet Let's Go teaching aids
Publications: books on mental handicap are published by the NSMHC

NAUTICAL AND BOATING

Brown & Perring Ltd   (Old Street/Moorgate)

Redwing House
36-44 Tabernacle Street EC2
253-4517

M–F 9:00–5:15

Brown & Perring sells nautical charts, but a portion of their business is in the field of nautical books as well. The shipping industry (vs. the pleasure boating public) is their principle clientele, with the result that **Brown & Perring**'s stock is comprised of commercial and technical marine publications and their recent move means that all titles are readily available.

Nautical almanacs, Admiralty, IMCO, OCIMF, ICS and HMSO publications are constantly stocked. The shop claims to be able to get virtually all technical nautical publications in print, including restricted nautical publications when possible and appropriate, such as Admiralty charts.

An interesting service which **Brown & Perring** offers is the compilation of 'case histories' for old or antique nautical instruments.

Non-book material: nautical charts   ships' stationery   lights (indeed anything needed for a ship)
Services: mail order   special order

J. D. Potter   (Aldgate)

145 Minories EC3
709–9076

M–F 9:00–5:30

atlases   automation   construction   electronics   encyclopedias
fiction   history   knots and splices   mathematics   model boats
navigation   physics   pilotage   racing   radar   radio signals   sailing
sea stories   seamanship   signalling   voyages   yacht design

J. D. Potter specializes in new books on sailing, yachting and boat racing. The shop is an agent for Admiralty publications and, though most of the shop space is devoted to books, marine instruments and equipment are available as well. Marine law, engineering and insurance are especially well represented.

Services: mail order   special order (general subject areas as well)
Catalogue: complete catalogue annually   specialized lists

PERFORMING ARTS

Divertissement   (Angel)

18 Arlington Way EC1
837-9758

Appointment advisable (or via Reads, Charing Cross Road)

art   ballet   collecting   decorative arts   film   literature   memoirs
music   opera   plays   stage history

A few doors down from the Sadlers Wells Theatre is **Divertissement**, a second-hand bookshop specializing in books about the performing arts, especially dance. Theatre ephemera, playbills, programmes, a large selection of 78 r.p.m. records and posters are also available.

Non-book material: see above
Services: mail order   special order
Catalogue: specialized lists

RELIGIOUS

The Bible Society Bookshop   (Mansion House)

146 Queen Victoria Street EC4
248-4751

M–F 9:00–5:00

Located in one room in Bible House, the shop carries English and foreign language bibles and bible related literature. It has a sizable section of books and pamphlets designed for children.

Non-book material: posters   cards   gifts
Services: mail order   special order
Catalogue: complete list annually
Publications: The Bible Society publishes the *Good News Bible*

Christian Literature Crusade (St Paul's)

St Paul's Shopping Centre
Cathedral Place EC4
248-5528/6274

T–F 9:30–5:30   Sat 9:30–5:00

ground floor:

archaeology and atlases   Banner of Truth   bible study   bibles
biography   Christian home   Christian living   church growth
church history   commentaries   concordances   courtship and marriage   daily readings   evangelism   Greek and Hebrew   healing
missionary   Old and New Testaments   prayer   prophecy   renewal
sermon aids   theology   tracts

basement:

bible stories   biography   children's books   children's talks   missionary   object lessons and games   prayer books   teaching aids   teenagers' books

Appropriately located next to St Paul's Cathedral, the **Christian
Literature Crusade** bookshop is a large shop selling new books on all
aspects of Christianity, from religion in daily life to academic texts on
theology and comparative religion. The downstairs of the shop is
devoted largely to children's books and teaching aids. Also available
is a wide range of journals on Christianity and evangelism.

Non-book material: cards   cassettes   posters   records
Services: mail order   special order (in field of Christian books)
Publications: the shop does joint publications with Hodder and
Kingsway publishers

Protestant Truth Society (Blackfriars)

184 Fleet Street EC4
405-4960

M-F 9:00–5:30

Banner of Truth   bibles   biography   children's books   church
history   commentaries   contemporary church   daily readings   death
and life   Evangelical Press   Holy Spirit   Lakeland Series   Old and
New Testaments   PTS publications   Pickering and Inglis

preaching   religion and society   sects and other religions   US publications

PTS is a bookshop selling new books on all aspects of the Christian faith.

Non-book material: cards   stationery
Services: mail order   special order

TRAVEL GUIDES

Geographia   (Blackfriars)

63 Fleet Street EC4
353-2701

M–F 9:00–5:25

Travel guides for travel budgets of all sizes together with maps for practically every area of the world are **Geographia**'s speciality.

Non-book material: maps
Services: mail order
Catalogue: Geographia publications
Publications: Geographia publish maps and travel guides

LONDON EC
Second-hand Bookshops

The Clarke-Hall Bookshop   (Blackfriars)

Bride Court EC4
353-4116

M–F 10:30–6:30

anthropology   architecture   astronomy   biography   crafts   economics   fiction   health   history   illustrated books   Samuel Johnson   literature and letters   local history   military history   poetry   politics   psychology   religion   sciences   sociology   transport   travel

This is a general second-hand and antiquarian shop which is usually bustling at lunch-time, the attraction being shelves of review copies of new titles and second-hand books. The specialities of the shop, however, are late 19th century illustrated books – children's, art, natural history, etc. – the work of Samuel Johnson, his contemporary writers and his circle of friends as well as modern works. A few doors down the court is the Clarke-Hall Print Shop specializing in 19th-century topographical prints, cartoons and Victorian ephemera.

Non-book material: see above
Services: mail order   search service in all fields
Catalogue: Johnson illustrated books

Leather Lane Book Centre (Farringdon)

69 Leather Lane EC1
405-1270

M–F 9:30–5:30

antiques   art   children's books   classics   cookery   fiction   horror music   natural history   photography   science fiction   sports/games transport   travel guides

Most books here are remaindered and therefore sell at reduced prices. There are, however some new paperback titles, including sections on authors such as Tolkien, Steinbeck, and J. Herbert.

Services: mail order

LONDON EC
Antiquarian Bookshops

J. Ash   (Bank)

25 Royal Exchange EC2
(Threadneedle Street)
626-2665

M–F 10:00–5:30

art classics fiction history illustrated books literature modern
first editions natural history poetry sports topography (London)

Located opposite the Bank of England, the shop's stock reflects the
interests of the professional-class, 'local' population of bankers,
stockbrokers and lawyers. The rather small premises hold a good
amount of literature, mainly from 1800 to modern first editions, world
history and London topography, among other subjects.

Non-book material: engravings   maps   prints
Services: mail order   search service   framing service
Catalogue: modern first editions listed annually

EAST LONDON
General Bookshops

Barker and Howard Limited   (Shadwell)

102–310 Watney Street E1
790-5081

M–F 9:00–5:00   Sat 9:30–12:30

antiques biography children's books classics cookery crafts
DIY fiction gardening health humour illustrated books literature natural history philosophy photography reference religion
romance science fiction travel guide war

Established in 1829 as a newsagents and library supplier, **Barker and Howard** have recently opened a general bookshop to fill a need for such a shop in this area. With a stock carrying both hardbacks and paperbacks, and with a particularly good children's section, it is a welcome addition to the firm's activities.

Non-book material: see above
Services: mail order   special order

Centerprise
(Dalston Junction—British Rail)

136 Kingsland High Street E8
254-9632

T–W 10:30–5:30   Th 10:30–2:00   F 10:30–5:30   Sat 10:30–5:30

Africa   biography   black history and culture   British politics
children's books   cookery   crafts   crime   DIY   environment
Europe   feminism   fiction   film   gardening   health and sex   history   hobbies   horror   humour   Ireland   literacy   literature   local interest (biography, fiction, history, photography, pottery, politics)   music   mysticism   occult   poetry   politics   resources   social sciences   sports   thrillers   travel guides

The **Centerprise** bookshop is one of London's best examples of how books can form the nucleus of a community centre. Local shoppers, school kids and workers usually fill the shop, showing genuine interest in the books, journals and activities of the centre – so **Centerprise** is doing something right. Many of the **Centerprise** titles are politically oriented toward local politics, black, feminist and minority rights, and labour issues. The selection of children's books incorporates multiracial perspectives alongside classic fairy tales and fiction. Sections on Ireland, black America and the West Indies reflect the community's interest in political and social questions beyond the perimeters of London. Local history, fiction and poetry by authors from East London, and illustrated books about the area, comprise the section of 'local interest' titles – many of which are published by **Centerprise**.

Meeting rooms available for use by the community, a writers' workshop, a youth centre and the Hackney Reading Centre are also based at **Centerprise**, and a snack and coffee bar next to the bookshop, which also acts as an advice centre.

Non-book material: badges   cards   posters
Services: mail order (**Centerprise** publications only)   special order   supplies schools, colleges etc.
Catalogue: Centerprise publications
Publications: books of local writers' works, history, adult literacy schemes and issues of local interest are published by **Centerprise**

Fanfare Bookcentre   (Walthamstow Central)

2 Chingford Road E17
527-4296

M–F 9:30–5:30   Sat 10:00–5:00

accounting   automotive engineering   bibles   biology   building business   chemistry   children's books   classics   computing   cookery   crafts   current affairs   economics   electronics   fiction   gardening   geography   health and child care   history   humour   law mathematics   music   natural history   nursing   Pelican, Penguin physics   plays   poetry   politics   reference   science fiction   sociology   sports   technical   travel guides

General fiction and non-fiction, children's books and student text books are the three general areas in which **Fanfare** stocks books. Recently it has developed an extensive section on computing. This retail shop exists because of the success of their college bookstalls, but on Chingford Road there is an entire room (be it however small) devoted to a range of children's books, while the front of the shop holds general titles.

Non-book material: stationery   computers
Services: special order

Gallery Book Store
(Hackney Central—British Rail)

25 Lower Clapton Road E5
986-3753   985-6955

M 11:00–1:00   T–Sat 11:00–6:00

New, remaindered and second-hand books form a small part of the offerings of this store which is, in its most important function, an art gallery for the community of East London. Despite small premises, the shop and gallery reflect the owner's friendliness, energy and cultural interests. Books can be found at the front of the shop, including titles on popular fiction, science fiction, local history and authors, poetry and biography. Old theatre programmes are a speciality of the shop, and books about the theatre will become more prominent in the future.

At the rear of the shop is a small gallery, with frequently changing and unusual exhibitions. The Association of Little Presses was showing the work of small presses from all over the UK when I stopped by. The work of mental health patients may be the subject of the next show and hopes for the future include exhibits of multi-media work. The gallery is often used for poetry readings in the evenings.

Amid all this are selected paintings, illustrations and sculptures for sale, but nothing is priced over £100. Artists interested in exhibiting their work should contact the shop.

Non-book material: see above
Services: mail order (poetry and theatre programmes only)
Catalogue: poetry list   theatre programmes list

Paperbacks Centre
(Upton Park)

389 Green Street E17
470-1388

M–Th 9:00–6:00   F 9:00–6:30   Sat 9:00–6:00

art biography children's books classics cookery crime and thrillers economics fiction health history labour and unions Lenin literature Marx music Pelican, Penguin philosophy politics reference science fiction sexual politics sports and games travel guides

This is one of three **Paperback Centres** carrying a general range of new books, but with particular emphasis on books about politics, the labour movement, unions and individual rights. Located in a working-class area the shop stocks titles which are relevant to the lives of those in the neighbourhood, but it also caters to the interests of football supporters who flock to nearby Upton Park during the season. Football programmes are sold in the shop and they hold book signing sessions with personalities like Trevor Brooking.

Non-book material: calendars
Services: mail order   special order
Publications: New Park Publications publishes books on political issues, and produces a series of Newsline Reports which focus on current political 'hot spots' throughout the world.

W. H. Smith   (East Ham)

125 High Street North E6
552-4875/4876

M–Sat 9:00–5:30

W. H. Smith   (Leyton)

41 The Mall E15
534-5955

M–Sat 9:00–5:30

Richard Tudor   (Highams Park—British Rail)

135 Station Road E4
524-5518

M–W 9:30–5:00   Th 9:30–1:00   F–Sat 10:00–5:00

adventure fiction   biography   children's books   cookery   fiction
games   gardening   health   history   humour   language teaching
literature   natural history   pets   reference

This is a very small general bookshop which also doubles as a picture gallery. Most of the books are paperbacks, although hard-cover illustrated books are available.

Non-book material: paintings   wrapping-paper
Services: special order   photocopying and litho printing

Thap Community Bookshop (Whitechapel)

178 Whitechapel Road E1
247-0216

T–F 9:30–6:00   Sat 9:30–5:00

alternative technology   anarchy   anthropology   bicycling   biography   children's books   cookery   economics   education   fantasy   fiction   gardening   health and medicine   history   housing   humour   Ireland   language teaching   local interest (biography, fiction, history, photography, plays, poetry)   Marx/Russian history   nuclear power   poetry   politics   popular music   prison and crime   reference   rural Britain   science fiction   sexual politics   sociology   travel guides

THAP (Tower Hamlets Arts Project) **Community Bookshop** is one of two of the most exciting bookshops and community centres in London (the other is Centerprise). Each title in the shop is obviously chosen for its relevance to the East London community (with an emphasis on the arts and writing) from multiracial children's readers to books on realistic alternative technologies to urban gardening and contemporary literature from the Third World as well as the West. The books in the section 'local interest' feature photographic histories of East London, the poetry of local writers, fiction about East London (often by local authors) and books on race relations and local politics. All in all, **THAP** books are not just a mishmash of alternative literature and radical politics, but well chosen titles for a diverse audience.

The **THAP** has another dimension which includes aid for local authors and artists, helping them to work and be published, exhibited and staged. Workshops at the centre include writing, theatre, poetry and photography, as well as the children's workshop which has now split into teams of four, each making a super 8mm film. Printing facilities are open at the **THAP Bookshop**, consisting of a litho machine and professional advice on artwork, layout and paste-up.

'Controlled Attack' is another **THAP** group of writer/performers involved with street theatre – in short, the **THAP**s activities are wide-ranging, creative and distinctly community oriented.

Non-book material: prints and original work by local artists and illustrators
Services: mail order   special order
Publications: THAP Publishing publishes poetry by local writers, as well as an anthology of those in the TH Worker Writers Group

The Whole Thing   (Stratford)

53 West Ham Lane E15
534-6539

M 9:30–5:30   T 9:30–1:00   W–F 9:30–5:30   Sat 9:30–5:00

African fiction   alternative technology   Caribbean fiction   children's books   cookery   crafts   diet and nutrition   education   environment   fiction   gardening   health   history   Indian fiction   Ireland   labour and unions   literature   local interest   Marxism   nuclear energy   philosophy   poetry   politics   psychology   social issues   South American politics   women's issues

The Whole Thing is a community oriented co-operative which specializes in new books about political and social issues, but also has a good selection of black and Third World fiction. There are a variety of pamphlets and magazines on a range of subjects, from women to education to Ireland, and the tone of the stock as a whole is politically left-of-centre. A wholefood shop is also part of the co-op.

Non-book material: badges   cards   posters
Services: mail order (Page One Publications only)

97

EAST LONDON
Speciality Bookshops

EDUCATION

Newham Parents' Centre (Upton Park)

747 Barking Road E13
472-2000

M–W 9:30–5:30   Th 9:30–6:00   F 9:30–5:30   Sat 10:00–5:00

This is a small shop on the ground floor of the Newham Parents' Centre, specializing in educational books and play materials for children. Indeed, improving the quality of education for adults and children in the borough is the function of the centre. Five general subject areas characterize the shop's stock: developmental books for pre- and early readers; pleasure books for children; titles for adults including science fiction, thrillers, art books and philosophy; classic works of drama, poetry, literature and non-fiction; reference books from dictionaries to cookbooks.

The staff of the centre are involved in a variety of education activities, including community publishing, outreach schemes, play groups, career advising, and literacy programmes and the centre has a worker for young families.

Non-book material: games   play material
Services: mail order   special order
Publications: Parents' Centre Publications publishes information about community education and literacy issues and programmes

JUDAICA AND HEBRAICA

R. Golub & Son Ltd (Aldgate East)

27 Osborn Street E1
247-7430

M–Th 10:00–5:30   F 10:00–1:00   Sun 10:00–2:00

art biography culture and civilization economics Engels fiction
Hebraica Hebrew language teaching Hebrew texts history holidays Israel Judaica legends literature Marx memoirs music

philosophy politics prayer religion Talmudic studies Torah – tradition and commentaries travel guides war and Holocaust

R. Golub is London's largest bookshop specializing in Judaica and Hebraica. With new books on a variety of subjects, including Israeli politics, Jewish culture and faith, the Holocaust and the relevance of Marxism to the future of Israel, **R. Golub** has a refreshingly enlightened view of books which are relevant to their field of speciality. Traditional and classical Hebrew texts are available, as well as books on subjects relevant to orthodox and reformed Judaism.

Non-book material: religious requisites
Services: mail order special order home delivery of books to London areas: N, NW and E
Catalogue: comprehensive catalogue available

NAUTICAL AND BOATING

Kelvin Hughes Charts and Maritime Supplies

31 Nansell Street E1
481-8741

M–F 9:00–5:30

almanacs business cruising law medicine piloting racing reference radio single-handed sailing

Kelvin Hughes has a stock of new books on sailing and boating, some of which are geared to the pleasure-boating public or amateur boat-racing enthusiast, while other titles are in fields of interest to those in the shipping industry. The shop has a large range of Admiralty charts and publications, as well as nautical and marine supplies, including those necessary for yachting.

Non-book material: see above
Services: mail order special order

London Yacht Centre Ltd (Liverpool Street)

13 Artillery Lane E1
247-0521

M–F 9:00–5:30   Th (March–Sept.) 9:00–7:00

beginning yachting   cruising   design and construction   dinghies
meteorology   navigation   off-shore safety   power   racing   reference
ropework   sails   singlehanded sailing   voyages

In a corner upstairs in the **London Yacht Centre** are new books on
yachting and sailing. Admiralty charts for the channel are available,
and the shop can order charts for waterways in the rest of the world.
The rest of the shop is taken up with boating equipment and clothing.

Non-book material: charts   logs and maps for the British Isles and
Continent
Services: mail order   special order

POLITICAL

Freedom Bookshop (Whitechapel)

84b Whitechapel High Street E1 (Angel Alley)
247-9249

T–Sat 10:00–5:00   Th 10:00–8:00 (generally closed for lunch 1:00–2:00)

anarchy   communism   decentralization   ecology   education   feminism   individual rights   libertarianism   utopias

This small shop is difficult to find – off Whitechapel High Street on
Angel Alley on the second floor – and is really the administrative
offices of the anarchist press, Freedom Publishers. Individuals can,
however, buy books here. Books here are newly published titles on
anarchist concerns in a capitalist society.

Non-book material: badges   posters
Services: mail order   special order
Catalogue: complete list of new titles annually
Publications: Freedom publishes books and journals on the subject
of anarchy

RAILWAYS

Willen Limited (Leyton)

Howard House
Howard Road E11
556-7776

M–F 9:15–5:15

Specializing in the subjects of guns, railway history and hairdressing (!), **Willen** is actually a showroom and distributor for new titles in these fields, although individuals are welcome to drop in to look at and purchase books.

Services: mail order   special order
Catalogue: guns   railways   hairdressing – each listed annually

RELIGIOUS

All Things New (Upton Park)

12 Green Street E7
471-9857

T–Sat 9:00–6:00

bible stories   bibles   children's books   education   faith   Middle East   problem solving with faith   religion   social issues   South East Asia   spirituality   Third World and religion

The small stock of new books at this Christian bookshop in East London reflects the shop's interest in the areas of missionary and evangelistic issues. Books in the languages of Urdu, Gujarati, Hindi and Punjabi are also stocked, and the literature is interdenominational in nature. A counselling room is also on the premises and the staff seem to be more involved in missionary work than selling books.

Non-book material: cards   posters   stationery
Services: special order

UNIVERSITY BOOKSHOPS AND TEXT BOOKS

Dillons at Queen Mary College
(Mile End)

Mile End Road E1
980-2554

M–T 9:00–5:00   W 9:00–4:30   Th–F 9:00–5:00

astronomy biochemistry biology chemistry computers economics engineering English literature genetics geography history
mathematics microbiology Pelican/Penguin philosophy physics
plays politics sociology women zoology

This branch of **Dillons Bookshop** is located in the main building of
Queen Mary College and stocks student textbooks.

Non-book material: cards   posters   stationery
Services: special order

EAST LONDON
Second-hand Bookshops

Norman Lord
(Wood Street—British Rail)

Antique City Market
98 Wood Street E17

M–W 9:45–5:15   F–Sat 9:45–5:15

This shop, which is close to a large, free car-park, has a general stock
from the eighteenth century onwards, with prices ranging from 50
pence to £150 and more, and its antiquarian side is continuing to
grow. As well as having a large selection of literature, travel and
topography, natural history and gardening are covered and there is a
large section of biography, autobiography and the performing arts. A
number of association copies can usually be found here.

Non-book material: antiquarian maps and prints
Services: mail order

Paul Minet's Bookshop   (Tower Hill)

Ivory House
St Katharine's Dock E1
481-2842

M–F 8:00–6:00   Sun 9:00–6:00

art biography British Isles children's books cookery economics
fiction gardening history literature London maritime military
history natural history politics Scotland technical travel
accounts and guides

Paul Minet's second-hand shop (a branch of World of Books on
Sackville Street W1) is located in the newly refurbished St Katharine's Dock complex. With a view of the quiet yacht haven, this small
shop has exposed brick walls, a flag stone floor and classical music to
soothe the most harried sightseer. Biography, literature and maritime
history are the strongest sections in this general bookshop.

Services: see entry for World of Books, 30 Sackville Street, W1
Publications: Minet Reprints publishes reprints in specialized
fields (e.g. lace making)

NORTH LONDON
General Bookshops

The Angel Bookshop   (Angel)

102 Islington High Street N1
226-2904

M–Sat 9:30–6:00

antiques art biography children's books classics collecting
cookery drama fiction hardback fiction literature music natural history paperbacks photography poetry travel guides

Because the Camden Passage Antique Market is only a few steps from
the door of this general bookshop, **Angel** carries a large stock of books

103

about antiques and collecting. The shop has a nice children's section as well as cookery and wine. It also boasts very good coverage of new hardback fiction and non-fiction titles.

Non-book material: calendars   children's friezes   children's cassettes
Services: mail order   special order

Bookmarks (Finsbury Park)

265 Seven Sisters Road N4
802-6145/8773

M-T 10:00–6:00   W 10:00–7:00   Th–Sat 10:00–6:00

ground floor:

African fiction   anarchism   art   black studies   British history cookery   diet and health   economics   education   fascism   feminism feminist fiction   fiction   film   gardening   imperialism   Ireland literary criticism   literature   local presses   music   philosophy poetry   politics   racism   rights   science   science fiction   sexual politics   socialist theory   the State   theatre   travel

first floor:

Africa   Asia   children's books   economic history   Engels   Europe international issues   labour history   Latin America   Lenin   Marx media   Middle East   psychology   remainders   social sciences   trade unions   Trotsky   USA   USSR

second-hand – general, including:

fiction   politics   social science   general non-fiction

Bookmarks is one of the few alternative bookshops to make aggressive use of means other than a shop premises to sell books and disseminate information. The shops runs a quarterly book club – Bookmarx – which offers the best of new socialist books at low prices delivered to your door. Also affiliated with the shop is the Trade Union Bookservice, whose aim is to make new books, booklets and pamphlets on trade union issues and history available to trade unionists and others interested in the movement, outside the major cities.
  Bookmarks is affiliated to the Socialist Workers Party and has set up (at Seven Sisters Road) a publications and agitprop section of the

party called Socialists Unlimited, which organizes the production and distribution of pamphlets, books, posters and recordings. These items are listed with **Bookmarks** publications and SWP publications in a regular catalogue.

Finally, **Bookmarks** organizes an annual Socialist Bookfair, held in Camden Town, at which UK, French, Irish, German and Dutch socialist publishers exhibit their wares.

The shop itself is a specialist bookshop with two floors of varied stock and obvious strengths in their areas of labour relations and trade unionism. They also carry a large number of journals, magazines and newspapers.

Non-book material: cards   badges   posters
Services: mail order   special order
Catalogue: Bookmarks, SWP and SU publications   specialized lists (e.g. feminism)   Bookmarx book club   Trade Union Bookservice
Publications: see above

Canonbury Bookshop   (Highbury and Islington)

(Islington Books Ltd)
268 Upper Street N1
226-3475

M–Sat 9:00–6:00
(Art Dept: closed Thurs afternoon)

ground floor: general

antiques   classics   cookery   dance   fiction   film   gardening   health   history   humour   language teaching   literature   local history   music   natural history   photography   poetry   pregnancy and child care   psychology   reference   theatre   thrillers   transport   travel guides

basement: children's books

classics   fairy tales   fiction   Ladybird   non-fiction   novels   nursery rhymes   poetry   Puffin   transport

2 doors down: art

antiques   applied art   collecting   dance   fine art   history   music   photography

The **Canonbury Bookshop** is a general bookseller with two areas of specialization – children's books and art. Two doors down at No. 271 are art books, while downstairs in the main shop you will find a range of children's books, passing on the stairs a marvellous mural. The shop offers facilities to keep children occupied while mums are browsing. The shop also specializes in local history (Islington, Highbury and Highgate) and carries a large selection of general fiction and non-fiction.

Non-book material: artists' materials   cards of local scenes games   stationery   children's wooden toys and jigsaws   party gifts
Services: mail order   special order
Publications: Islington Books Ltd has published one title about Islington and greeting cards of local scenes

Crouch End Bookshop (Highgate)

60 Crouch End Hill N8
348-8966

M–F 9:00–6:00   Sat 9:30–6:00

second-hand:

arts   biography   children's books   fiction   literary criticism   literature   military history   natural history   poetry   theatre   travel   UK guides

new:

anthropology   archaeology   art   astronomy   bibles   child care   children's books   classics   cookery   Corgi, Pan, Penguin   crafts   crime   drama   fiction   film   history   literature   mathematics   music   philosophy   poetry   politics   psychology   reference   science fiction   sexual politics   travel guides

With a general selection of new and second-hand books, the **Crouch End Bookshop** has quite a good section on sexual politics and alternative political literature, and also carries a range of feminist, gay and leftist political magazines and newspapers.

Non-book material: a bit of ephemera
Services: mail order   special order   wants lists accepted

Faculty Books

98 Ballards Lane NW3
346-0145

M–Sat 9:30–5:30

antiques   art   astrology   biography   children's books   classics
cookery   drawing and painting   economics   feminism   fiction
games and crafts   gardening   health and child care   history
humour   literature   literary criticism   mathematics   military history   music   mysticism   natural history   occult   Penguin   philosophy   plays   poetry   psychology   reference   sociology   sports
theatre   travel guides   young adults

This general bookshop is one large, airy room with particularly good
sections of poetry, literary criticism and children's books. For the first
few weeks after publication, newly released titles are displayed
separately.

Services: mail order   special order
Note: There are 2 branches of **Faculty Books** at:
Middlesex Polytechnic, The Burroughs NW4
202-3593
M–W 10:00–4:00
and All Saints, Tottenham
801-9894
M–F 11:00–5:00
Both shops carry academic textbooks

Fagin's Bookshop

62 Chase Side N14
882-5690

M–F 9:30–5:30   Sat 9:00–5:30

art   biography   children's books   classics   cookery   crafts   drama
economics   education   fiction   film   gardening   health   history
literary criticism   literature   music   natural history   Penguin   philosophy   photography   plays   poetry   politics   psychology   reference   religion   revision aids for students   science fiction   sociology
transport   travel guides

Fagin's is a medium size general bookshop with current hardcover and paperback titles. Contemporary fiction and children's books form the largest sections of the stock, and the shop carries a few A-level student textbooks among the selection of non-fiction.

Non-book material: cards
Services: special order

Highgate Bookshop   (Highgate)

9 Highgate High Street N6
340-5625

M–Sat 9:30–5:30

art biography children's books classics cookery economics
education fiction history illustrated books literature music
mysteries natural history Penguin philosophy poetry politics
psychology reference sexual politics sociology travel guides
women

As one might expect in well-heeled Highgate, this general bookshop is very complete and well-stocked, with good sections of literature, fiction and children's books, and coverage of the social sciences. There are no second-hand or remaindered books, nor magazines.

Services: mail order special order

Muswell Hill Bookshop   (East Finchley/Highgate)

72 Fortis Green Road N10
444-7588

M–Th 9:30–5:45 F 9:30–6:30 Sat 9:30–5:30

antiques art astronomy biography child care cosmology classics cookery crafts crime drama education fantasy fiction
films games and sports gardening health history literature
Marxism medicine music natural history non-fiction Penguin,
Picador, Pelican philosophy poetry politics psychology reference religion science fiction socialism theatre transport travel
guides women

Muswell Hill is fortunate to have such a well stocked general bookshop, with an especially large Penguin section, while having a tendency throughout the shop towards the leftist and alternative approaches to issues and literature.

Non-book material: bookmarks   cards   cassettes   records   (BBC only)   wrapping paper   maps   specialist left-wing magazines
Services: mail order   Post-a-Book   special order

W. H. Smith   (Highgate)
9 The Broadway N8
340-1928

M–Sat 9:00–5:30

W. H. Smith   (East Finchley and then bus)
766 High Road N12
445-2785

M–Sat 9:00–5:30

W. H. Smith   (Palmers Green/Southgate—British Rail)
5 Alderman's Hill N13
886-4743

M–Sat 9:00–5:30

W. H. Smith   (Silver Street–British Rail)
104 Fore Street N18
807-7637

M–Sat 9:00–5:30

W. H. Smith   (Wood Green)
110 High Road N22
889-0221

M–Sat 9:00–5:30

NORTH LONDON
Speciality Bookshops

AVIATION

The Aviation Bookshop   (Archway)

656 Holloway Road N19
272-3630

M–Sat 9:30–5:30

aerodynamics aeronautics air battles aircraft markings construction DIY flight history and development of aircraft Iron Curtain maritime aircraft military model aircraft reference rockets
space technical

The shop's name is a dead giveaway, as new (about 80% of the stock)
and second-hand books about aviation and aircraft are the only books
here. I was told that if there's a book published on aviation the shop
has it and if this claim won't actually fly, they do carry the majority of
English and American aviation titles as well as titles in German,
French, Italian and Japanese (in which the photographs are said to
be most popular).

  A wide range of aviation magazines and journals are sold and back
issues are often available.

Non-book material: photographs posters slides aeromodellers'
plans
Services: mail order special order search service in field
Catalogue: complete annual catalogue

W. E. Hersant Ltd   (Highgate)
(The Chomley Bookshop)

228 Archway Road N6
340-3869

M–W F 9:30–1:00 2:00–5:30 Sat 9:30–1:00 2:00–5:00

speciality:

aviation military naval

general:

atlases   children's books   cookery   dictionaries   literature   Penguin

The bulk of **The Chomley Bookshop**'s stock is new and second-hand books on all historical aspects of aviation, the military and the world's navies. These books come from publishers throughout the world. In addition, the shop has magazines and journals specializing in these areas and some remaindered books.

What general books are in stock take up relatively little space in the shop and might be there to keep spouses and children occupied while the aficionados indulge their specialized interest.

Services: mail order   special order   search service
Catalogue: aviation   military   naval

BLACK STUDIES

New Beacon Bookshop   (Finsbury Park)

76 Stroud Green Road N4
272-4889

T–Sat 10:30–6:00

African fiction and non-fiction   Afro-American fiction and non-fiction   anthropology   Caribbean fiction and non-fiction   children's books   colonization   cookery   economics   education   history   individual rights   literary criticism   literature   music   philosophy   poetry   politics   science   social issues   sociology   Third World   women

New Beacon Bookshop specializes in current titles about and from Africa, the Caribbean and Afro-America (from Brazil to the US to Canada). Journals, magazines and newspapers on politics, social issues, women and education are available, and they have a large general stock of books as well. School texts for use by children of Caribbean, African, Bangladeshi and Pakistani origin are a peculiar speciality, and they carry a wide range of general children's books.

Non-book material: cards   posters
Services: mail order   special order (any book in print)
Catalogue: selected lists (e.g., children's books, African literature)
Publications: New Beacon Books Ltd publishes books on African politics, history, etc.

Operation Headstart Books and Crafts

25 West Green Road N15
800-2389

M–F 9:30–6:00   Sat 9:30–6:00

Africa   Afro-America   art   black studies   children's books   civil rights   cookery   history   law   literature   music   plays   poetry politics   religion   sociology

Operation Headstart specializes in new books on black studies in the UK and abroad. Titles on political and social issues are especially prominent, but the shop also has African, Caribbean and black American fiction.

Non-book material: cards   crafts   gifts
Services: mail order   special order

CHILDREN'S BOOKS

Children's Bookshop

29 Fortis Green Road N10
444-5500

M–F 9:15–5:45   Sat 9:15–5:15

astronomy   bible stories   biography   classics   dictionaries   encyclopedias   fairy tales   fiction   football   hobbies   horses   Ladybird music   nursery rhymes   poetry and verse   Puffin   puzzle books reading schemes   science fiction   songbooks   sports   transport young readers

Walking into this colourful shop is, in itself, enough to make one want to have kids. The shop is devoted to new books for children from infancy up to twelve, and their goal is to make reading enjoyable. The staff are happy to give advice on reading schemes, new books and books in specialized interest areas.

Non-book material: cassettes   cards   birthday cards
Services: mail order   special order

DECORATIVE BOOKS

Wade Galleries (Angel)

12b Charlton Place N1
226-3803

W Sat 10:00–5:00

Wade Galleries is an antique shop dealing with, among other things, books with fine bindings which are used for decorative purposes. If you need to fill a lovely, antique shelf, **Wade Galleries** can fix you up with the desired number of attractively spined volumes to create that studied air of erudition. The content of their books is less importance to the dealers than the condition and colour of the spine. I did notice, though, that the books were predominantly literary or historical, English and French, and from the 18th and 19th centuries.

Non-book material: antiques
Services: mail order (reluctantly)

ENERGY AND ENVIRONMENT

Sun Power (Finsbury Park)

83 Blackstock Road N4
226-1799

M 12:00–6:00   T–Sat 10:00–6:00

alternative energy sources   alternative medicine   astrology   children's books   cookery   crafts   diet and health   drugs   education   energy   environment   feminism   fiction   gardening   love and sex   mysticism   natural history   nuclear energy   occult   social issues   transport

Sun Power is a small community bookshop which specializes in books on energy (anti-nuke), the environment and related subjects.

Non-book material: crafts   recently opened wholefood section
Services: mail order   special order
Catalogue: selected annual list on environment and energy
Publications: the shop has published a pamphlet on nuclear waste transport

FEMINIST

Sisterwrite

190 Upper Street N1
226-9782

T–W F 10:00–6:00   Th 10:00–7:00   Sat 11:00–6:00

birth and child care   black and Asian women   children's books
education feminism fiction health history Jewish women les-
bianism literary criticism literature media myths, matriarchy
and religion non-Western women older women poetry politics
science fiction and fantasy science, technology and ecology sexuality and psychology violence against women women's liberation
women's rights working-class women young women

Sisterwrite is a feminist co-operative selling new books by and about
women, as the many notices in the shop make clear. Their literature
section is excellent as is the coverage of minority and non-Western
women. What feminist history has been written is available and I was
pleased by the inclusion of a section on myths, matriarchy and
religion (those often insidious oppressors). An excellent range of UK
and US feminist magazines, papers, booklets, pamphlets, etc. is also
available, and there is a small second-hand section of books on
feminism.

Non-book material: cards posters records jewellery
Services: mail order   special order   library order
Catalogue: 1982–83 catalogue comprising complete stock up to
mid-1981. Write for information

HISTORY

The History Bookshop

2 The Broadway, corner of Macdonald Rd &
Friern Barnet Road N11
368-8568

W–Sat 9:30–5:30

ground floor:

education history (aviation, economic, general, military, naval, UK)
London mountaineering philosophy politics Scotland transport travel Wales

basement:

architecture art building chess cinema detective fiction European history fiction gardening and landscapes illustrated books literary criticism literature modern first editions music natural history plays poetry social sciences theatre theology

One could do much worse than spend a morning or afternoon getting to this bookselling outpost in North London where the speciality is second-hand (and some antiquarian) history books. Military, local history and travel are the largest subject categories in the stock, but books on economic, political and social history are also on the shelves. Titles on transport, guides to the English counties and London can be found on the ground floor as well. (There are a few imported new titles in these areas.)

In the basement are books on a range of general subjects, and these shelves no doubt hold one or two collectors' items in each category. Of special interest is the collection of illustrated books, many of which are interesting examples of obscure printing, engraving and book-making techniques. As a group, the illustrated books provide a telling history of the evolution of printing and book-making from the mid-19th century.

The staff at **The History Bookshop** is as unusual as their stock. They seem less concerned with the money you spend than with your interest in and pleasure from the books on hand.

Non-book material: maps prints (antiquarian and later) antique china glass *objets d'art*
Services: mail order special order: any book in print from UK or US and Germany
Catalogue: a separate list for military history
Publications: The History Bookshop occasionally publishes German and English historical monographs

ISLAM

The Muslim Bookshop   (Finsbury Park)

233 Seven Sisters Road N4
272-5170 263-3071

M–F 9:30–5:30 Sat 10:00–6:00

children's books Christians economics faith government health and welfare history human rights Islam Middle East politics prayer prophets Quran reference religion social responsibility society sociology understanding Islam women worship

The Muslim Bookshop is part of Muslim Information Services, an organization which is very active in the Muslim community promoting the perpetuation of Islamic faith and culture. The bookshop is for Muslim and non-Muslim alike, with new books in English, Arabic and Urdu on all aspects of Islam, including interesting titles on current political issues and the culture of the Islamic world. There is a large section on the Quran, the text of which is also available on cassettes.

Muslim Information Services also operate from the premises and keep a wide variety of literature on the Middle East and Islam.

Non-book material: cards   cassettes   educational aids   posters   video-cassettes and films
Services: mail order   special order
Catalogue: selected list
Publications: MWH publishes books on Islam, from *The Dilemma of Muslim Psychologists* to the *IQ Islamic Quiz Book* and educational material

JUDAICA AND HEBRAICA

Hebrew Book & Gift Centre   (Stoke Newington—British Rail)

18 Cazenove Road N16
254-3963

M–Th 9:30–6:00   F 9:30–3:00   Sun 10:00–2:00

biography   cookery   culture   faith   folklore   Hebraica   history   holidays   Judaica   law   religion   Talmudic studies   Torah

The **Hebrew Book & Gift Centre** specializes in new books on Judaism, especially on religious heritage and the orthodox Jewish faith. Many of the religious books – Talmudic and Torah studies and commentaries – are in Hebrew, while the English language books are concerned with Jewish culture, history and religious life. Fiction by Jewish authors, or about Israel and Judaism, is not, however, a strong element in the shop's stock.

Non-book material: gifts   religious requisites
Services: special order

MARITIME

Anthony J. Simmonds Books

(Highgate)

214 Archway Road N6
341-2934

F–Sat 10:00–5:00

Simmonds sells new, second-hand and antiquarian books about the sea, though its focus is less oceanographic than on the literature of exploration, travel, trading, yachting, sailing and naval and maritime history. Although the business is primarily mail order, the shop is open to the public two days each week, at which time books from the catalogue can be seen and bought. New books come from publishers around the world, including a few private press publications from the USA. There are a limited number of remaindered books available as well.

Services: mail order   special order   search service
Catalogue: specialized lists   short lists bi-monthly

MODERN FIRST EDITIONS

Edna Whiteson

(Arnos Grove)

343 Bowes Road N11
361-1105

M-T Th Sat 10:00–5:00   F 10:00–6:00

art   biography   cookery   fiction   gardening   literary criticism modern first editions   music   natural history   plays   politics   transport   travel

Edna Whiteson is a second-hand bookseller specializing in modern first editions and 20th century literature. The selection of general fiction and non-fiction is strong as well, and the shop also carries a large selection of 19th-century prints and maps.

Non-book material: see above
Services: mail order   search service for modern first editions
Catalogue: modern first editions

POLITICAL

CND Bookshop

227 Seven Sisters Road N4
263-5673

T–F 10:00–6:00   Sat 10:00–4:00

This bookshop, set up by CND to cater for the increasing interest in nuclear disarmament, also helps to fund the campaign by selling a wide range of books on all aspects of the subject.

Non-book material: badges jewellery mugs postcards posters records stickers T-shirts
Services: mail order   special order
Catalogue: complete list of all anti-nuclear titles, with quarterly supplements
Publications: CND publishes various books and pamphlets as well as cards and posters

Housmans Bookshop

5 Caledonian Road N1
837-4473

M–F 10:00–6:00   Sat 10:00–5:00

ground floor:

child-birth and child rearing children's books cookery (vegetarian) drama feminism film and media gay/lesbian general fiction health Marxism philosophy poetry psychology radical politics reference books sub-culture/music

downstairs:

anarchism anti-militarism ecology education Gandhi Ireland nuclear issues pacifism peace education peace studies reduced books South Africa Third World

Housmans, a pacificist bookshop owned by *Peace News* Trustees, opened in 1945 and has continued to specialize in books related to non-violence, anti-militarism and the peace movement. To support this core of politically-oriented titles, the shop sells a limited range of general titles. The staff, however, are very much involved with the main stock of alternative literature, and are generous with their time and knowledge. (The shop, collectively run, is a member of the Federation of Radical Booksellers.)

Non-book material: a wide range of magazines, newspapers and pamphlets on radical subjects and concerns stationery postcards posters badges stickers records etc.
Services: mail order special order
Catalogue: regular lists are issued on such subjects as peace education, feminism, anti-militarism
Publications: Housmans publishes pamphlets on such topics as pacificism as well as the annual *Peace Diary*. It also acts as UK distributor for Black Rose Books, Bradford School of Peace Studies, Bewick, Exitstencil Press, Navijavan, Porter Sargent, Ralph Myles and Telos

New Era Books (Finsbury Park)

203 Seven Sisters Road N4
272-5894

M–W 10:00–6:00   Th 10:00–7:00   F–Sat 10:00–6:00

Africa anti-imperialism Asia children's books China class struggle classics of revolutionary writing communism Engels Ireland labour Lenin literature Mao Tse-Tung Marx Middle East political philosophy revolution socialism Stalin Third World women worker's rights

New Era Books is independently operated, but stocks new books in line with the politics and philosophy of the Revolutionary Communist League of Britain. The shop specializes in progressive literature from the Third World, and as they are the wholesalers for the Foreign Language Press in Peking, the shop has unique access to anything published in China. The bookshop also stocks an extensive selection of material of Irish interest. Also on sale is a range of booklets on politics and community issues, magazines and newspapers, many from Third World countries. Yet despite the overt political identity of **New Era**, the shop also serves the needs of the neighbourhood as a general bookseller.

Non-book material: cards T-shirts gifts from China crafts paints and brushes posters paper cuts fans

119

Services: mail order   special order
Catalogue: mail order and trade list for wholesalers

The Other Bookshop (Angel)

328 Upper Street N1
226-0571

M–T 10:00–6:00   W 12:00–7:00   Th–F 11:00–7:00   Sat 10:00–6:00

Africa black studies Eastern Europe economics ecology England, Scotland, Wales feminism fiction gay rights general fiction individual rights Ireland labour/trade union youth Marxism Middle East race relations revolution sexual politics socialism sociology South-East Asia Soviet Union theatre Trotsky Western Europe

As a Marxist shop, **The Other Bookshop** deals with political and social economics in all areas of the world, as well as individual and collective rights. The books are new, with special areas of concentration such as sexual politics, gay rights, black studies and literature about Ireland. Lots of pamphlets, booklets and magazines are available on all subjects, from all parts of the world.

Non-book material: badges calendars cards posters T-shirts
Services: mail order   special order
Catalogue: list of Socialist League publications
Publications: The Socialist League publishes pamphlets and journals

RAILWAYS

Model Railway (Manufacturing) Co. Ltd (King's Cross)

12 & 14 York Way N1
837-5551

M–Sat 9:30–5:30

This shop primarily sells model railway equipment but has a section of new books about railway history, stations, steam wagons, liveries and road transport.

Non-book material: model railway and transport detail pieces
Services: mail order, home and abroad   special order
Publications: MRMCO Ltd publishes books on wagons and liveries

RELIGIOUS

SCM Bookroom   (Dalston Junction–British Rail)

26–30 Tottenham Road N1
249-7262

The **SCM Bookroom** in its move from Bloomsbury continues to stock
an excellent range of books on Christianity, philosophy and theology,
among other topics. There are some bargain books, either slightly
damaged or remaindered, and a few recently out-of-print titles. Most
of the shop's business is done by mail order and the staff says that it
can get any theological title currently in print.

Services: mail order   special order
Catalogue: annual comprehensive list
Publications: SCM Press publishes standard works on religion and
political theology, as well as prayer and educational titles

SCIENCE FICTION

Fantasy Centre   (Highbury & Islington)

157 Holloway Road N1
607-9433

M–F 10:00–6:00   Sat 10:00–5:00

For collectors of post-war science fiction, fantasy and horror books,
Fantasy Centre is a treasure trove of (unbelievably) moderately
priced hardbacks, paperbacks and magazines. In one large room are
second-hand books and magazines and a small, but up-to-date
selection of new titles. Sci-fi fanatics will drool over the collectors'
section at the back of the shop which holds rare first editions (some of
which are signed) and vintage magazines.

   Standard 19th-century sci-fi writers are kept, but the majority of
the stock is post-1945.

Services: mail order   wants lists accepted
Catalogue: selected list every month

TEXT BOOKS

Austin Parish Ltd
(Archway)

162 Archway Road N6
340-2575

M–F 9:00–5:30

This is a full service, academic text bookshop supplying libraries, schools and other shops with books in all subject areas, but **Austin Parish** is also happy to help individual customers. While most of the shop's stock is geared to the United Kingdom's university-level education system, the staff are very good about tracking texts from all over the world (although they do not handle any out-of-print material).

Non-book material: Audio-visual teaching aids cards cassettes posters
Services: mail order special order on request the shop will complete subject lists of the available stock

NORTH LONDON
Second-hand Bookshops

Bonaventure
(Highgate)

259 Archway Road N6
341-2345

T–W 10:30–6:00 F 10:30–6:00 Sat 10:30–1:00

This general second-hand shop, which also keeps a number of antiquarian titles, covers such subjects as English literature, history and fiction but has an emphasis on travel around the world.

Non-book material: maps and prints
Services: mail order wants lists accepted

Camden Passage Antique Market   (Angel)

Camden Place N1

market days: W and Sat

Scattered around the arcades at Camden Passage are a number of
booksellers whose stands and stocks may change location from week
to week. Of particular note, though, is **Martin Stone** (usually found
early Saturday mornings along the Camden Passage pavement near
Carrier's restaurant) who specializes in collectors' science fiction and
detective fiction. Nearby is **Ian Sinclair** whose special interest is
second-hand contemporary poetry and the beat poets of the 1950s
and 60s.

Fisher & Sperr   (Highgate)

46 Highgate High Street N6
340-7244

M–Sat 10:00–5:30 (hours may vary)

basement:

economics politics sociology sports

ground floor:

art chess children's books classics economics fiction film
gardening geography history humour illustrated books law
literary biography, criticism, history literature London mountaineering music natural history occult ornithology Penguin &
Pelican philosophy poetry psychology topography travel guides

first floor:

art topography travel accounts

second floor:

Judaica medicine military history modern first editions

Fisher & Sperr is a large general second-hand and antiquarian shop,
neatly laid out on four floors, in a charming 17th century listed
building – one of the oldest in Highgate. The shop's stock is
particularly strong in the areas of literature and topography. It is a
fine shop to browse in and prices range from £1.00 up to thousands.

Non-book material: engravings and prints (including local scenes)
Services: mail order   search service   framing service
Catalogue: occasional special list
Publications: Fisher & Sperr have published a pamphlet about the
history of Highgate Village

Whetstone Books   (Totteridge/Arnos Grove)

368 Ackleigh Road North N20
368-8338   455-8667

T–W F 10:00–2:00   Sat 10:00–5:00

This small, full corner-shop puts many larger ones in central London
to shame. Certainly it makes a trip to this corner of London more
than worth its while. The stock is general but of a high quality, the
limited space meaning that the friendly, knowledgeable owner cannot
keep rubbish. All in good condition, the stock ranges from cookery,
history, topography and biography to fiction, foreign literature and
hobbies. Especially good are the sections of poetry and of Penguins
and Pelicans – many of these are the sought-after, out-of-print titles.
There is an interesting section of Everyman and the original World's
Classics series. All of the books are at prices considerably lower
(indeed, often as much as two-thirds) than one would pay in more
central London. Its lower rents mean that Totteridge could well
become a focus for the second-hand book trade if Mr Carty's excellent
shop is anything to go by.

Non-book material: a few prints and postcards
Services: mail order   occasional specialized lists   search service

NORTH LONDON
Antiquarian

G. W. Walford   (Highbury and Islington)

186 Upper Street N1
226-5682

M–F 9:30–5:00 (appointment sometimes advisable)

A general stock of fine, rare and antiquarian, rather than routine second-hand, books is kept here with some emphasis on economics, illustrated books, natural history, sciences and travel, as well as a number of sets of standard literary authors.

Services: mail order
Catalogue: frequent, general

NORTH WEST LONDON
General Bookshops

Belsize Bookshop   (Belsize Park)

193 Haverstock Hill NW3
794-4006

M–F 9:30–6:30   Sat 9:30–5:30

art astrology biography children's classics cookery crime drama essays fiction guides health history humour medical Pelicans poetry Picador reference science fiction social sciences sport travel

In a relatively small space the **Belsize Bookshop** manages to contain an excellent range of titles, a large proportion of which are in paperback; the owner, however, is extremely keen to promote new fiction and a good number of these are in recent hardback. Being close to the hospital means that a useful amount of medical books is stocked.

Non-book material: some literary magazines such as the *London Review of Books*   maps
Services: rapid special order   mail order

C. & L. Booksellers

13 Sentinel Square
Brent Street NW4
202-5301/6288

M–Sat 9:30–5:30

art   BBC language teaching   business   children's books   classics collecting   cookery   crafts   crime   dictionaries   economics   fiction film   gardening   health   literature   military history   natural history   Pelican, Penguin   sciences   sculpture   sports   technical textbooks: O and A level   transport   travel guides

C & L is a general bookshop selling new and remaindered books (from 50p) with a section of academic textbooks and study aids.

Non-book material: cassettes   records   stationery
Services: mail order   special order

Compendium

234 Camden High Street NW1
485-8944

M–W 10:00–6:00   Th 11:00–6:00   F–Sat 10:00–6:00

ground floor:

acupuncture   art   astronomy   Black and Third-World fiction   blues, country, folk, jazz   Bronze Age   civilizations (Egyptian, Mayan, North American)   Indian cookery   diet and nutrition   drama criticism   education   family therapy   feminism: anthropology, black women, fiction   film (criticism, theory, history)   Gestalt   health history   Indian philosophy and religion   literary criticism   magic

mysticism mythology natural history numerology occult Oriental philosophy and religion   plays   poetry   pregnancy and childbirth psychic literature psychology rock 'n' roll history religion
sexuality social work symbolism tarot transactional analysis
TV and media women's rights

basement:

architecture   building   communities   ecology and environment
economics gay literature husbandry health history linguistics
modern fiction   nuclear power   philosophy   politics   semiotics
semiology travel

Compendium is at the top of the list of London's alternative
bookshops, in terms of size, the depth of their stock and the range of
the subject areas they cover. The books in the major sections are
ordered by individual buyers who bring substantial knowledge to the
areas in which they specialize. Poetry, literature, feminism, philosophy and politics are particularly strong sections, and a wide range of
magazines, specialist journals, pamphlets, booklets, etc. are kept in
all major subject areas. The shop specializes in American paperback
books in all subject areas, but the shop does take seriously its role as
an alternative bookshop with, for example, sections on Mayan and
Native American civilizations.

   With **Compendium**'s growth in size and range has come a rise in
their public's expectations of what the shop is able to supply in
addition to books. One buyer told me that the telephone rings all day
with questions about workshops, meetings, marches and films which
the public *thinks* **Compendium** will know about; not realizing that
the shop doesn't function formally as an information centre.

Non-book material: postcards   political posters
Services: mail order   special order
Publications: Compendium has, in the past, produced English
Language editions of foreign texts and may publish in the future

English Continental Book Market Ltd   (Hendon Central)

57a Brent Street NW4
202-9248

M–F 9:00–5:30   Sat 9:00–12:00

academic textbooks   antiques   art   children's books   cookery
fiction gardening health and beauty literature reference sports
travel guides

127

Belying its name, this is a small general shop in the front of the offices of a book export company. Most of their business is mail order, but the shop is open to individual customers.

Services: mail order   special order

High Hill Bookshops Ltd (Hampstead)

6 Hampstead High Street NW3
435-2218

M–Sat 9:30–6:30

general:

antiques archaeology architecture art biography cinema classics cookery crafts Eastern philosophy and religion fiction gardening health history humour literature local history music natural history nostalgia occult philosophy photography plays poetry and verse politics reference science fiction Shakespeare TV and movie guides travel guides women

children's books:

arts Asterix bible stories board books chess classics Dr Seuss early learning early readers fiction games geography history hobbies Ladybird music myths natural history poetry pop-up books pre-school readers puzzles reference sports transport younger tales

High Hill in Hampstead has a wealth of current titles for adults and children. Reflecting the literary and artistic personality of the village are the constantly changing displays in the window of new biographies, letters, memoirs, fiction, essays, art books and literary criticism. One room of the shop is devoted to hardcover titles, one to paperback books and one to children's books in which there are colourful and informative titles for children of all ages and reading levels. **High Hill** is an extraordinary high street bookshop in the depth and range of its stock.

Services: mail order   special order

The Kilburn Bookshop (Kilburn Park)

8 Kilburn Bridge
Kilburn High Road NW6
328-7071

M–F 9:30–6:30   Sat 9:00–5:30

alternative religions   astrology   biography   black studies   business studies   children's books   classics   cookery   cosmology   crime drama   education   fantasy   feminism   fiction   gardening   health history   humour   Ireland   literature   mysticism   natural history occult   poetry   politics   psychology   reference   religion   science fiction   sports/games   thrillers

The Kilburn Bookshop is in a neighbourhood which will, I hope, help to support and form the shop's identity. The shop is relatively small but bright and open and it carries an interesting selection of titles. In addition to the general stock of new books, which includes a good section of sci-fi and fantasy books, are growing sections on feminism, Ireland, black culture and leftist politics, reflecting the ethnic and political mix of the area. A useful range of political, feminist and community magazines, journals and papers are sold as well.

Non-book material: cards   wrapping paper
Services: mail order   special order

Owl Bookshop (Kentish Town)

211 Kentish Town Road NW5
485-7793

M–Sat 9:30–6:00

art   biography   British history   children's books   classics   cookery current affairs   economics   education   feminism   fiction   gardening   health   literary criticism   literature   music   natural history philosophy   photography   plays   poetry   politics   psychology   reference   science fiction   sociology   thrillers   travel guides   women's literature   world history

This is a spacious, general bookshop, whose stock reflects a special interest in literature and children's books, with better than average

129

holdings in the arts and social sciences. The **Owl Bookshop** is one of the better, medium-size general shops that I've found and is far stronger on academic books than most shops of this size.

Services: mail order   special order

Primrose Hill Books   (Chalk Farm)

134 Regents Park Road NW1
586-2022

M–Sat 10:00–6:00

art   automobiles   children's books   classics   cookery   fiction
gardening   literature   natural history   photography   plays   poetry
psychology   reference   social sciences   travel accounts

This general shop has an unusual combination of new, second-hand and antiquarian titles. The books are divided according to price and type; new books ('up-market' paperbacks and hardcover titles, children's books, art cookery, etc.) are in the front room, antiquarian (18th, 19th and 20th-century literature and travel accounts, primarily) are located in the back room of the shop and general second-hand books are located downstairs. With the recent closure of the neighbourhood's only other second-hand and antiquarian bookshop, **Primrose Hill Books** is trying hard to fill the void which resulted in the fields of second-hand and antiquarian bookselling. (It also keeps a stall in the Portobello Road on Saturdays.)

Services: mail order   special order   search service   book binding & repair service

Regent Bookshop   (Camden Town)

73 Parkway NW1
485-9822

M–Sat 9:00–6:30   Sun 12:00–5:00

adventure & crime   architecture   art   biography   Britain   children's books   classics   cookery   economics   education   fiction

film   health   history   literature   Penguin   philosophy   poetry
psychology   reference   science fiction   sciences   sociology   travel
guides

The **Regent Bookshop** is a straightforward, friendly neighbourhood
shop selling a good range of general paperback and hardcover titles.

Non-book material: cards   stationery   wrapping-paper
Services: mail order (infrequent)   special order

W. H. Smith   (Kilburn/Willesden Green)
82 Walm Lane NW2
459-0455

M–Sat 9:00–5:30

W. H. Smith   (Swiss Cottage)
Harben Parade
9 Finchley Road NW3
722-4441

M–Sat 9:00–5:30

W. H. Smith   (Hendon Central)
379 Hendon Way NW4
202-8420/8439

M–Sat 9:00–5:30

W. H. Smith   (Brent Cross)
Brent Cross Shopping Centre NW4
202-4226

M–F 10:00–8:00   Sat 9:00–6:00

131

W. H. Smith (Kilburn Park)

113 Kilburn High Road NW6
328-3111

M–Sat 9:00–5:30

W. H. Smith (Mill Hill)

29 The Broadway NW7
959-1316

M–Sat 9:00–5:30

W. H. Smith (Golders Green)

22 Temple Fortune Parade NW11
455-2273

M–Sat 9:00–5:30

Strathmore Book Shop (St John's Wood)

145 Park Road NW8
722-6166

M–F 8:30–5:30

children's books   classics   cookery   fiction   gardening   literature
Pelican, Penguin   poetry   reference   travel guides

Strathmore is a general bookshop selling, among other subjects, 'up-market' paperback fiction and literature (no doubt for the up-market neighbourhood), as well as a selection of children's books.

Services: mail order   special order

Swiss Cottage Books Ltd   (Swiss Cottage)

3 New College Parade
Finchley Road NW3
586-1692

M–Sat 9:30–6:00

ground floor:

art biography child care classics crime education fiction film
health literature music non-fiction Pelican, Penguin philosophy photography plays poetry politics psychology science
fiction sociology

lower floor:

children's books cookery crafts and DIY Far East history
hobbies humour literary criticism Middle East natural history
reference religion sport travel guides

This is a general bookshop with excellent psychology and sociology
sections, as well as a good range of literary criticism and children's
books.

Non-book material: calendars posters
Services: special order

Writers and Readers Bookshop   (Camden Town)

144 Camden High Street NW1
267-0511   485-3883

M–Sat 10:00–6:00

This bookshop below the offices of the enterprising **Writers and
Readers Publishing Co-operative** contains a wide range of titles
with a political emphasis, such publishers as The Women's Press,
Virago, Gay Men's Press and **Writers and Readers** itself being
prominent. It is especially notable for its cookery, art theory and
children's sections, making a pleasant, useful addition to the area's
bookshops.

Non-book material: 'Fotofolio' postcards
Services: special order mail order library and bookstall supply readings film shows

133

Publications: Writers and Readers is a publisher especially notable for its titles on art theory and its fiction (including some in translation).

Writer's Cramp   (Hampstead)

17 Flask Walk NW3
435-4741

M–Sat 9:30–6:00   Sun 11:00–6:00

astrology   classics   fiction and biography   feminist and Virago fiction   feminist literature   humour   local and London history meditation   mysticism   occult   poetry   self-realization   yoga

basement:

children's books   cookery (including vegetarian) and diet   home medicine   homeopathy   keep-fit   mother-and-child

This small bookshop has recently changed its emphasis from a general stock, while retaining a useful amount of books from fiction to local history. In such space it cannot of course compete with High Hill and other local shops. However, its new emphasis on such topics as home medicine and meditation, as well as general health from jogging to pregnancy gives the shop an aspect not matched anywhere in the area. The enthusiastic owner will supply any book not in stock extremely quickly form his wholesaler. The children's section, filling at least half of the basement, is especially useful.

Non-book material: cards   postcards
Services: special order   mail order

NORTH WEST LONDON
Speciality Bookshops

BUSINESS

The Business Bookshop   (Baker Street)

72 and 74 Park Row NW1
723-3902

M–F 9:00–5:30

accounting analytical techniques behavioural sciences education
finance law macro- and micro-economics management marketing organizational and work study Penguin personnel production reference statistics

This is a bookshop naturally specializing in books on business. There
are no remainders, second-hand or out-of-print books, but new titles
come from the UK, US, the Netherlands and France and cover the
expected range of practical and theoretical business subjects.

Non-book material: a bit of stationery
Services: mail order special order express delivery
Catalogue: monthly bulletins in business, technical, EEC, director-
ies and reference
Publications: Alan Armstrong Ltd produces reference material for
libraries and also owns this bookshop

CHESS

Game Advice   (Kentish Town)

1 Holmes Road NW5
485-2188

T–Th 9:30–2:00 3:00–5:30 F 9:30–2:00 3:00–7:00 Sat 9:30–5:30

baby and child care card games chess children's books cookery
education health hobbies individual rights poetry songs travel
guides

This is a toy and game shop as well as a bookshop. New, second-hand
and antiquarian books are available on three floors, and along the
staircases from one floor to the next.

Antiquarian and second-hand specialities are chess and cookery, but there are interesting children's story and picture books as well.

Non-book material: games and toys
Services: mail order   special order   search service in field

CHILDREN'S BOOKS

Hampstead Book Corner   (Edgware Road)

Alfie's Antique Market
Stands 111–113
13 Church Street NW8
724-2320

T–Sat 10:00–5:00

This is one of the few shops in London which specializes only in second-hand and antiquarian children's books. Children of all ages will find something of interest here – fairy tales, classics, accounts of voyages and exploration, or 19th-century illustrated stories. The majority of the stock is from the 19th and 20th centuries.

Services: mail order   search service in field
Catalogue: complete stock lists three to four times annually

EAST ASIA

East Asia Company   (Mornington Crescent)

103 Camden High Street NW1
388-5783

M–Sat 10:00–5:30

ground floor: English language

acupuncture   archaeology   art   ceramics   crafts   cookery   family structure   history   Imperial Chinese civilization   Japan   literature martial arts   philosophy   politics   religion   South-East Asia

basement: Chinese language books in above areas, also language teaching books and readers

East Asia has an extensive range of activities selling new, out-of-print and antiquarian books on East Asia and other countries, publishing both the East Asia Bibliography which contains detailed notes on new books about East Asia and language teaching books, as well as selling sophisticated acupuncture books and equipment.

Non-book material: acupuncture charts and equipment   cards   cassettes   crafts   gifts   prints   records   paintings   *objets d'art*
Services: mail order   special order   wants lists accepted
Catalogue: East Asia Bulletin   specialized lists
Publications: see above

FOLK TRADITIONS

The Folk Shop   (Camden Town)

Cecil Sharpe House
2 Regent's Park Road NW1
485-2206

M–Sat 9:30–5:30 also open on Sat evening and other selected evenings

festivals   folk crafts   folk customs   folk dancing   folk music   history   Ireland   Scotland   traditions   US folk traditions

Although this is only a small shop on the premises of the English Folk Dance and Song Society, there is a lot of information available about the history and practice of folklore, history, song and dancing in the UK and, to a lesser degree, in the USA. The books here are new; there are magazines about dancing and music, as well as song books and folk song records.

Non-book material: crafts   folk instruments   music   records
Services: mail order   special order in field
Catalogue: large annual list of 'folk' books and song records
Publications: The English Folk Dance and Song Society publishes books and records

GREECE

Kimon Bookshop (Mornington Crescent)

87–88 Plender Street NW1
387-8809

M–Sat 9:00–8:00

Kimon sells books about, and from, Greece, Cyprus and Turkey. A very friendly Greek couple run the shop and stock new (and a few second-hand) titles in ancient and modern Greek and English. All aspects of ancient and contemporary Greece are covered, including books on literature, drama, mythology, military history, politics and philosophy. The front of the shop is also a newsagent's counter selling Greek newspapers and magazines in addition to the regular UK fare.

Non-book material: crafts decorative items ceramics paintings
Services: mail order special order search service
Catalogue: infrequent specialized lists
Publications: **Kimon** has published a guide to London in Greek

ISLAM

Islamic Book Centre (Warren Street/Euston)

120 Drummond Street NW1
388-0710

M–Sat 10:00–6:00

art calligraphy history philosophy politics

On the premises formerly occupied by Hawthornden Books the **Islamic Book Centre** sells Islamic religious books primarily in the areas listed above, the first such shop in the centre of London.

Non-book material: Quranic cassettes rugs posters cards postcards
Services: mail order special order

JAPAN

OCS Bookshop   (Camden Town)

67 Parkway NW1
485-4201

T–F 10:00–6:00 Sat 9:00–6:00 Sun 10:00–6:00

OCS carries new books in Japanese about Japan and the Far East. Language teaching books are the only titles in English, but for those who can read Japanese the rest of the books cover every aspect of history, art, culture and politics in Japan. The shop imports all its books and is the distributor for the Japanese Government Printing Office.

Non-book material: cards
Services: mail order special order

JUDAICA AND HEBRAICA

J. Aisenthal   (Golders Green)

11 Ashborn Parade
Finchley Road NW1
455-0501

M–F 9:00–6:00

art biography children's books civilization cookery ethics faith Hebrew language teaching history holidays Israel Jewish authors literature music prayer books religious philosophy religious practice Talmudic studies Torah

Aisenthal is a bookshop selling new books on all aspects of Jewish culture, religion and politics. The shop's stock is generally pro-Zionist, but **Aisenthal** carries books for those interested in reformed as well as orthodox Judaism. About 50% of the books are in English, the rest in Hebrew.

Non-book material: religions requisites
Services: mail order special order

Jerusalem The Golden

146a Golders Green Road NW11
458-7011   455-4960

M–Th 9:30–6:00   F 9:30–2:30 – Summer 4:30   Sun 10:00–2:00

art biography children's books civilization cookery ethics Hebrew language teaching history holidays Israel Jewish authors literature politics prayer books religious philosophy religious practice Talmudic studies Torah

The majority of titles at this Jewish bookshop are in English and focus on subjects of interest and importance to the movement of Reformed Judaism. There are some religious and secular titles in Hebrew, and books are imported from the US and Israel.

Non-book material: cassettes records gift items religious requisites
Services: mail order special order

Menorah Print & Gift Centre/ Hebrew Booksellers

227 Golders Green Road NW11
458-8289

M–F 9:30–1:00   2:00–6:00   Sun 9:45–1:00

biography child raising commentary and analysis cookery culture and civilization ethics faith Hebrew language history holidays Jewish life literature music philosophy religion Torah

Few of the books here are in English, most are religious texts in Hebrew imported from the US and Israel. The emphasis in all subject areas is on orthodox Judaism and the preservation of the laws of the Torah.

Non-book material: religious requisites

LANGUAGE TEACHING

LCL Benedict Ltd   (Camden Town)

65 Camden Town NW1
267-3673   267-3247

M–F 9:30–6:00

Language teaching texts and courses are the specialities of **LCL Benedict**. Approximately 50% of their stock is devoted to books for teaching English as a foreign language, while the rest of the titles are on learning a wide variety of foreign languages including Serbo-Croatian, Vietnamese, Mandarin Chinese and Urdu. As with all shops specializing in this field, **LCL Benedict**'s books are usually sold in conjunction with audio-visual learning aids and are most useful to the home student.

Non-book material: audio-visual language teaching aids
Services: mail order   special order in field
Catalogue: monthly to subscribers

MEDITATION AND PSYCHOLOGY

Changes Bookshop   (Kilburn Park)

242 Belsize Road NW6
328-5161

T–F 10:00–6:00   Sat 10:00–5:00

astrology body-work therapy Buddhism family therapy Freud
groupwork holism Jung mythology non-clinical psychologies
psychoanalysis spiritual issues transactional analysis Zen

Brian Wade, who used to work at Compendium, has brought **Changes** to London from Bristol because of the strength of mail order interest from the capital. Mail order remains important for him, and he issues a two-monthly newssheet (£1 for 6 mailings) and occasional subject catalogues. The shop stocks second-hand books within its subject area and will look out for customers' out-of-print wants. It also offers a bookstall service to appropriate conventions. The friendly atmosphere doesn't change; there's free coffee, and a box of toys for the children.

141

Non-book material: meditation & psychological tapes, magazines
Services: mail order   special order
Catalogue: subject catalogues   two-monthly newssheet   bookstall

MILITARIA

Ken Trotman   (Hampstead)

2–6 Hampstead High Street NW3
794-3277

M–F 9:00–5:30   Sat 10:00–5:00

Until recently **Ken Trotman** was a mail order business, but the shop
is now open to the public during regular hours throughout the week.
New, second-hand and antiquarian books about military history are
the speciality of the shop. The antiquarian stock is continuing to grow
and subjects include armour, uniforms, weapons, tanks and artillery,
as well as general military history and campaign accounts.

Services: mail order   special order   search service in field
Catalogue: regular specialized lists of books on military history

POLITICAL

Bellman Bookshop   (Tufnell Park)

155 Fortress Road NW5
485-6698

M–Sat 10:00–5:00

Africa: economics, politics, society   Americas: economics, politics,
society   anthropology   Asia: economics, politics, society   British
history   children's books   classics   cookery   drama   Europe: economics, politics, society   fiction   folk traditions   Ireland and IRA
language teaching   Marxism and Lenin   myths   poetry   psychology   reference   social history   travel guides

This is the bookshop of the Communist party of Britain (M-L),
selling new books which are curiously divided between general
subjects and communist literature. I was treated to an extended
ideological harangue from the woman who was staffing the shop. In

spite of the staff's enthusiasm, the stock is scanty, though **Bellman** is one of the few places which has literature from the Communist Party of Ireland.

Non-book material: badges cards games posters
Services: mail order   special order
Catalogue: a listing of Party publications and related political titles
Publications: see above

PRIVATE PRESS PUBLICATIONS

Basilisk Press and Bookshop   (Chalk Farm)

32 Englands Lane NW3
722-2142

M–Sat 9:30–5:30

architecture art calligraphy children's books gardening Hawk Press Hippopotamus Press horticulture literature maritime natural history Northern House Permanent Press poetry and verse printing Taurus Press Thornhill Press Triton Press

This is the only shop in the world to deal exclusively with current private press publications. **Basilisk** carries books, booklets, leaflets and pamphlets, mostly of poetry and verse, literature, natural history or art, all of which are beautifully designed and printed. The above listing is only a smattering of the presses which are represented, most of which are from the USA.

The shop also exhibits and sells original wood cuts and engravings from the illustrated books which they stock, and since one speciality of the shop is natural history, there are often lovely floral and fauna prints.

Non-book material: original calligraphy cards hand-marbled paper
Services: mail order   special order
Catalogue: selected listing (fee)
Publications: Basilisk Press publishes in the fields of natural history, history of landscape and illustrated literature

RELIGIOUS

Friends Book Centre   (Euston)

Friends House
Euston Road NW1
387-3601   ext. 23

M–F 9:30–5:30   (Sats occasionally – ring for details)

alcoholism   children's books   Christianity   comparative religion
cookery   Eastern religions   elderly   faith   fiction   non-fiction   non-
violence and peace   Pelican and Penguin   Quaker faith   social issues
and responsibilities

The **Friends Book Centre** carries general literature on religion with,
predictably, a specific concentration on literature about the Quaker
faith. Ninety per cent of the books are new, although the Centre does
have second-hand and rare books on Quaker topics and religion.

Non-book material: cards   posters   maps   guides
Services: mail order   special order   search service for out-of-print
and rare Quaker titles
Catalogue: annual new title list of books on Quaker faith   second-
hand book list in process   list of Swarthmore lectures, including
out-of-print   Quaker poster lists
Publications: The Religious Society of Friends publishes a variety
of books in the field of religion and Quaker Faith

Methodist Church Overseas Division   (Baker Street)
Bookshop

25 Marylebone Road NW1
935-2541

M–F 9:00–5:00

bibles   children's books   China   commentaries   contemporary
issues   dictionaries   ethics   evangelism   faith   family   Far East
Middle East   missions and missionaries   political and social change
prayer   religion and Third World

This is a small shop with new books covering Christian and religious
subjects from evangelism and missionaries to the history of the high

church. The staff are friendly, helpful and respond quickly to mail order requests.

Non-book material: cards   cassettes   jewellery   posters   records   song books   jewellery
Services: mail order   special order
Publications: Cargate Press occasionally publishes books on religion

Mustard Seed   (Camden Town)

21 Kentish Town Road NW1
267-5646

M–Sat 10:00–7:00   (hours may vary; often open later)

bibles   children's books   C. S. Lewis   family   inspirational biography   pregnancy and child care   religion

This small shop sells new books about Christian-based alternatives to the conventional church. A community fellowship is run in conjunction with the shop, for those who are disaffected with the church and are looking for a locally based alternative group.

Non-book material: cards   embroidered butterflies   posters
Services: mail order   special order
Publications: Mustard Seed produces leaflets on Christian issues

SPCK Church Bookshop   (Great Portland Street)

Marylebone Road NW1
387-5282   second-hand dept. ext. 23

M–Th 9:00–5:30   F 9:00–5:00

new books:

bibles   children's books   Christian education   church history   commentaries   comparative religion   evangelism   Fontana, Hodder & Stoughton, Lion, Penguin   monuments and cathedrals   Old and New Testament   prayer   religious philosophy   theology   Third World

145

antiquarian and second-hand books:

apocrypha bible background Byzantine church history church
unity collections of authors commentaries comparative religion
essays French, German, Hebrew, Latin texts hymns and music
lectures Middle Ages missions moral and pastoral theology
patrology philosophy prayer, liturgy, worship psychology re-
formation religious biography religious denominations religious
poetry and literature sermons social order and the church spiritual life theology

The long list of categories in **SPCK**'s second-hand antiquarian
department is evidence of their extraordinary stock – to my mind, the
finest religious holdings in London.

In the new book section of the shop the scope of Christian
education material is particularly broad, geared to young learners as
well as adults, but a fine range of all recent Christian and religious
titles is sold here.

Non-book material: cards cassettes creche figures films post-
ers slides tapes
Services: mail order special order search service
Catalogue: new books listing only
Publications: Religious books are published under the imprints of
SPCK, Sheldon and Triangle; and the shop distributes Abingdon and
Seabury in the UK

RUDOLF STEINER

Rudolf Steiner Bookshop   (Baker Street)

35 Park Road NW1
723-4400

M–F 10:00–6:00 Sat 10:00–1:30 during school term

art art history children's books meditation occult Penguin
philosophy Rudolph Steiner

This small shop sells new books, primarily of and about Rudolf
Steiner's work, but with a selection of books on other general subject
areas as well. Athough run independently from the Rudolph Steiner
Bookshop on Museum Street, WC1, the two shops are affiliated
through the Anthroposophical Association and share the speciality of
Steiner's life and work. Journals here are connected to Steiner in some
way, and are mostly in German.

Non-book material: cosmetics elixirs paints postcards prints shampoos
Services: mail order   special order in any field
Publications: Rudolph Steiner Press

THEATRE HISTORY

Offstage Theatre Shop and Gallery

(Chalk Farm/Camden Town)

37 Chalk Farm Road NW1
485-4996

T–Sat 10:00–6:30   Sun 12:00–6:00

ballet and dance biography children's theatre cinema criticism music hall play texts puppet theatre reference stagecraft television theatre history

The ground floor of this recently-opened shop has new books covering all aspects of the performing arts, together with a second-hand department and a few antiquarian titles; upstairs is a gallery displaying a collection of theatre designs both by 19th- and early 20th-century designers. Outside exhibitions, talks and play-readings are also held.

Non-book material: cards magazines stage designs and prints theatre and cinema posters
Services: mail order   special order   wants lists accepted

NORTH WEST LONDON
Second-hand Bookshops

Book Bargains (for the Spastics Association)

(Camden Town)

73 Camden High Street NW1
no phone

M–F 9:30–5:30   Sat 9:00–5:00

art biography biology children's books cookery crafts fiction film literature natural history · politics sports travel guides

147

Book Bargains is a newly opened shop carrying only remaindered books, which means that the composition of the shop's stock varies almost weekly. The shop does, however, maintain a speciality in bargain price children's books, from young adults' fiction to toddlers' picture books, and gives special discounts on these books to schools.

The Corner Bookshop   (Chalk Farm)

Camden Lock
Chalk Farm Road NW1
no phone

Sat–Sun 10:00–6:00

Africa   art   astronomy   biography   cookery   fiction   gardening   health   heraldry   history   letters   literature   London   Middle East   music   natural history   topography   travel guides

This is a second-hand and antiquarian bookshop which is always packed with market browsers on Saturdays and Sundays. The stock is general, with illustrated books from this century and the last, travel guides, a bit of literature and a reasonably large section of books about London. Prints, book plates, engravings and water-colours of theatre scenes, landscapes, animals and people, are also plentiful and pleasant to leaf through.

Non-book material: see above
Services: mail order (through shop in Hertfordshire)

Eric & Joan Stevens Booksellers   (West Hampstead)

74 Fortune Green Road NW6
435-7545

Sat 10:00–6:00 and by appointment

anthologies   art   bibliography   biography   cinema   cookery   economics   feminist history   fiction   history   Israel   law and crime   literary criticism   literature   Middle East   modern first editions   music   natural history   photography   plays   poetry   psychology religion   sexual politics   theatre   thrillers   travelogues   women writers

What a shame that this shop is not open more hours during the week because in the relative desert north of central London this general bookshop is something of an oasis. There are two main rooms filled with second-hand books, a few remainders and review copies, and some antiquarian titles.

The shop specializes in literature, art, poetry and feminism, the latter being a solid section of literature by women or about sexual politics and feminist history – most unusual in a second-hand shop in London. The section of literary criticism is also good and there is a nice selection of modern first editions.

Non-book material: cards
Services: mail order   search service
Catalogue: five specialized catalogues yearly (e.g. feminism, literature, art, poetry)
Publications: Eric and Joan Stevens privately publish (indeed, they privately *print*) original poetry and contemporary writing

The Flask Bookshop (Hampstead)

6 Flask Walk NW3
435-2693

M–Sat 10:00–6:00

ground floor:

antiques   archaeology   architecture   art   collecting   drama fiction   gardening   history   literary biography   literary criticism literature   modern first editions   music   natural history   Penguin philosophy   poetry   porcelain   psychology   Shakespeare

basement:

Americana   architecture   art   education   history   politics and wars psychology   sculpture   sociology   stage history

This is my favourite Hampstead bookshop because, though there is the feeling of a 19th-century bookseller's pride in his stock, the shop's contents are far from stuffy. The general collection of second-hand books and a large number of review copies is marked by an excellent section of reduced-price art books, a small but select section of modern first editions and a literary criticism section which is substantial and up to date, not full of jumble sale cast-offs.

Because of the regularity with which the shop gets review copies, newly published fiction, biography and art, for example, can often be found here at reduced prices. The owner is also an author (he has written on collecting modern first editions, P. G. Wodehouse and Jerome) and the shop keeps a small Wodehouse section. The bias of the shop is toward the humanities, with a twist here and there, and the stock changes regularly.

Non-book material: Hampstead prints
Services: mail order

Gabriels Bookshop   (Willesden Green)

47 Walm Lane NW10
451-2047

M–F 10:00–6:30   Sat 9:30–6:00

accountancy biography children's books classics cookery crafts crime dance economics engineering fiction: English, French, Spanish film and TV history medicine plays romance science fiction sociology westerns

There is a strange mix of books in this shop, including second-hand text books in the sciences, new and second-hand romance, fiction and sci-fi in English and Spanish, a collection of second-hand film, TV, detective and romance magazines and a section of children's books.

Non-book material: games and puzzles
Services: mail order

George Greer Books   (Edgware Road)

87 and 95 Bell Street NW1
262-7661 and 724-0876

T–Sat 10:30–5:45

Africa art biography Christianity economics English classics fiction French and German texts gardening history hobbies literature local guides military history poetry politics reference witchcraft

These two shops, of which no. 87 has been recently modernized, are nicely ordered, with general, second-hand stock and a few remainders and review copies. All the books are in good condition and at reasonable prices.

Non-book material: engravings ephemera maps prints
Services: wants lists accepted

Lionel Halter   (Mill Hill Broadway—British Rail)

7 Hale Lane NW7
959-2936

M–F 9:00–5:30   Sun 10:30–1:00

annuals art biography boxing children's books cookery fiction film gardening history Judaica literature natural history reference religion theatre travel and topography

This shop, a little awkward to reach by London Transport, is close to a British Rail station. Its stock is general and its prices resonable, with more valuable books kept in a cupboard towards the back, both in hardback and paperback. As well as a useful, specialist section on boxing, it has a number of sets of encyclopaedias and standard authors, as well as transcripts of such topics as the Nuremberg Trials.

Non-book material: postcards magazines
Services: mail order photocopying and general printing
Catalogue: occasional lists on general and specialized topics

A. A. Miles   (Edgware Road)

105 Bell Street NW1
733-8455

M–Sat 10:30–6:00

This jumbled, nay chaotic, general second-hand bookshop is run by an ailing gentleman with an interest in industrial history, art and

151

architecture. Books can be found from 50p or so, at what is said to be Marylebone's second oldest bookshop.

Services: wants lists accepted

Phase One Books (Finchley Road)

1 Midland Crescent
Finchley Road NW3
435-4634

M–Sat 10:30–6:30

This is a small general second-hand shop whose moderately priced stock changes almost fortnightly. The owner buys one large collection of books, the contents of which may be fiction, natural history, science, travel or Czech cookery, to name only a few possible subject areas.

Services: mail order   search service

Richard Law Booksellers (Kilburn)

35 Cricklewood Broadway NW2
752-9494

M–Sat 7:30–5:00

business economics education fiction gardening geography
history mathematics medicine sciences sociology

This is a small, grubby, disorganized second-hand bookshop (there are also some new titles and remaindered books) with nothing noteworthy about the scanty stock, although most titles are in the fields of the social sciences and science. The owner is personally interested in 'utopias' and says he wants to sell books that make people happy, but I was happy to get out of the shop.

Services: mail order   special order

Stanley Smith and Keith Fawkes   (Hampstead)

1–3 Flask Walk NW3
435-0614

M–Sat 10:00–5:30

anthropology antiquities architecture art ballet biography children's books classics cookery crafts crime dictionaries and grammar drama essays exploration and travel fables fiction folklore gardening history interior design literature local history marine life modern first editions music: classical/contemporary natural history Penguin philosophy poetry and verse science fiction sociology stage history theology thrillers transport

Approximately 20% of the books here are antiquarian, the rest being second-hand in a wide range of subject areas. The shop is a good stop for browsers, it is relatively large, its shelves are well marked and the contents are nicely organized. Also, the flavour of old village Hampstead floats in from historic Flask Walk. Strong sections among the books are literature (French, German and Spanish in translation, as well as English) exploration and travel, art and biography.

Non-book material: occasionally engravings and prints
Services: mail order
Catalogue: antiquarian titles listed bi-annually

The Village Bookshop   (Belsize Park)

46 Belsize Lane NW3
794-3180

M–Sat 11:00–5:30

archaeology architecture art astronomy biography children's books crime detective fiction fiction food Germany history illustrated books Judaica literature: English, French, German military history modern first editions mountaineering music natural history philosophy photography poetry psychology sport theatre topography travel war women

There is a large general stock with noteworthy sections of Victorian illustrated and children's books, literature and modern first editions.

The two partners buy their stocks separately and one of the owners has a special interest in books on all aspects of Germany, both in German and English, and has filled a good half of a wall with titles on the subject.

Services: mail order

Walden Books (Chalk Farm)

38 Harmood Street NW1
267-8146

Th–Sun 10:30–6:30

aeronautics architecture astronomy biography children's books cookery economics education fiction film gardening humour languages literary criticism literature modern first editions music natural history Penguin philosophy poetry psychiatry psychology railways romantic fiction sciences sociology sports

Located on the ground floor of the owner's home, this general second-hand bookshop takes on the comfortable air of its context, and customers can browse through a large stock of paperbacks in a variety of subject areas. The books are bought quite selectively by the owner and the stock changes from week to week, with 19th- and 20th-century literature as the main area of interest.

Services: mail order   search service (antiquarian books as well)
Publications: the owner has photocopies of his own poetry, free of charge

Walm Lane Bookmart (Willesden Green)

62 Walm Lane NW10
no phome

M–T 10:30–6:00   W 10:30–7:00   Th 10:30–1:00   F 10:30–7:00
Sat 9:30–6:00

adventure classics crime detective fiction education fiction horror romance science fiction thrillers war westerns

154

This is a second-hand book exchange which gives 50% credit on books bought here and returned for exchange. The usual paperback range of science fiction, romance, war novels and westerns is augmented by a few text books, paperback literature and classics, and a bit of hardback fiction. The shop also has some remaindered books and occasionally gets review copies.

Services: wants lists accepted

NORTH WEST LONDON
Antiquarian Bookshops

Archive Bookstores   (Edgware Road)

83 Bell Street NW1
402-8212

M–Sat 10:00–6:00

dictionaries gardening history literature magic medicine military history music Penguin travel accounts witchcraft

This antiquarian and second-hand shop is run by a man who seems to know good books and also knows how to restore them well. A lovely hour's browse can easily be had here and I found the prices reasonable, the shop well ordered and the books and business well cared for. The specialities are historical and illustrated books, as well as books on music. The shop also runs a stall, during the weekends, at the Camden Lock Market, Chalk Farm Road, NW3.

Non-book material: maps   music
Services: mail order   search service   restoration of fine bindings

Bibliopola

Alfie's Antique Market
Stands 109–110
13 Church Street NW8
723-0429

T–Sat 10:30–5:30

ancient history   classics   cookery   English literature   history
limited editions   modern first editions   natural history   private
presses   travel accounts and guides

This nicely organized general antiquarian bookshop stocks books in
the noted categories, including 16th- and 17th-century Italian and
Latin texts and 19th-century illustrated books. The books are in good
condition and prices reflect their fine quality.

Services: mail order   search service
Catalogue: selected lists are planned

WEST LONDON
General Bookshops

Athena

The Trocadero, Coventry Street, W1

M–Sat 10:00a.m.–11:00p.m.   Sun 12:00–11:00

art   cookery   fiction   gardening   home decoration   sport   teach
yourself   travel guides

The Pentos Group, who own Dillons, have opened the **Athena** shop
in the Trocadero – the new tourist complex in Piccadilly. Obviously,
it caters for the tourist market: in its general stock, long opening hours
and planned design – a large, spacious shop, brightly-lit and air-
conditioned.

Non-book material: Athena poster and card gallery
Services: gift-wrapping

The Baker Street Bookshop   (Baker Street)

35 Baker Street W1
486-6959

M–F 9:30–5:30   Sat 10:00–1:00

antiques   archaeology   architecture   art   biography   buses and
trams   business and management   canals   child care   children's
books   cinema   classics   collecting   cookery   cosmology   crime
ecology   economics   education   fashion   feminism   fiction   gardening   health   history   humour   languages   literature   music and
stage   natural history   Penguin   philosophy   photography   plays
poetry   politics   psychology   railways   reference   religion   royal
family   science fiction   sciences   Sherlock Holmes   sociology   sport
and games   transport   travel

Owned by the Devon publishing group, David and Charles, **The
Baker Street Bookshop** is basically a general bookshop, but has
larger-than-usual sections on various modes of transport and their
histories. There is also a good sized record department in half of the
basement, which also contains the separate transport section.

Non-book material: calendars   cards   posters   records
Services: mail order   special order
Catalogue: David and Charles publications   Devon Book News
Publications: David and Charles is a general book publisher

Barker's of Kensington   (High Street Kensington)

63 Kensington High Street W8
937-5432

*M 9–00–5:30   T 9:30–5:30   W 9:00–5:30   Th 9:00–6:30
F–Sat 9:00–6:00*

biography   children's books   classics   cookery   crime   fiction   film
health   history   horror   literature   music   natural history   occult

157

recreation   reference   romance   science fiction and fantasy   travel guides

For a general department store, **Barker**'s has a large book section of current fiction and non-fiction. The hectic atmosphere of a busy department store, however, overflows into the book section, which makes a quiet hour's browse a near impossibility. Another problem is that the stock categories labelled in the shop are unreliable; books regularly appear under incongruous headings.

Non-book material: globes   maps
Services: mail order   special order

Booksmith
(High Street Kensington)

201 Kensington High Street W8
937-5002

M–Sat 9:30–8:00

art   astrology   biography   classics   fantasy   feminism   fiction history   humour   gardening   literature   natural history   reference romance   science fiction   travel guides

This is the largest of the **Booksmith** shops, with both new paperback titles, and a general range of (mostly hardcover) remaindered books. Current best-selling fiction, Penguins and Virago titles are among the full-price paperbacks. The range of subjects of the remaindered books changes weekly with new shipments of titles, but always a bargain can be found.

Catalogue: Bibliophile book club list

Buckinghams
(Piccadilly)

50 Piccadilly W1
734-1337

M–Sun 10:00–10:00pm

About a third of a general gift-shop (with stock ranging from deodorants to Jackson's tea-caddies) is given to books. These are

mainly paperbacks, with a few best-selling hardbacks, and are largely
thrillers, adventure stories and romance.

Bush Books   (Shepherd's Bush)

144 Shepherd's Bush Shopping Centre
Shepherd's Bush Green W12
749-7652

M–F 10:00–6:00   Sat 10:00–5:00

antiques and collecting architecture art biography children's
books cookery crime drama education environment feminism
fiction film gardening health and sex history humour languages literature music mysticism natural history philosophy
photography poetry politics psychology reference religion science fiction sport theatre travel

Bush Books stocks a general range of new books, including recent
best-sellers, a selection of books in the social sciences and a range of
children's books.

Non-book material: book and gift tags   cards   wrapping-paper
maps   some radical and literary magazines
Services: special order

Christopher Foss   (Baker Street)

120 Baker Street W1
935-9364

M–F 9:00–6:00   Sat 10:00–5:00

art astrology biography business child care children's books
classics cookery crafts crime and adventure economics education fiction film games health and medicine history humour
languages literature music natural history philosophy photography plays poetry psychology reference religion science
fiction sociology travel guides

159

For a small shop **Christopher Foss** has a surprisingly good range of subjects packed onto the shelves, together with a wide variety of postcards and greetings-cards.

Non-book material: stationery
Services: special order

Claude Gill Books (Bond Street)

10–12 James Street W1
no phone

M–W 9:30–6:00   Th 9:30–8:00   F–Sat 9:30–6:00

antiques art astrology beauty biography children's books cinema classics cookery crafts crime fiction gardening health humour literature music natural history non-fiction Penguin photography poetry reference science fiction sport TV/film transport travel guides

This branch of **Claude Gill** carries a general range of new titles, particularly paperbck fiction, but also has bargain tables of remaindered hardback books.

Non-book material: cards posters

Claude Gill Books (Tottenham Court Road)

19/23 Oxford Street W1
734-5340

M–Sat 9:30–8:00

antiques art biography children's books classics cookery crime fiction film gardening health history humour literature music natural history Penguin photography plays poetry references science fiction teach yourself transport travel guides

Along with a wide range of current fiction and non-fiction, this **Claude Gill** shop has a particularly good selection of poetry titles (the shop is run by a poet). About 12% of the stock is remaindered books, while the rest of the books are current general hardcover and paperback titles. Budget label records are also available.

Non-book material: cards   posters   records

Claude Gill Books. (Piccadilly Circus)

213 Piccadilly W1
no phone

M–Sat 9:30–8:00   Sun 11:00–7:00

ground floor:

biography classics crime fiction humour literature non-fiction
occult Pelican, Penguin science fiction teach yourself travel
guides

basement:

antiques art children's books cookery crafts DIY film gardening health music natural history photography plays poetry
sex sports and games transport

This **Claude Gill** branch has a broad range of new books, and in the spacious basement is a good number of remaindered books at bargain prices. Also available are budget label records.

Non-book material: cards   posters   records

Ealing Books (Ealing Broadway)

5 Central Buildings
The Broadway W5
579-3727

M–W 9:15–5:30   Th–F 9:15–6:00   Sat 9:15–5:30

antiques art biography child care children's books classics
cookery crafts crime economics fiction gardening health
history humour language teaching literary criticism literature
mathematics music mysteries photography plays poetry politics reference science fiction sciences travel guides

Located directly across from Ealing Broadway tube station, **Ealing Books** is a general bookseller stocking hardcover and paperback titles. The arts, literature and illustrated non-fiction are well represented, and there is also a section of text books in the sciences and humanities.

Non-book material: cards
Services: mail order   special order

Elgin Books (Ladbroke Grove)

6 Elgin Grove W11
229-2186

T–Sat 10:00–6:00

ground floor:

art   biography   classics   fiction   history   literature   poetry   politics   reference   travel guides

basement:

children's books   cinema   cookery   feminism   natural history   photography   science fiction   thrillers

Elgin Books is a distinctive looking bookshop just off the Portobello Road. On the ground floor, amid wall-to-wall carpeting and dark wood, is a fine selection of current hardcover and paperback fiction, literature and poetry with recent book reviews and news conveniently pinned up on a bulletin board on one wall. A spiral staircase at the front of the shop (though customers are asked to use the wider steps at the rear) winds down to a spacious basement full of children's books. Downstairs is a lovely table with chairs in which adults and kids can sit to read.

Services: mail order   special order

Hammick's Bookshop Ltd

(Hammersmith)

9 King's Mall W6
No phone available at press

M–Sat 9:00–5:30

A proposed new family bookshop, with all general interest subjects covered, full information was not available when going to press.

Non-book material: cards   wrapping-paper
Services: special order

Hatchards

(Piccadilly Circus)

187 Piccadilly W1
439-9921

M–F 9:00–5:30   Sat 9:00–1:00

ground floor:

antiques   art   astrology   astronomy   biography   business   cinema   cookery   energy   fiction   gardening   history   humour   language   literature   military   music   natural history   naval   occult   plays   poetry   politics   reference   sport and games   theatre   travel guides

first floor:

architecture   book binding   calligraphy   costumes   crafts   music: history and biography   pets   sailing   textiles   theatre

second floor:

children's books (classics, fiction, non-fiction, pictures, sciences)   classics   fine bindings   literature   plays   rare books   second-hand books

basement: paperbacks

biography   business   classics   cookery   crime   drama   fiction   history   humour   literature   music   nature and countryside   poetry   politics   psychology   science fiction   social sciences

Hatchards is one of London's largest general booksellers, with new and to a lesser extent, second-hand and antiquarian books in all

163

subject areas. Its recent expansion into the neighbouring premises has greatly increased the stock in some departments, especially the travel and paperbacks sections which are now a third larger. The children's section is also worthy of note. The staff throughout are helpful and knowledgeable.

Services: mail order   special order   search service
Catalogue: annual selected lists
Note: There is a smaller branch of **Hatchards** at Harvey Nichols department store in Knightsbridge SW1

G. Heywood Hill Ltd (Green Park)

10 Curzon Street W1
629-0647

M–F 9:00–5:30   Sat 9:00–12:00

antiques   architecture   art   biography   children's books   classics
cookery   crafts   design   fiction   graphics   history   humanities
jewellery   literature   music   natural history   philosophy   porcelain
pottery   sports and games   stage design   travel

Heywood Hill have a lovely combination of new, out-of-print and antiquarian books on the arts and humanities. The shop's holdings are particularly strong in fine art, 19th-century English literature, modern first editions and children's books (which take up most of the basement). The staff are knowledgeable, helpful and extremely industrious but the shop maintains an atmosphere from the era of the genteel 'gentlemanly booksellers'.

Non-book material: children's ephemera
Services: mail order   special order   search service for out-of-print and antiquarian   valuations
Catalogue: new book lists

The Kensington Bookshop Ltd (Notting Hill Gate)

140 Kensington Church Street W8
727-0544

M–F 10:00–6:00   Sat 10:00–5:00

antiques   archaeology   architecture   art   atlases   ballet   biography   business studies   child care   children's books   cinema   classics   cookery   crime and adventure   crossword   DIY   design   fiction   gardening   health   history   humour   language teaching   literature   militaria   motoring   music   mythology   natural history   occult   Pelican, Penguin   photography   plays   poetry   politics   recreation   reference   religion   science fiction   self-sufficiency   transport   travel guides   wines   women's studies

The Kensington Bookshop is a large, friendly shop selling a complete range of fiction and non-fiction, in hardcover and paperback. The children's books section includes fairy tales, classics, reference books and non-fiction titles on a variety of topics. For adults, there is an extensive selection of contemporary paperback fiction, illustrated travel and art books, among other subjects. Their lease expires in 1985 and they are hoping to relocate in the same area. Should this happen they will maintain their name.

Non-book material: cards   maps   wrapping paper
Services: mail order   special order
Catalogue: Christmas and summer selected lists

Liberty and Co.   (Oxford Circus)

210 Regent Street W1
734-1234

M–W 9:00–5:30   Th 9:00–7:00   F–Sat 9:00–5:30

art   biography   children's books   classics   collecting   cookery   fiction   gardening   history   hobbies   literature   music   natural history   Penguin   poetry   Reader's Digest books   travel guides

The book department at **Liberty** has, most notably, a general selection of new best-selling fiction and literature, illustrated books about Great Britain and the arts, and a section of children's books.

Non-book material: department store
Services: mail order   special order

Mandarin Books

22 Notting Hill Gate W1
229-0327

M–F 10:00–6:00   Sat 10:00–6:00

art biography childbirth cookery drama education energy
environment family fiction games history literary criticism
literature music natural history occult philosophy poetry
politics psychology reference religion science fiction

While you can find the newest, best-selling hardcover and paperback
books at **Mandarin**, the shop tends to carry less 'popular', somewhat
more obscure titles in the range of subjects outlined above. The
section on education is strong, with a well-chosen range of both
practical and theoretical titles. Books about energy and environmental issues, usually found only in large general bookshops, are available
at **Mandarin**, despite the shop's small space. Indeed, all manner of
good fiction and non-fiction are packed on to the shelves.

Services: mail order   special order

Paperbacks Centre

28 Charlotte Street W1
636-3532

M–Th 9:00–6:00 F 9:00–7:30 Sat 9:00–5:00

first room:

biography children's books classics cookery fiction health
humour literature Penguin plays poetry reference science
fiction

second room:

Africa and Caribbean China education labour history Latin
America Lenin literary criticism Marxism philosophy politics
psychology sciences sexual politics sociology Soviet Union

This is one of three shops owned by the socialist New Park Publishers.
General hardcover and paperback titles are at the front of the shop,
while books in the shop's speciality, left-wing and socialist literature
can be found in the rear of the shop. A good range of magazines and

newspapers on the arts, literature and radical politics is also available.

Non-book material: UK/London maps
Services: mail order   special order
Publications: New Park Publications publishes books on political issues, and produces a series of Newsline Reports which focus on current political 'hot spots' throughout the world

Quartet Bookshop   (Oxford Circus)

45/46 Poland Street W1
437-1019

M–F 10:00–6:00

art biography children's books classics cookery fiction film gardening health and medicine literary biography literature Marx Middle East music/jazz non-fiction Penguin photography poetry psychology Quartet Books Robin Clark Publications socialism sociology Third World Women's Press

Quartet is a general bookshop with a selection of new middle-of-the-road fiction and non-fiction. The shop's stength, however, lies in more radical political and literary areas. They stock a full range of Quartet, Robin Clark and The Women's Press publications, and these provide interesting titles in literature, jazz, sexual politics and sociology – to name a few of the diverse subject areas. There is also a limited range of alternative arts and political magazines.

Non-book material: cards
Services: special order
Catalogue: Quartet Books   Robin Clark   Women's Press
Publications: The shop is owned by Quartet Books, which also owns Robin Clark, The Women's Press and *Literary Review*

Riverside Studios Bookshop

(Hammersmith)

Crisp Road W6
741-2251

T–Sun 12:00–8:00

art biography children's books classics cookery dance drama
feminism film literary criticism literature music OUP, Panther,
Penguin, Quartet, Virago, Women's Press philosophy poetry
performing arts

Although the shop is small in size, and despite recent difficulties,
Riverside Studios continues to keep an appealing and selective stock
of mostly paperback titles. Contemporary fiction, titles on feminism
and children's books comprise the primary sections in their stock,
alongside a range of titles on the performing arts – titles which vary to
complement the theatre or dance programmes on offer at the studio.
A large range of literary, political and arts magazines are also
available.

In addition to the bookshop, **Riverside** operates two studios where
there are always film series or modern dance, theatre or ballet
companies performing. The separate art gallery has frequent exhibitions and there is a restaurant and bar in which to relax.

Non-book material: badges cards posters for events at **Riverside
Studios**
Services: mail order special order
Publications: a series of Riverside Interviews with people such as
Allen Ginsberg have been published by the Studios

Selfridges

(Bond Street or Marble Arch)

400 Oxford Street W1
629-1234

M–W 9:00–5:30 Th 9:00–7:00 Sat 9:00–5:30

antiques art BBC publications biography children's books
classics cookery crafts crime and thrillers drama fiction film
gardening historical romance history humour Ladybird medicine and health music natural history occult and horror poetry
reference religion romance science fiction sport and pastimes
theatre transport TV war

Selfridges book department carries a general range of new books, with a large selection devoted to children's fiction, picture books, crafts, etc. and is especially useful in the almost bookless Oxford Street.

Non-book material: department store
Services: mail order   special order

W. H. Smith

370 Chiswick High Road W4   (Chiswick Park)
995-9427

M–Sat 9:00–5:30

W. H. Smith   (Ealing Broadway)

21 The Broadway W5
567-1471

M–Sat 9:00–5:30

W. H. Smith   (Hammersmith)

16 King's Mall, High Street W6
534-5955

M–Sat 9:00–5:30

W. H. Smith   (High Street Kensington)

132 Kensington High Street W8
937-0236

M–Sat 9:00–5:30

W. H. Smith   (Notting Hill Gate)

192 Notting Hill Gate W11
727-9261

M–Sat 9:00–5:30

W. H. Smith (Ealing Broadway)

64 The Broadway W13
579-3461

M–Sat 9:00–5:30

Vanessa Williams-Ellis (Warwick Avenue)

4 Warwick Place W9
289-0071

M–F 10:00–6:00   Sat 10:00–5:00

biography   children's books   classics   cookery   fiction   gardening
health   literature   memoirs and letters   mysteries   non-fiction
plays   poetry   politics   reference   travel   women

One would hardly expect to find this charming, general bookshop on what seems to be a residential side street in Little Venice. **Vanessa Williams-Ellis** has a fine (if rather literary) selection of new paperback and hardcover literature, as well as a selection of books for children.

Many political figures and well-known public servants live in the neighbourhood of the shop, and recent non-fiction of interest to them (if not written by them) is always prominently displayed. A small selection of second-hand books is available. Recent book reviews are usefully displayed.

Services: mail order   special order   search service for out-of-print and antiquarian
Catalogue: four times a year   standing orders for annuals etc   regular, useful lists delivered locally

Waterstone's

88 Regent Street W1
734-0713/4

M–F 10:00–10:00   Sat 10:30–7:00   Sun 12:00–7:00

ground floor: .

antiques   art & architecture   biography & memoirs   classics
computers   dictionaries   fiction   languages   literary criticism   literature   photography   poetry   theatre & plays   travel   travel literature

basement:

business & economics   children's books   cookery   gardening
health   history   music   natural history   occult   philosophy   political science   psychology   reference   religions   sports & games

Non-book material: maps   postcards   records and cassettes (classical, jazz, language)
Services: mail order   search service and selected list for account
holders   **Waterstone's** credit card which can be used in all branches
and by telephone
Publications: literary diary   postcards   projected lists of art,
architecture and religion

Waterstone's

193 High Street Kensington W8
937-8432/3

M–F 9:30–10:30   Sat 9:30–7:00   Sun 12:00–7:00

basement:

business & economics   children's books   computer science   cookery
crafts   drama   gardening   health   history   natural history   performing arts   poetry   politics   psychology   reference   religion & philosophy   sport

ground floor:

biography & memoirs   fiction   literature   travel

first floor:

art & architecture (new & second-hand)   antiques   collecting

Waterstone's chain of five central London bookstores is the most important development of the London retail booktrade in recent years. Tim Waterstone has put range, imagination and good service back into heavyweight London book-selling. Each of his stores is an oasis of good layout, informed help and abundant stock. The managers are accessible, the staff is friendly and with an apparent sense of identification with its work. A distinctive feature of the chain is the range of services it offers, especially to account customers. Those who hold a charge account credit card can order books by telephone or post, have them gift-wrapped (as can the ordinary customer) and packed off worldwide. They become free subscribers to *Books and Bookmen*, are invited to book-signings and other special events, and can make use of the firm's search facility for out-of-print books. **Waterstone's** is casting its net wide: the music departments are strong; a literary diary is to be brought out each year; it has its own ranges of architectural and botanical postcards: and a projected imprint for art, architecture and religious books. The shelves of this branch hold about 50,000 titles, and the warehouse stock is moving towards half a million.

Non-book material: records and cassettes (classical, jazz, language)   maps   postcards   *London Review of Books, Books & Bookmen*
Services: mail order   search service and selected lists for account holders   **Waterstone's** credit card which can be used in all branches and by telephone.

WEST LONDON
Speciality Bookshops

ARCHITECTURE

London Art Bookshop Ltd   (High Street Kensington)
8 Holland Street W8
937-6996

M–Sat 9:30–6:00

administration   Africa and South America   alternative technology
American architecture   Baroque and Renaissance   building construction   building regulations   castles and country homes   church
architecture   classical architecture   counties   Eastern Europe and
Russia   exhibition catalogues   France   Georgian and Victorian
architecture   Greece and Southern Europe   housing   industrial
archaeology   interior design   Islamic and Oriental architecture
London and suburbs   medieval architecture   offices and shops
perspective and drawing   Scandinavia and Northern Europe   tour-
ism and restaurants   town planning   towns and cities   vernacular
architecture

Though small, this well organized shop specializes in new books on
all aspects of architecture. The wide range of subject areas within the
specialized stock is remarkable in a shop where an exhaustive survey
of Renaissance architecture can be found as well as a highly
specialized text on industrial archaeology. Indeed, almost all possible
divisions within the field of architecture are acknowledged. A few
second-hand books are available, and a selection of magazines and
journals on architecture and design is on hand.
   Across the street is the Academy Bookshop, which is under the
same ownership as the **London Art Bookshop**, and carries books on
fine and applied arts (see separate entry).

Services: mail order   special order
Catalogue: Academy Editions list
Publications: Academy Editions publishes books about architecture
and fine and applied arts

Royal Institute of British Architects Bookshop

(Great Portland Street
or Regent's Park)

66 Portland Place W1
251-0791

M–F 9:30–5:30

building types   carpentry   construction and structure   design data
energy conservation   estimating   gardens   history of architecture
history of design   interior design   interiors   land and leisure   legal
and contracts   planning: city, town, country   planting   reference
rendering   specifications   surveying

This is a small (but complete) shop, off the foyer of the **RIBA**
building, specializing in new books on architecture, design and
construction. Most of the material is geared toward professionals
working in these fields, though there are some illustrated books for the
lay reader.

Services: mail order   special order
Catalogue: complete list annually
Publications: RIBA Publications publishes books on: architects,
buildings, crafts and the visual arts   reports   building contracts and
forms

ART

Academy Bookshop

(High Street Kensington)

7 Holland Street W8
937-6996

M–Sat 9:30–6:00

antiques and collecting   art deco   art history and theory   art
nouveau   artists' monographs   calligraphy and printing   carpets and
rugs   ceramics   colour theory   county crafts and book binding
design manuals   design and pattern source books   early photography   ethnic crafts   furniture   gardens   glass   glassmaking   illustrations   illustrators and monographs   interior design   landscape design   metal work and jewellery   painting and drawing   paper
photography collections   photography criticisms and history   photography monographs   photography techniques   posters and post-

cards   pottery   prints and print making   sculpture   silver   textiles
wood

The **Academy Bookshop** is run in tandem with the London Art
Bookshop, but here the new books are on all aspects of fine and
applied arts. A particularly rich harvest of books on photography can
be found here, but even in the more specialized fields of carpets,
furniture, patterns and textiles, they stock a good range of titles. As in
the London Art Bookshop, the **Academy Bookshop** is distinguished
by the extraordinary range and depth of its holdings.

Services: mail order   special order
Catalogue: Academy Editions list
Publications: Academy Editions publishes books in the fields of .
architecture and the arts

Books and Things   (Notting Hill Gate)

Dolphin Arcade (Upstairs)
157 Portobello Road W11
no phone

Sat 9:00–4:00

Almost overflowing into the snack bar area are the second-hand
books of **Books And Things**. Late 19th century and 20th-century
books on the decorative and fine arts are the speciality of the shop.
Also available are modern first editions and a smattering of general
fiction and non-fiction.

Non-book material: ephemera   original posters and book illustra-
tions
Services: mail order   wants lists accepted
Catalogue: twice yearly list of general titles, art and illustrated
books and modern first editions
Note: **Books And Things** can also be found (with three other
booksellers) at the alleyway running alongside the Royal Academy of
Arts. W–F 11:00–5:00

Royal Academy of Arts (Piccadilly Circus)

Burlington House
Piccadilly W1
434-9052

M–Sun 10:00–6:00

The shop in the **Royal Academy of Arts** carries books on the fine arts, art history, genres, architecture, design and photography, many of which are related to current exhibitions. On hand, as well, are exhibition catalogues.

Non-book material: cards   glassware and pottery   posters   prints   slides of permanent collection   wrapping-paper
Services: mail order   special order   framing service
Publications: Exhibition catalogues are published by the **Royal Academy of Arts**

AUTOMOBILES

Connoisseur Carbooks (Chiswick Park)

32 Devonshire Road W4
994-6783

M–W 9:00–5:30   Th 9:00–8:00   F 9:00–5:30   Sat 10:00–4:00

body work and restoration   Brooklands publications   CB radios   collecting cars   commercial vehicles   customizing   history and general   models and modelling   motorcycles   off-road vehicles   'one make' books   racing   rallying   reference   technical   trucks

New books for car enthusiasts are the speciality of **Connoisseur Carbooks**. Shelves in the shop are packed with illustrated UK and US titles on all aspects of automobile collecting, racing and history, and there is a substantial section of books on individual makes of cars. What you won't find here are repair manuals, but the shop does carry books on technical aspects of car collecting.

Services: mail order   special order
Catalogue: complete list annually with frequent supplements
Publications: Motor Racing Publications publishes books on cars and trucks

BBC PUBLICATIONS

BBC Bookshop   (Baker Street)

35 Marylebone High Street W1
580-5577

M–F 9:30–5:00   Sat 9:30–12:30

BBC Broadcasting House   (Great Portland Street
                                        or Regent's Park)

Portland Place W1
580-4468   ext. 2303

M–F 9:30–5:00

architecture   art   children's books   cookery and nutrition   crafts and
hobbies   drama   education and literacy   engineering   gardening
health and welfare   languages   music   natural history and environment   politics and economics   religion   science

The main BBC shop is at Marylebone High Street, while there is a
stall in the foyer of the Broadcasting House. BBC Publications cover a
wide range of subjects, including educational material and books
derived from television series.

Non-book material: audio-visual language aids   journals   lectures
Services: mail order   special order (BBC titles only)
Catalogue: complete listing
Publications: see above

BLACK STUDIES

Grassroots Storefront   (Westbourne Park)

61 Goldbourne Road W10
969-0687

M–Sat 10:00–6:30

Africa   Afro-America   architecture   art   black studies   Caribbean
children's books   China   cinema   cookery   economics   education
environment   fiction   history   language teaching   Latin America
literature   music   poetry   politics   race relations   rights   women

As a community based black bookshop, **Grassroots** carries current
titles relevant to class and race relations in Britain, as well as fiction

and non-fiction by, and about, blacks from around the world. Magazines, newspapers and journals about community politics, Third World issues, individual rights and women's issues are also available, as is a range of children's books and learning material.

Non-book material: African and Caribbean arts and crafts
Services: mail order   special order
Publications: Grassroots publishes a newspaper

Walter Rodney Bookshop   (West Ealing – British Rail)

5a Chignell Place W13
579-4920

M–F 9:00–5:00

Africa Afro-American art biography children's books cookery crafts drama economics education fiction folk tales and legends history imperialism individual rights music myths poetry politics religion sociology Third World development West Indies

The name of the **Walter Rodney Bookshop** commemorates a scholar and political activist from Guyana. The shop specializes in new books about and by black people and is committed to literature with a multiracial perspective on the world – the primary concern of Walter Rodney in his lifetime.

Non-book material: cards   crafts   posters
Services: mail order   special order
Catalogue: Bogle-L'Ouverture Publications
Publications: Bogle-L'Ouverture Publications publishes books about and by black people, including the work of Walter Rodney

CARTOGRAPHY

Jonathan Potter Ltd   (Green Park)

1 Grafton Street W1
491-3520

M–F 9:30–5:30   Sat 9:30–11:30

This shop, which specializes in prints of London, maps and atlases pre-1850, has an excellent selection of more modern reference books on all aspects of cartography. Many of these are out-of-print and modern first editions.

Non-book material: see above
Services: mail order   special order
Catalogue: comprehensive list issued once a year

CHILDREN'S BOOKS

Young World   (High Street Kensington)
(Children's Book Centre Ltd)

229 Kensington High Street W8
937-6314

M–Sat 9:30–6:00

ABC readers   arts and religion   Beatrix Potter   crafts   Dr Seuss fairy tales   fiction (ages 5–8)   fiction (ages 8–11)   geography ghosts   history   humour   Ladybird   natural history   new recommended fiction   non-fiction series   nursery rhymes   picture books poetry   pop-up books   reference   science   science fiction   sports and hobbies

With new toys on the ground floor and books downstairs, this brightly decorated, slightly crowded shop should delight any child who happens in for a look round. Books are categorized according to age group – one to five years, five to eight years, fourteen to one hundred years! – and within each section is a range of fiction and non-fiction titles.

Non-book material: cards   games   posters   presents   toys
Services: mail order   special order
Catalogue: recommended book lists once every two years

M. and R. Glendale

Grays Antique Market
Stand 121
58 Davies Street W1
629-2851

M–F 10:00–6:00

Walking into the shop of **M. and R. Glendale** is like walking into a
world of fine detail and precise decorative purposes. Their beautifully
bound and arranged books are mainly for children and collectors of
(Victorian) children's books and ephemera, but they also carry titles
on women's rights, cookery, domestic history, colour plate and
illustrated books, and such obscure subjects as flush toilet construction! Also featured are entertainment items – games, puzzles, etc. –
made of paper.

Non-book material: paper ephemera
Services: mail order   search service   will respond with offers to
specific book(s) requests

COOKERY AND FOOD

Books for Cooks

15 Blenheim Crescent W11
221-1992

M–Sat 9:00–5:00

This shop which opened in 1983 has a stock of about 2,500 food, diet
and cookery books, both new and, on the basement floor and outside,
second-hand. There's an amusing sprinkling of such titles as *The
Moveable Feast* and *The Pie and the Patty-pan* for the browser of the
second-hand.

Services: mail order   special order   book binding

EDUCATION

Foyles Educational Bookshop (Marble Arch)

37 Upper Berkeley Street W1
262-4699/5310

M–F 9:00–5:30

ground floor:

architecture   art   biography   business   child care and family
classics   cookery   crime   economics   fiction   Fontana, Pan, Panther,
Peacock, Pelican, Penguin, Puffin, Sphere   history   languages
music   natural history   philosophy   photography   plays   poetry
politics   reference   travel guides   war

basement:

children's books:

alphabet and counting   arts and crafts   Batsford books   classics
encyclopaedias   fiction   geography   history   hymn books   Ladybird   literature   mathematics   Macdonald reference   music   readers   theology   transport

text books:

adult education   business   careers   drama   economics   English
grammar   geography   history   language teaching   law and politics
mathematics   Open University   poetry   psychology   sciences
sociology   teaching   technical

This shop is not run by the management of **Foyles** on Charing Cross
Road; in fact there is no connection between the two businesses. The
Educational Bookshop carries a stock of general books on the
ground floor, while downstairs is an extensive range of children's
educational material. Also in the basement is a wide selection of O, A
and University level text books in all academic subject areas, and
there is a large section of Oxford University Press titles on language
courses and teaching.

Non-book material: educational aids
Services: mail order   special order

181

ELECTRONICS, TECHNOLOGY AND MEDICINE

The Modern Book Co.   (Edgware Road)

9–21 Praed Street W2
402-9176

M–F 9:00–5:30   Sat 9:00–1:00

accounting art building communications computers cookery
economics electronics engineering fiction gardening hi-fi and
audio hydraulics management mathematics medical microprocessors natural history non-fiction nursing Pelican, Penguin
photography radio and TV reference sport structures technical transport travel guides

This spacious shop specializes in new technical and medical books,
and also carries general fiction and non-fiction. The shop is particularly proud of its selection of books on radio and TV, computers,
electronics, hi-fi and audio equipment and microprocessors. In these
technical areas, **The Modern Book Co** stocks the latest US, as well
as UK publications. I have found no other shop in London with as
wide a range of technical books on modern electronic equipment.

Services: mail order   special order
Catalogue: numerous lists in specialized areas

ESPERANTO

The British Esperanto Association Inc.   (Holland Park)

140 Holland Park Avenue W11
727-7821

M–F 9:30–6:00

Located in the administration offices of **The British Esperanto
Association**, this is the only Esperanto bookshop in Britain. Three
hundred current titles are in stock, including Esperanto language
teaching books, and magazines and journals are available as well.
Approximately 50% of the titles are in technical subject areas (e.g.,
construction and the sciences) while the other half of the stock is in
the field of the humanities. Original literature in Esperanto is
available as well as Esperanto works translated into English.

Non-book material: badges   cassettes   records (language and entertainment)
Services: mail order   special order
Catalogue: complete list of titles

FAMILY

The Catholic Marriage Advisory Council Bookroom

(Holland Park)

15 Lansdowne Road W11
727-0141

M–F 9:30–5:00

The bookroom at the **Catholic Marriage Advisory Council** carries new books on the subjects of the family, marriage, family counselling, child raising, psychology, sociology, sex and sex education. Despite this being run by a Catholic organization, the titles in the bookroom have less to do with religion than with the psychology of human sexual and social behaviour.

Non-book material: book marks   cassettes   posters
Services: mail order
Catalogue: complete book list
Publications: the **CMAC** publishes booklets and pamphlets on marriage and the family

Family Planning Association Book Centre

(Goodge Street)

27–34 Mortimer Street W1
636-7866

M–F 9:30–5:00

abortion   birth control   breast feeding   children's information books   fertility   history   medical   nursing   population control pregnancy and childbirth   psychology   sex and marriage   sex education   sex technique   sociology

As part of the Family Planning Association, the **Book Centre** stocks new books, leaflets, fact sheets, studies and reports on all aspects of family planning in the UK.

Services: mail order   special order
Catalogue: selected annual list
Publications: the **FPA** has published the book *Learning to Live with Sex* and various studies, facts sheets and reports

FRENCH LITERATURE

Hachette Bookshop   (Piccadilly Circus)
4 Regent Place W1
734-5259

M–F 9:30–6:00   Sat 9:30–1:00

art   children's books   classics   classiques larousse   commerce
cookery   dictionaries   drama   economics   fiction   history   language
teaching and course books   literature   livres de poche   philosophy
politics   psychology   science   travel guides

Hachette is London's main source for new French books on all subjects. The shop is run by a French staff who are energetic about stocking the most recent publications from across the channel. For the most part, their clientele's native language is English, so the books are geared towards language teaching and the educational market with books on French history and culture, in English, available as well.

The management strives to get new French publications at attractive prices adding, at most, 5% on the list price of a book published in France. There are occasions, however, when imported titles can be bought for the same price as in France, or even less.

Through their unique relationship with French distributors **Hachette** is able to stock books and magazines on topics such as football and travel to be found nowhere else in London.

Non-book material: language teaching materials
Services: mail order   special order
Publications: Continental Publishers has been inactive but hope to revive publishing activities

GERMANY

The German Book Centre Ltd   (Baker Street)

52 Manchester Street W1
935-3441/3481

M–F 9:00–6:00   Sat 10:00–5:00

This shop specializes in new books about, or from, Germany. All aspects of Germany are covered and these books are kept in stock, available to customers off the street.

Non-book material: language cassettes and records
Services: mail order   special order
Catalogue: German Book Centre Ltd only
Publications: Eric Maylin Ltd publishes limited-edition books in the field of natural history

HEALTH

Wholefood of Baker Street   (Baker Street)

24 Paddington Street W1
486-2756

M 8:45–6:00   T–F 8:45–6:30   Sat 8:45–1:00

agriculture   childbirth   cookery   ecology   farming   gardening
nutrition   reflexology   therapies   vitamins   yoga

Wholefood is a bookshop as well as greengrocer, grocery shop and butcher. Most of the books are new though they have a shelf full of out-of-print titles, and all of the titles are concerned with nutrition, agriculture and horticulture.

Non-book material: see above
Services: mail order   special order in field
Catalogue: selected list

INDIA

Publications India (Warren Street)

112 Whitfield Street W1
388-9832

M–Sat 11:00–7:00

art culture fiction folklore history language teaching literature philosophy poetry politics religion sociology

This shop specializes in new books about India, in English and Hindi,
imported from India and Pakistan. The political section is quite good,
and there is a solid selection of language teaching books from India,
Pakistan and Bangladesh. Also available are a variety of journals and
magazines published in India.

Non-book material: cassettes records videotapes
Services: mail order special order
Catalogue: complete annual list with supplements every 2 months,
free of charge
Publications: Star Publications, one of the largest publishers in
India, produces books in Hindi

JAPAN

Japanese Publications Centre (Piccadilly Circus)

5 Warwick Street W1
439-8035

M–F 10:00–6:00   Sat 10:30–6:00

The majority of books here are imported from Japan, in Japanese,
covering all aspects of the country and its history. A few titles on art,
history, healing arts, religion, language and the martial arts are in
English. Magazines, comics and children's books are available, and
there are a few second-hand books.

Non-book material: cards fans gift items prints
Services: mail order special order

LANGUAGE TEACHING

Keltic (Notting Hill Gate)

140 Kensington Church Street W8
229-8560

M–F 10:00–5:30   Sat 10:00–1:00

adult language courses   commercial English   English as a foreign
language   English for specific uses   practice books   primary language course   reading   reading comprehension   reference   secon-
dary language courses   speaking   teachers' manuals   writing

Located at the bottom of a staircase at the rear of the Kensington
Bookshop, **Keltic** is a small, uncluttered shop specializing in teaching
books for English as a foreign language. Students and teachers alike
will find a complete range of current titles from the major language
text publishers. Like the Kensington Bookshop, their lease expires in
1985 and they are hoping to relocate in the same area.

Non-book material: cassettes   records   video-tapes   wall charts
journals
Services: mail order   special order
Catalogue: selected lists of titles

Linguaphone (Oxford Street)

207–209 Regent Street W1
734-7572

M–F 9:00–5:30   Sat 10:00–4:00

The **Linguaphone** Institute has developed, and sells, comprehensive
language teaching courses for home use. Included in a course package
are cassettes or records, text book, course handbook, self-correcting
written exercise book, and an oral exercise book. The Institute also
offers an advisory service via the post for student questions and
written work. Languages include German, French, Spanish, Italian,
Persian, Arabic, Chinese, Norwegian – 32 in all.

Non-book material: see above
Services: mail order
Publications: course material is published by **The Linguaphone
Institute**

MEDICINE

Kimpton's Medical Bookshop

(Great Portland Street Regent's Park)

205 Great Portland Street W1
580-6381

M–F 9:00–5:30   Sat 9:30–5:00

49 Newman Street W1
580-4250

(Goodge Street)

M–F 9:30–5:30   Sat 9:30–1:00

205 Great Portland Street:

acupuncture anaesthesia anatomy biochemistry cancer cardiology dentistry dermatology dictionaries dietetics ear, nose, throat embryology endocrinology forensic medicine gastroenterology geriatrics haematology histology hospitals immunology medical genetics medicine microbiology neurology nursing nutrition obstetrics occupational medicine ophthalmology orthopaedics pathology paediatrics pharmacology physiology physiotherapy pregnancy and baby care psychology and psychiatry public health radiology respiratory medicine rheumatology sexology speech therapy statistics surgery toxicology tropical medicine urology and renal veterinary sciences

49 Newman Street W1:

All the above with the exceptions of dentistry, speech therapy and veterinary sciences

As the list shows, a great deal can go wrong with the human and animal body. **Kimpton's,** one of the leading specialist booksellers and library suppliers, stocks works on almost all cures; most of its stock is directed towards the medical and paramedical professions, but there is an amount for the layman to experiment with as well. The main shop, at Great Portland Street, is large with a wide range of titles for undergraduates, postgraduates, and nurses (it is close to the Royal College of Physicians); the smaller shop is opposite the Middlesex Hospital Medical School and its stock is aimed more at the undergraduate and nursing markets.

Services: mail order   special order   visits to medical meetings and schools of nursing for the display and sale of books   the Teviot subscription agency is able to handle orders for all British and international periodicals and journals

188

Catalogue: Kimpton's monthly Book News; specialized subject-lists
Publications: Kimpton's and Teviot Scientific publish books in the field of medicine

MIDDLE EAST

Al Saqi Books   (Queensway)
26 Westbourne Grove W2
229-8543

M–Sat 10:00–6:00

academic texts   art   biography   business   children's books   culture and civilization   economics   education   fiction   history   linguistics literature   music   philosophy   poetry   politics   reference   religion science   sociology   technical

The emergence and success of **Al Saqi** reflects the interest and growth of the Middle Eastern population in London. With the exception of language teaching and English language titles, relevant to the Middle East, all the books here are in Arabic languages. New, second-hand and antiquarian books are sold and the shop prides itself on a comprehensive coverage of subject areas for the interests of a diverse clientele. A Middle East centre is being constructed in the building in which **Al Saqi** is located.

Services: mail order   special order
Catalogue: one catalogue per year, with general supplements

Hosains Books   (Marble Arch)
25 Connaught Street W2
262-7900

T–F 10:30–5:30   Sat 10:30–1:00

art   biography   culture   history   literature   religion   travel

Hosains specializes in second-hand, antiquarian and rare books about the Middle East, Central Asia, North Africa, India and Islam;

189

most of which are in English. A few of the titles are set apart by cards with detailed explanations of their history and significance. Art, travel and illustrated books and literature form the largest portion of the stock, while the basement houses additional books, as well as Persian and Indian miniatures and oriental prints.

Non-book material: see above
Services: mail order   search service in field
Catalogue: selected lists four or five times a year
Publications: Nash Publications plans to publish oriental works

MILITARIA

Tradition   (Green Park)

5A–5B Shepherd Street W1
493-7452

M–F 9:30–5:30   Sat 9:30–3:30

Tradition carries solely books on military history, uniforms, equipment, weapons and campaigns. They have new titles on uniforms, especially, as well as out-of-print and antiquarian books about the military, such as 18th-century army lists.

Non-book material: new and antique military figures
Services: mail order   special order in field

Under Two Flags   (Bond Street)

4 St Christopher's Place W1
935-6934

T–Sat 10:00–5:00

military campaigns   military equipment   military history   models and miniatures   model soldier painting   uniforms   weapons

Under Two Flags is a charming small shop in the shopping precinct at St Christopher's Place. The shop specializes in new books on military uniforms and model soldiers and stocks titles in the related subject areas of military history and weapons. Only a portion of the

shop is concerned with books, though, as model soldiers and prints
are also sold.

Non-book material: see above
Services: mail order   special order in field

MODERN FIRST EDITIONS
AND ILLUSTRATED

Charlotte Robinson Bookshop   (Piccadilly Circus)

35 Great Pulteney Street W1
437-3683

M–F 11:00–6:00

Amid the encircling gloom and glitter of the surrounding area the
Charlotte Robinson Bookshop is most welcome. Run in a co-
operative with Peter Jolliffe (who also operates at Words Etcetera)
and Clearwater Books, as well as a fourth partner who will be joining
presently, the shop brings together an excellent, beguiling collection
of modern first editions and illustrated books as well as a fair
proportion of children's illustrated. Much of the stock is fiction
(including some detective stories), but poetry, biography and literature are covered as well. Notable is the section of books by the
increasingly-popular Henry Williamson, and the collection of titles
concerning the First World War. Many of the books have their
original dust-wrappers and if the prices at first might seem a little
expensive it should be remembered that the first-edition market is
continuing to grow, and that even original issues by post-war writers
fetch high prices, the first printing of so recent a novel as Martin
Amis's *Other People* realizing more than the cover-price.

Non-book material: none
Services: mail order
Catalogue: all the partners issue regularly

MUSIC

Boosey and Hawkes Music

(Oxford Circus)

295 Regent Street W1
580-2060

M–Sat 9:00–5:00

biography counterpoint dictionaries harmony musical instruments and teaching opera libretti popular music theory

The majority of this shop is devoted to sheet music, musical scores and songbooks (including educational songbooks for children), in both classical and popular music. There is a limited selection, mainly of hardback books about composers, conductors, theory and music analysis, and a few specialized music journals are available.

Services: mail order
Publications: Boosey and Hawkes publishes sheet music and allied music books

Brian Jordan Music Books

(Holland Park)

60 Princedale Road W11
229-8676

M–F 10:00–1:00   2:30–6:30   Sat 10:00–5:00

Brian Jordan carries both new music books (about 25% of total stock) and music scores. Academic and reference books on early (pre-1800) music, instruments and composers are the speciality of this small shop. Music and dance history, musicology, music theory and early treatises about music are other subjects on which the shop stocks books.

Non-book material: lute and viol strings   sheet music
Services: mail order   special order (general books as well)
Catalogue: Brian Jordan publications only
Publications: Brian Jordan, with Early Music Centre Publications, publish lute and viol music

Chappell

50 New Bond Street W1
491-2777

M–F 9:30–6:00   Sat 9:30–5:00

ballads   ballet   biography   dictionaries   history   hymns   instruments   jazz   opera   rock

Chappell sells sheet music, hi-fi and electronic equipment and musical instruments, but the shop also has a selection of new books about music and dance.

Non-book material: see above
Services: mail order   special order
Publications: Chappell publishes books about music

The Chimes Music Shop

65 Marylebone High Street W1
935-1587

M–F 9:00–5:30   Sat 9:00–2:00

biography   composition   criticism and analysis   dance   dictionaries   harmony   history   instruments   music notation   music reading   opera   orchestration   sight reading and singing   song   teaching   theory

The Chimes Music Shop has one of the most diverse stocks of new music books in London. They cater to all levels of ability and interest in music and instruments, carrying everything from elementary teaching guides to specialized texts.

Non-book material: records   scores   sheet music   song books
Services: mail order   special order

Music Book Centre

(Goodge Street)

78 Newman Street W1
636-9033

M–F 9:30–5:30

This small, modern shop is part of the publishing concern, Music Sales Ltd, and about 80% of the titles (all of which are new) are their own. The shop does, however, carry music books from other publishers. All the books and song books deal with contemporary music and music personalities – rock, jazz, blues, popular, contemporary classics.

Services: mail order
Catalogue: books and song books
Publications: music books by Music Sales Ltd, Wise Publications and Omnibus Press

Music Boutique

(Piccadilly Circus)

70 Shaftesbury Avenue W1
437-6144

M–Sat 9:00–6:00 (often later)

At the top of this narrow building is a shop specializing in books about pop music 'from Abba to Zappa'. Its general stock of biographies and discographies also contains a large number of guides and tutors to individual instruments as well as song-books. Especially notable is a large section of Beatles collectables which at present is expanding further.

Non-book material: guitar-polish strings cassettes, etc.
Services: mail order   special order
Catalogues: general English and American issued

Peters Music Shop   (Oxford Circus or Tottenham Court Road)

119 Wardour Street W1   Soho
437-1456
434-3642 (Oxford University Press music books)

M–F 9:30–5:30

biography   counterpoint   dictionaries   harmony   history   instruments   opera   orchestration   theory

Peters Edition sells mostly sheet music and scores, but has a
selection of new books about composers, performers, and music
theory and history. There is also a separate section which stocks
music books published by Oxford University Press.

Non-book material: scores   sheet music
Services: mail order   special order
Publications: Peters Edition publishes books on music

Schott & Co. Ltd   (Oxford Circus).

48 Great Marlborough Street W1
437-1246

M–F 9:00–5:00

biography   classical music   counterpoint   dictionaries   harmony
musical instruments and teaching   opera   theory

A small portion of the stock of **Schott & Co.** consists of new books
about music, though their primary business is selling classical and
opera scores, and musical instruments.

Non-book material: see above
Services: mail order
Catalogue: Schott & Co. publications listed six times yearly
Publications: Ernst Eulenburg Ltd publishes books and sheet music

NATURAL HISTORY

Harriet Truscott Books (Notting Hill Gate)

Portobello Antiques Arcade
139–149 Portobello Road W11
no phone

Sat 7:00–3:30

Harriet Truscott has a medium-sized stall in the Portobello Antique Arcade which is stocked with antiquarian and second-hand books. Natural history, travel, art and a general stock of non-fiction are the specialities of the stall.

Services: mail order   search service

NEW ZEALAND

Whitcoulls Ltd (New Zealand) (Piccadilly Circus)

6 Royal Opera Arcade W1
930-4587

M–F 9:00–5:00   Sat 9:30–12:00

biography culture fiction history lifestyle literature New Zealand Government publications poetry travel guides

This is both a book and gift shop specializing in the history and culture of New Zealand. Most of the books are imported, all are new, and there are a few New Zealand magazines.

Non-book material: art cards crafts gift items records slides tapes
Services: mail order   special order
Catalogue: complete list of stock annually
Publications: Whitcoulls Publishers Ltd publishes literature and fiction by New Zealand writers

NUMISMATICS

Mayfair Coin Co. (Piccadilly Circus)

73 New Bond Street W1
629-8633

M–F 9:30–5:30

Although the primary business here is selling coins and medals, **Mayfair Coin Co.** has a very small selection of standard reference books on English and foreign coins. Aside from an occasional second-hand book, the shop stocks mainly current numismatic titles.

Non-book material: coins   military medals
Services: mail order   special order

B. A. Seaby Ltd (Oxford Circus)

11 Margaret Street W1
580-3677

M–F 9:00–5:00

bibliography   military history   military decorations and medals
mint reports   naval history   naval decorations and medals   numismatic handbooks   numismatic history: worldwide   private collections' catalogues   uniform history

Seaby specializes primarily in new, recently out-of-print, and rare books and journals, in a variety of languages, on all aspects of coins and paper money from ancient to modern times. Also featured are books on naval and military history. **Seaby**'s main activity, though, is the buying and selling of coins.

Non-book material: coins   medals
Services: mail order   special order (out of field as well)   search service for out-of-print and antiquarian
Catalogue: new and rare book lists are produced quarterly
Publications: B. A. Seaby Ltd publishes new books, semi-annuals and reprints exclusively on coins and medals

POLAND

Polonez (Shepherd's Bush)

129/130 Shepherd's Bush Shopping Centre
Shepherd's Bush Green W12
749-3097   743-2391

M–W 9:00–5:00   Th 9:00–1:00   F 9:00–5:00   Sat 10:00–5:00

Everything in **Polonez** is from, or about, Poland. Most of their books are imported from Poland (in Polish), although titles concerning Poland which might not be found in that country are probably available here at **Polonez** (this odd situation arises because books published in Poland often go out of print quickly, becoming unobtainable behind the Iron Curtain, yet may sit on Western booksellers' shelves for many months). Western classics in translation and English language books about Poland are the spheres of Western influence in this shop. In the areas of out-of-print and antiquarian books, **Polonez** is able to obtain books through the antiquarian department of Poland's national book distributor. The shop can order periodicals from a list of over 200 Polish publishers.

    Polonez is also a gift shop featuring imported items from Poland including prints, records, crafts and folk art.

Non-book material: see above
Services: mail order   special order   search service in field
Catalogue: specialized lists are produced frequently

POLITICAL

The Poland Street Book Centre (Oxford Circus)

9 Poland Street W1
437-1984

M–F 9:30–5:30

biography drugs government and politics (UK) health housing labour Liberal Party Northern Ireland oil social issues Soviet Union state research TV women work

The building here, which is wholly a subsidiary of the Joseph Rowntree Social Service Trust, houses a number of political and public interest groups each of whose publications are sold in this small shop on the ground floor. The books are new, but the majority of the material consists of reports, studies, information booklets, newspapers and pamphlets. The organizations represented are: Acton Society, APTEC (Appropriate Technology Ltd), Artists Union, British Society for Social Responsibility in Science, BSSRS Publications Ltd, Counter Information Services, Friends of the Earth, Joseph Rowntree Social Service Trust, Low Pay Unit, Minority Press Group, Public Interest Research Centre Ltd, Social Audic Ltd, Socialist Environment and Resources Association, Socialist Health Association, State Research, Third World Publications, Youth Aid.

Non-book material: badges
Services: special order
Publications: from the organizations listed above

POTTERY

The Craftsmen Pottery Shop   (Oxford Circus)

William Blake House
8 Marshall Street W1
437-7605

M–F 10:00–5:30   Sat 10:30–5:00

ceramic techniques   Chinese ceramics   clays   glazes   health and safety   history   kilns   porcelain   pottery   raku   stoneware

This spacious shop, in a corner of the modern building which houses The Craftsmen Potters Association, is primarily a display space for members' work. There is a selection of new books on all aspects of applied ceramics and pottery, as well as the history of ceramics, pottery, porcelain and stoneware around the world. There are also ceramics magazines and exhibition catalogues.

Non-book material: see above
Services: mail order (books and pottery tools)   special order regular monthly evening meetings with speakers on pottery exhibitions
Catalogue: book list regularly
Publications: The Craftsmen Potters Association publishes a bimonthly magazine, *Ceramic Review*; an illustrated directory of members' work, *Potters*, and *The Ceramic Review Book of Glaze Recipes*

PUBLISHERS' BOOKSHOPS

The Literary Guild Bookshop   (Goodge Street)

89 Newman Street W1
637-0341

M–F 10:00–6:00

arts best-sellers biography children's books classics cookery
fiction gift books history literature natural history new titles
reference

Only members of the W. H. Smith/Doubleday book clubs can
purchase books here. All titles are hardback and available through
the Guild's mail order service, and the shop does attempt to stock
books from past book offerings. The Literary Guild can be joined
here, and details of the other clubs are available.

Services: mail order   back order
Catalogue: separate catalogues for each club, produced quarterly

Reader's Digest   (Green Park)

25 Berkeley Square W1
629-8144

M–F 9:00–5:30

art cookery DIY gardening household language teaching
motoring natural history reference transport travel guides

The majority of books here are new **Reader's Digest** titles, although
other UK publishers are carried. Two of their more useful sections
are those devoted to English language teaching and travel guides.

Non-book material: calendars cards posters records
Services: mail order   special order: **Reader's Digest** titles
Catalogue: Reader's Digest publications
Publications: Reader's Digest publishes new titles in a variety of
fields

RELIGIOUS

A. R. Mowbray & Co. Ltd   (Oxford Circus)

28 Margaret Street W1
580-2812

M–W 9:00–5:30   Th 9:00–6:00   F 9:00–5:30   (December: M–W 9:00–6:00   Th 9:00–7:00   F 9:00–6:00   Sat 11:00–3:00)

lower ground floor: paperbacks

children's books   crime   fiction   literature   Penguin, Pelican   reference   science fiction

ground floor:

antiques   archaeology   art   biography   business   classics   cookery   crafts   drawing and painting   fiction   film   gardening   health   history   humanities   literature   music   natural history   photography   plays   poetry   printing   publishing   reference   secretarial   sports and pastimes   theatre   travel guides   yoga

gallery:

bible   church requisites   fine bindings   hymn and song books   prayer books   records   second-hand books   theology

first floor:

biography   children's books   church history   commentaries   concordances   confirmation   dictionaries   lexicons   Mowbray paperbacks   Penguin   prayer   religion   saints   sermons   spiritual reading   theology

Mowbray's is a two-part shop. Half is a general bookshop with good coverage of the arts, humanities and children's books, while the gallery and first floor house books on the shop's speciality, religion and theology.

Non-book material: cards   church stationery   records   religious requisites
Services: mail order   special order
Catalogue: Mowbray's publications only
Publications: Mowbray publishes religious and theological books

Scripture Union Bookshop (Bond Street)

5 Wigmore Street W1
493-1851

M–T 9:00–5:30   W 9:30–5:00   Th 9:00–7:00   F–Sat 9:00–5:30

apologetics bible characters and background bibles biography
children's books Christian life Christian service the church
church history commentaries C. S. Lewis daily readings devotional doctrine ethics evangelism fiction healing Holy Spirit life of Christ music morality Old and New Testament prayer
prophecy

Scripture Union is a religious bookshop with an emphasis on
evangelical titles and subjects, though many of the books are
concerned with practical approaches to daily Christian life. A corner
of the shop is devoted to material for children, including teaching
aids, prayer and assembly books, and bible games and puzzles.

Non-book material: audio-visual material cards cassettes re-
cords teaching material
Services: mail order (infrequent) special order
Catalogue: Scripture Union publications
Publications: Scripture Union publishes books about the church
and Christian life

SPORTS

Turf Newspapers Ltd (Green Park)

55 Curzon Street W1
499-4391

M–F 9:00–5:00   Sat 9:00–12:00

biography breeding courses fiction horses racing sale figures
statistics Timeform training

This retail bookshop in the publishing offices of **Turf Newspapers**
sells new titles about horse breeding and racing with a few related
equestrian subjects. Much of the material is statistical, concerned
with the present racing season, but the shop also stocks less utilitarian
books, like all of the Dick Francis mysteries.

Non-book material: calendars cards diaries prints table mats
video films of horses and horse races
Services: mail order   special order
Catalogue: selected list
Publications: Turf Newspapers Ltd publishes reference books and
other books about racing

THEATRE

French's Theatre Bookshop (Goodge Street)

52–56 Fitzroy Street W1
836-7513

M–F 9:30–5:30

audition material   biography   children's theatre   illustrated theatre
history   libretti   musical plays   one-act plays   play texts   technical
theatre history   vocal scores

French's, London's oldest theatre bookseller, has recently moved
from its elegant Covent-Garden premises to these larger ones where it
continues to offer a comprehensive stock and service. Only new books
are stocked and these do include titles in the more technical areas,
such as stage management, design and lighting. The staff will help to
find out whether a title is in print, and the shops carries a useful stock
of theatre magazines, both current and back-issues, from the UK and
US.

Non-book material: dialect recordings   musical scores   postcards
sound-effects   spoken-word records
Services: mail order   special order   a variety of amateur rights for
play productions are handled   musical scores and libretti are for hire
Catalogue: many on specialized subjects
Publications: play texts and audition material are published by
Samuel French

TRAVEL

Bernard Shapero

Grays Antique Market
Stand 125
58 Davies Street W1
493-0876

M–F 10:00–6:00

Downstairs in Grays Antique Market will be found what is perhaps the UK's largest dealer in second-hand Baedecker travel guides. **Bernard Shapero**'s shop is only a cubby-hole, but the owner has a marvellous selection of second-hand and antiquarian travel and guide books, general illustrated books and shelves of rare Baedeckers. If what you want is not on the shelves, chances are the shop's search service can turn it up.

Services: mail order search service in speciality and general second-hand antiquarian
Catalogue: guidebooks listed twice yearly

Gabriel Byrne

Westbourne Antique Arcade
113 Portobello Road W11
no phone

Sat 9:00–4:00

Antiquarian books on travel and topography are the speciality of **Gabriel Byrne**, though there are also a few natural history, illustrated and medical books.

Services: mail order

The Travel Bookshop Ltd

(Ladbroke Grove)

13 Blenheim Crescent W11
229-5260

T–F 10:00–6:00   Sat 10:00–5:00

The Travel Bookshop moved to these larger premises in 1982. It lives up to its name with a well-organised selection of titles, arranged by country. Within each section are not solely travel guides, but all manner of books on subjects relevant to the particular country, including cookery, crafts, architecture, fiction and history.

Non-book material: maps
Services: mail order   special order   search service
Catalogue: selected lists two to three times yearly

UNIVERSITY BOOKSHOPS AND TEXTBOOKS

Acton Book Centre

(Acton Town)

144 Churchfield Road W3
992-6029

M T 9:00–6:00   W 9:00–2:00   Th–Sat 9:00–6:00

biology chemistry children's books classics commerce cookery economics education electronics fiction language teaching law mathematics natural history Open University Panther, Pelican, Penguin photography plays poetry psychology reference science fiction statistics typing zoology

Acton Book Centre is a general bookshop with a useful emphasis on academic books.

Non-book material: stationery
Services: mail order   special order

WEST LONDON
Second-hand Bookshops

Any Amount of Books   (Hammersmith)

103–105 Hammersmith Road W6
603-9232

T–Sat 11:00–7:00

ground floor:

architecture   art   classics   cookery   education   fiction   film
gardening   history   illustrated books   language teaching   law
legends   literature   memoirs   music   myths   non-fiction   Penguin
philosophy   photography   plays   poetry (first editions)   politics
psychology   religion   science fiction   sociology   sports   theatre
travel

basement:

arts   children's books   foreign language literature   history   medicine   novels   thrillers   travel

Any Amount of Books is a cut above most general second-hand
bookshops. Two floors house a general stock of titles, with particularly good sections of literature, poetry and travel books. Prices are
extremely reasonable, and scattered among the second-hand books
are a few new titles at reduced prices, including review copies and
remainders.

Non-book material: a gallery next door has been opened selling
prints and lithographs   book-plates   art books
Services: mail order   wants lists accepted
Catalogue: of art, first editions and literature twice a year

The Book Gallery   (Bond Street)

127 Grays Antique Market
58 Davies Street W1
408-1239

M–F 10:00–6:00

Four dealers, Sarah Baddiel, Michael Flower, Sue Lowell and Tony
Ward, take it in turns to work at a shop in this market just off Oxford

Street, where a varying number of dealers can often be found; each specializes, together forming a shop covering golf and juvenile books, motoring and transport, modern first editions and general literature from the nineteenth century onwards, topography and mountaineering, and natural history. Each of the dealers is able to contact the others by telephone should a customer need more information on a certain area.

Non-book material: prints   motoring and golf ephemera
Services: mail order   search service

W. A. Foster
(Chiswick Park)

134 Chiswick High Road W4
995-2768

M–W, F–Sat 10:00–6:00 (occasionally closed for lunch)   Th 10:00–1:30

183 Chiswick High Road W4
994-1610

M–Sat 11:00–4:00 (closed Th)

archaeology   architecture   art   biography   children's books   cinema   classics   collecting   cookery   economics   fiction   gardening   geology   health   humour   literary criticism   literature   music   mysteries   natural history   plays   poetry   psychology   railways   reference   religion   sailing   social sciences   stage history   travel   accounts and guides

Both of the **Foster** shops carry a general selection of second-hand books, as well as a few antiquarian titles. The combined contents of the shops make for a large stock of books with particularly good sections of literature and children's books.

Non-book material: cards   engravings   prints

Gaby Goldscheider
and Helga Wellingham

Collectors' Corner
Portobello Road W11
no phone

Sat 8:00–4:00

These two booksellers based in Windsor have joined to run a small stall in the Portobello Road on Saturdays. The general stock is particularly strong on art, biography and topography, all of which is in excellent condition and reasonably priced.

Non-book material: prints
Services: mail order

Notting Hill Books

132 Palace Gardens Terrace W8
727-5988

M–W 10:00–6:00   Th 10:00–1:00   F–Sat 10:00–6:00

Africa   ancient world   architecture   art   biography   British topography   China and South-East Asia   cinema   cookery   crafts education   English literary criticism   English literature   fiction French literary criticism   French literature   gardening   general history   German literary criticism   German literature   Latin America   London   Middle East   music   natural history   philosophy plays   poetry   politics   psychology   Russian literary art   Russian literature   sociology   theatre   travel   USA   USSR   women

Publishers' remainders, review copies and a few second-hand titles comprise the stock of this friendly shop where the speciality subjects are art, history, poetry, literature and literary criticism. Half-price paperbacks are available, and here the selections of literature and literary criticism offer especially good choice and value as the cover price, rather than the current price, is the basis for the reduction.

Seal Books

2 Coningsby Road W5
567-7198

W–Sat 10:00–5:30

Africana archaeology art astronomy biography children's books classics cookery crafts economics education fiction French literature gardening health history literature music natural history philosophy photography poetry politics psychology reference religion sociology topography translations travel

Seal Books is one of Ealing's little treasures. Second-hand books pack the shelves of this rambling but cozy bookshop. English literature, modern first editions and Africana are the specialities of the shop, and they also have large sections of cookery books, French literature and titles on religion. The woman who runs the shop also has a nearby bookroom which she opens by appointment.

Services: mail order

Sky Books

119 Shepherd's Bush Road W6
603-5620

M–Sat 10:30–6:30

crime fiction horror romance science fiction thrillers

Sky Books is one of many book exchange shops sprouting all over London. Any books bought at the shop can be returned for a 50% credit towards your next purchase. Second-hand paperback science fiction, horror stories and thrillers comprise most of the stock of **Sky Books**. There are also UK and US comics and science fiction magazines.

Non-book material: see above
Services: mail order occasionally search service for American comics

World of Books

(Piccadilly Circus)

30 Sackville Street W1
437-2135

M–Sun 10:00–6:00

ground floor:

antiquities archaeology art biography British royalty British topography children's books collecting cookery crime dance economics essays Far East fiction film gardening history hobbies humour linguistics literary criticism literature medicine military history music natural history naval history occult philosophy plays poetry politics psychology science and technology science fiction sociology theology travel guides

basement: (*T–F 10:00–6:00*)

Ferret Fantasy (George Locke):
detective fiction fantasy horror science fiction

Graham Weiner
sciences

World of Books is a vast, general second-hand bookshop specializing in biography and with large history, travel and fiction sections with some remainders. Its cookery section is particularly notable. **Ferret Fantasy** specializes in science fiction and fantasy books and magazines, while **Graham Weiner**'s interest is in the field of science books.

As with most second-hand shops, the stock at **World of Books** turns over regularly, replenished from new purchases as well as from the owner's large volume of warehoused stock.

Catalogue: travel and cookery lists six times yearly

Wyvern Bookshop

(Turnham Green)

148 Devonshire Road W4
995-6769/995-5005

W–Th 9:30–12:00 Sat 10:00–6:00

extensive railway collection (by appointment only) industrial history transport

A small general antiquarian and second-hand bookseller stocking some titles other than those the owners specialize in. The books are in good condition. This newly-opened shop acts as an outlet for Robert Humm who previously only worked from home.

Catalogue: railways, buses, trams and trolleys

WEST LONDON
Antiquarian Bookshops

Andrew Edmunds   (Oxford Circus or Piccadilly Circus)
44 Lexington Street W1
437-8594

M–F 10:00–6:00

This shop specializes in 18th and early 19th-century prints of social and political caricature and decorative scenes. There is a small selection of antiquarian books on illustration, caricature, history and decorative prints.

Non-book material: see above
Services: mail order   wants lists accepted in field of art

Bernard Quaritch Ltd   (Piccadilly Circus)
5 Lower John Street W1
734-2983

M–F 9:30–5:30   Closed 1:00–2:00

art, colour plate and illustrated books   bibliography and palaeography   early printed books and manuscripts   English literature   natural history   philosophy and human sciences   private press books, standard sets and children's books   science, medicine and technology   travel

Quaritch is one of the grand old antiquarian booksellers in London. The shop was founded in 1847 by Bernard Quartich who built his business into the largest bookselling enterprise in the world. The vast collection of catalogues he produced from his stock during his 50 years as a bookseller carried the stamp of his interests in natural history, oriental learning, fine art, incunabula, illustrated manuscripts, early English literature and cartography – to name but a few areas.

Today, the staff, though no longer all in the family, are still producing up to 10 catalogues yearly, reflecting an extensive stock of general antiquarian books. I was disappointed, though not surprised, to find that the physical layout of the shop does not encourage browsing, as most of the books are kept out of sight or locked in cases. The staff, however, are very happy to attend to 'specific' browsers and willingly spend an afternoon with serious bibliophiles.

Services: mail order   search service   auction service   sale by consignment   appraisal
Catalogue: many on specialized subjects

Brian Bailey   (Notting Hill Gate)

Westbourne Antique Arcade
113 Portobello Road W11
229-1692 (home number)

Sat 9:00–4:00

art   collecting   fiction   French literature   illustrated books   literature   military history   natural history   poetry   reference   topography   travel

Brian Bailey specializes in antiquarian illustrated books, although the stock in his stall in Portobello Road has a selection of general second-hand and antiquarian titles.

Non-book material: maps   prints
Services: mail order

Caissa Books   (Bond Street)

Grays Antique Market
Stand A18/19
1–7 Davies Mews W1
629-3644

M–F 11:00–6:00   (Sat 8:00–4:00, Stand 20, 290 Westbourne Grove W11)

Australia   chess   children's books   military   travel

Caissa in the basement is a general second-hand and antiquarian bookseller, though they specialize in collector's books about chess from the 16th century to the present (though most, however, are from the mid-19th century). Other areas of interest are illustrated travel books about Australia and a selection of children's books.

Services: mail order   wants lists accepted for chess books   search service for general books
Catalogue: chess books, four to six lists annually

Charles Sawyer   (Green Park)

1 Grafton Street W1
493-3810

M–F 9:00–5:30 Sat 9:00–11:30 (except Bank Holidays)

Churchill   colour plate books   early printed books   English literature   fine bindings   natural history   original works of book illustration   private press books   rare Africana   sporting

Sawyer is an old and established London dealer in antiquarian and rare books 'suitable for a gentleman's library from Caxton to 1900', so on a number of counts a large portion of the population will probably not become **Sawyer** clients. But for those gentlemen with libraries, **Sawyer**'s books are in fine condition, most are truly rare – and dear. One of the specialities of the shop is books by, about and owned by Churchill. Africa, especially South Africa, is another area of interest.

Non-book material: illustrations   prints   maps of Africa
Services: mail order   search service
Catalogue: lists issued annually
Publications: Charles J. Sawyer has published prints of Africa, and has done a small book on Kyd, the illustrator

Christopher Mendez

(Oxford Circus or Piccadilly Circus)

51 Lexington Street W1
734-2385

M–F 10:00–5:30

This is primarily an antiquarian print shop, but bound volumes of 16th through 18th-century continental prints and engravings are sold. A few new books about prints and print making are also available.

Services: mail order
Catalogue: prints and occasional books

Demetzy Books

(Notting Hill Gate)

Westbourne Antique Arcade
113 Portobello Road W11

Sat 10:00–5:00

architecture   art   classics   collecting   crafts   early illustrated books   medical literature   modern first editions   natural history   travel

Demetzy carries second-hand and antiquarian books. Illustrated books and literature comprise most of the stock.

Services: mail order   wants lists accepted

Henry Sotheran Ltd

(Piccadilly Circus)

2–5 Sackville Street W1
734-1150

M–F 9:00–5:30

second-hand and antiquarian:

archaeology   architecture   art   astronomy   atlases   autographs   bibles (rare)   bibliographies   black studies   botany   British topography   children's books   cinema   classics   colour plate   cookery   costume   fiction   gardening   heraldry   history   literary criticism

literature   modern first editions   mountaineering   natural history
philosophy   poetry   religion   sporting   travel

new books:

art   collecting   general remainders   natural history   reference

Sotheran's was founded in 1761 in York, which makes it the
country's oldest surviving booksellers, and moved to London in 1815.
It has an illustrious history behind it. H. C. Folger of New York
acquired much of his renowned Shakespeare Collection with **Sotheran**'s help. Charles Dickens was a regular customer of the shop and, on
his death, Dickens's library was purchased by **Sotheran**. Many of the
items are still in the shop's possession.

No business can rest on past laurels though, and **Sotheran**'s
continues to sparkle in this century. The shop carries new, remaindered, second-hand and antiquarian books, so it is possible to find a
50p book next to a rare £2,500 bible.

Whatever the price, each book is there to be looked at, taken out of
their beautiful bookcases, leafed through and appreciated. To me,
this is the wonder of **Sotheran** – books aren't locked away, prices are
marked on the back flyleaf (a custom once general but now unique to
Sotheran) and the staff are happy to let people wander around.

The shop also has an extensive collection of prints and maps, and
English hand-coloured engravings in all subject areas.

Not too many book lovers could walk by the lovely, tall windows of
this shop front and pass by the contents.

Non-book material: see above
Services: export dept., catering for libraries and institutions and
acts as an agent for periodicals   mail order   special order anything
in print   search service   framing service   binding and restoration
Catalogue: numerous lists on specialized topics
Publications: Henry Sotheran Ltd publishes fine books on natural
history

E. Joseph   (Bond Street)

1 Vere Street W1
493-8353

M–F 9:30–5:30 (phone for Saturday hours)

Formerly in the Charing Cross Road, **E. Joseph** now operates from a
suite where the firm continues to sell fine and rare books with some

emphasis on illustrated works, press books, fine bindings, colour plate books, as well as Victorian and early 20th-century watercolour paintings. As before, it is perhaps the first place to try for sets of standard authors, such as the *Waverley* novels, bound in cloth or leather. There is also an interesting stock of general literature.

Non-book material: see above
Services: mail order   search service
Catalogue: various always available

Levrant Rare Books   (Notting Hill Gate)

Panton Gallery
159 Portobello Road W11
no phone

Sat 9:00–5:00

children's books   cookery   early English literature   fine bindings
magic   poetry   UK history

The tightly packed shelves of this orderly shop hold a general stock of rare and antiquarian books. Second-hand books or modern first editions will not be found here.

Maggs Bros Ltd   (Green Park)

50 Berkeley Square W1
499-2007/2051

M–F 9:30–5:00

Maggs Bros, which since November 1982 has been bookseller by appointment to the Queen, is the last of London's grand 19th-century antiquarian booksellers still to be family-run (it now has a fifth generation at work here). The shop on Berkeley Square is a listed, blue-plaque house with five floors of medium- to high-priced antiquarian books in all subjects.

  Each general department is run by a seasoned book buyer and scholar in the field, each of whom seems to be more than happy to spend time with any customer who shows genuine interest in books. Somehow amid the grandeur of lovely bookcases filled with (almost) priceless volumes, the shop maintains an atmosphere of friendliness which always makes me feel as though I'm walking into someone's home. And chances are, you will run into one member of the Maggs family if more than a half hour passes by before you leave.

The special interest of one of the family is the literature of exploration and travel, especially the voyages of Captain Cook, and there are also beautiful books in the area of natural history and art.

Non-book material: ephemera engravings maps prints autographs Indian miniatures illuminated manuscripts
Services: mail order search service valuations bid on commission
Catalogue: numerous specialized catalogues
Publications: Maggs Bros Ltd has published reprints on exploration, natural history and bibliography and other areas

Marlborough Rare Books Ltd   (Piccadilly Circus)

35 Old Bond Street W1
493-6993

M–F 9:30–6:00

Marlborough, which has recently expanded into more general books as well, specializes in antiquarian books on fine and graphic arts, including architecture, calligraphy, bibliography and illustrated books. The stock ranges from the rarest specimens of early printing to mid 19th-century engraved and bound illustrations. The staff are knowledgeable and gracious.

Services: mail order search service in fields binding repair valuation bid on commission
Catalogue: separate lists on architecture, bibliography and calligraphy, illustrated books, fine and applied arts

217

Mellor & Baxter   (Bond Street)

Grays Antique Market
Stand 367
58 Davies Street W1
629-7855/6

M–F 10:00–6:00

In this renovated indoor market behind South Molton Street are a
number of specialized second-hand and antiquarian booksellers.
Mellor & Baxter concentrates on early (16th through 18th-century)
medical and scientific books, as well as antiquarian illustrated travel
books and atlases. Also on hand is some antiquarian English
literature mainly of the 18th and 19th centuries.

Services: mail order   search service
Catalogue: annual general catalogue   short lists of medical/science
books

Peter Eaton (Booksellers) Ltd   (Holland Park)

80 Holland Park Avenue W11
727-5211

M–Sat 10:00–5:00

ground floor: antiquarian

antiques architecture art classics cookery economics heraldry
history: general, naval and military literature medicine music
natural history occult religion sets science sport travel

basement: second-hand

anthropology architecture art biography British topography
drama economics fiction film foreign literature history literary
criticism literature London history music occult philosophy
poetry psychology reference science sociology theatre theology travel

Peter Eaton is a lovely light and airy shop in which the cheapest
stock is kept in the basement, and rises in price – always reasonable –
as one ascends. 'General' is the only word to describe the range of
stock on both floors, all of which is in good condition and well

labelled. 'Distinctive' is hardly too strong a word for the interior of this shop, with a multi-level ground floor and soft, natural lighting throughout. The atmosphere is serene, and spending a few hours here with the shop's diverse stock is certainly pleasurable.

Non-book material: manuscripts
Services: mail order
Catalogue: occasional specialized lists
Publications: Peter Eaton has published bibliographies in the past

Timothy Shaw   (Warwick Avenue)

1 Lanark Place W9
289-1200

M–W 10:00–5:00   F–Sat 10:00–5:00

architecture business exploration France French literature history literary history literature London manuscripts mysticism natural history poetry religion sciences technical travel

Timothy Shaw and his wife have now moved from the City to this elegant shop in Maida Vale. Their stock of antiquarian books, which continues to attract many of their customers from the previous location, has become a little smaller but remains full of highly desirable volumes, all of which are in excellent condition. They have also started to sell remainders, but these are certainly not the run-of-the-mill chain-store sort; these are general, high-quality titles with some emphasis on literature and history. This friendly shop, Mr Shaw deeply knowledgeable and enthusiastic about his excellent stock, is one of the most pleasant to visit in London.

Services: mail order   search service (occasionally)
Catalogue: detailed lists regularly issued

SOUTH WEST LONDON
General Bookshops

Army & Navy   (Victoria)

101–105 Victoria Street SW1
834-1234

M–Th 9:00–5:30   F–Sat 9:00–6:00

antiques   art   biography   children's books   classics   cookery
crafts   film   gardening   history   humour   illustrated books and
special editions   languages   literature   natural history   naval and
military   reference   sport   theatre   transport   travel accounts and
guides

This is quite a large and complete book department for a general
department store. Hardcover and paperback fiction and non-fiction
are carried, with illustrated and gift books overflowing out of the
shelves onto tables.

Non-book material: department store
Services: mail order   special order

Balham Food and Book Coop   (Balham)

92 Balham High Road SW12
673-0946

M–T 9:30–6:30   Th–F 9:30–6:30   Sat 9:30–5:30

anarchy   animals and pets   anthropology   child raising   children's
books   cosmic solutions and theory   crime   drama   essays   feminist
fiction and poetry   fiction   film and TV   health   Hinduism   history
homeopathy   horror and fantasy   I Ching   Irish fiction and politics
Islam   law and disorder   legends   linguistics   literacy   literature
Marxism   media   mysticism   nutrition   occult   photography
poetry   politics   psychic phenomena   psychology   Qabalah   racial
politics   science   science fiction   self-sufficiency   sexual politics
sociology   stress   Sufism   Third World fiction and politics   UK
trade unions   yoga

If the variety of current titles at the **Balham Food and Book Coop** have any one thing in common it is that they are all non-racist and non-sexist, including the wide selection of children's books. Different areas of radical politics figure prominently in the stock, as do titles on alternative medicine, Eastern philosophies and general nutrition. Good selections of feminist, Irish and Third World fiction are available, as well as journals and newspapers on politics and community issues.

Adjoining the bookshop is a food shop and a vegetarian cafe.

Non-book material: badges cards posters
Services: special orders

Battersea Arts Centre Bookshop

(Clapham Junction
– British Rail)

Old Town Hall
Lavender Hill SW11
223-6557–9

W–Sun 11:30–9:30

architecture art biography children's classics cookery and food
crafts feminism fiction film history humour literature music
philosophy photography poetry politics reference sociology
theatre and stage travel women's presses

Although Battersea has been acquiring something of an overspill population from Chelsea in recent years it still lacks bookshops, which makes this good one in **Battersea Arts Centre** (in the Old Town Hall, at the top of Theatre Street, where Bertrand Russell delivered 'Why I am not a Christian' in 1927) all the more useful. Its general stock, which is largely in paperback, has a large children's section as well as an emphasis on the arts and stage, literary fiction, poetry and the various women's presses. Run highly knowledgably and enthusiastically, it is very much a part of the Arts Centre, organizing, for example, a stall of books outside the cinema and holding a literary festival. A number of authors, such as Ian McEwan, Paul Theroux and Graham Swift, live in the area and the shop promotes their books vigorously, in hardback as well.

Non-book material: cards   a good range of literary and political magazines maps postcards

221

Services: mail order   special order   travelling bookshops to schools, etc.   school supply   mailing list sent to members of Battersea Arts Centre

Belgravia Books   (Victoria)

43 Elizabeth Street SW1
730-5086

M–F 10:00–6:00   Sat 10:00–1:00

This is a small general bookshop crammed with the latest – and best – hardcover and paperback titles in subjects such as literature, fiction, music, art, history, biography, sociology and psychology. There is a good number of children's books, and the stock is generally above average in the quality and content of the books.

Services: mail order   special order

Berger & Tims   (Victoria)

7 Bressenden Place SW1
828-8322

M–F 9:30–5:30

art   biography   classics   collecting   cookery   fiction   gardening
health   history   hobbies   literature   music   natural history   poetry
reference   sports   thrillers   travel guides

Berger & Tims is a very nicely stocked general bookshop carrying a range of paperback and hardcover fiction and non-fiction. Conveniently located just around the corner from Victoria Station, the books here certainly offer an excellent range of new titles which makes a better choice than the usual station kiosk fare.

Services: mail order   special order

Bolingbroke Bookshop
(Clapham South)

147 Northcote Road SW11
223-9344

M–T 9:30–5:30   W 9:30–12:30   Th 9:30–8:00   F–Sat 9:30–5:30

art   architecture   business   children's   classics   cookery and food
crime   essays   fiction   history   humour   languages   military
music   photography   poetry   reference   religion   travel

A welcome addition to the largely bookless Battersea and Clapham is
this shop close to the excellent Northcote Road market. Its stock is
concentrated on paperbacks, but a range of hardbacks, especially in
new titles, is also kept.

Non-book material: cards   maps   wrapping-paper
Services: mail order   prompt special order (also by telephone)

Books Etc.
(Knightsbridge)

147 Brompton Road SW3
584-6152

M–T 9:00–6:00   W 9:00–7:30   Th–Sat 9:00–6:00

antiques   art   astrology   biography   children's books   classics
cookery   crafts   crime   ecology   economics   fiction   film   games
gardening   geography   health and child care   history   humour
literature   music   mythology   natural history   occult   Pelican,
Penguin   philosophy   photography   plays   poetry   politics
psychology   reference   religion   science fiction   sex   sociology
sports   travel guides   women's issues

This large branch of the **Books Etc.** chain also sells records.

Non-book material: cards   records   wrapping-paper
Services: special order

223

Books Etc.   (Victoria)

66/74 Victoria Street SW1
828-8849

M–T 9:00–6:00   W 9:00–7:30   Th 9:00–6:00

antiques   art   biography   children's books   classics   cookery
crafts   crime   film   games   gardening   health and child care
history   humour   literature   music   mythology   natural history
photography   plays   poetry   politics   psychology   reference   sex
sociology   sports   travel guides   women's issues

This branch of **Books Etc.**, often to be found, as an increasing
number of bookshops are, playing pop music has a prominent section
of thrillers near the door, no doubt to catch the Victoria station
commuters. Reduced books are often found here, either damaged
copies or remainders.

Non-book material: cards   wrapping-paper   magazines
Services: special order

Broadway Books   (Fulham Broadway)

15 Jerdan Place SW6
385-8334

M–Sat 10:00–6:00

antiques   art   architecture   biography   children's books   cinema
cookery   crafts   fiction   gardening   history   humour   illustrated
nature   photography   reference   sport   transport   travel   wine

This remainder shop belongs to West London Books, a firm which
specializes in taking quantities of books for sale at offices and
factories. The turnover, both in paperback and hardback, is therefore
rapid. While some of the books are the sort that are only published to
be remaindered, there is a number of interesting titles to be found.

Non-book material: maps   wallcharts
Services: see above

Fielders

54 Wimbledon Hill Road SW19
946-5044

M–Sat 9:00–5:30

antiques art BBC publications biography biology business
chemistry children's books classics collecting cookery crafts
economics fiction film gardening geography geology history
law literature military history music natural history paperbacks photography physics plays poetry and verse reference
science fiction sports travel guides

Fielders carries current paperback and hardcover titles and has
particularly good sections of children's books, travel guides and
paprback fiction.

Non-book material: stationery artists' materials maps
Services: mail order special order
Catalogue: Christmas

The Gloucester Road Bookshop

123 Gloucester Road SW7
370-3503

M–F 8:30a.m.–10:30p.m.   Sat–Sun 10:30–5:30

antiques archaeology architecture art biography cinema classics cookery crafts detective fiction fiction film gardening
health history humour literature science music natural history nostalgia philosophy photography plays poetry politics
reference science fiction travel guides women

The old bookseller in *The Human Factor* could remember the days
when people would queue for a new World's Classic; it is likely that
queues will form outside this shop, owned by the Greene family,
which, together with Waterstone's appears to be pioneering book-
buying as the best evening's entertainment in the area. A high level of
stock is maintained — it is the sort of shop one had always hoped
would open in the area. There are plans to expand into the basement.

225

Non-book material: postcards
Services: special order

Harrods Book Department (Knightsbridge)

Knightsbridge SW3
730-1234

M–T 9:00–5:00   W 9:30–7:00   Th–F 9:00–5:00   Sat 9:00–6:00

general:

antiques archaeology architecture art bibles biography business classics collecting cookery crafts drama Everyman Library fiction film and TV fishing and yachting health French texts gardening health and childcare history humour language teaching literature London medicine military history music natural history pets photography poetry politics prayer books psychology reference religion science fiction sports teach yourself theatre thrillers transport travel guides wine

children's books:

Beatrix Potter cartoon books classics fairy tales fiction up to nine fiction over nine first readers foreign languages general knowledge geography history hobbies Ladybird music nature nursery rhymes painting poetry pre-school reference

Harrods has a very large book department with new paperback and hardcover titles. Children's books have an entire room of their own with a range of books for all ages and reading levels. For adults there is a wide selection of illustrated books about Britain, art, antiques, food, wine and sports, a section of Penguin classics and new fiction, as well as sections of recent hardcover titles in politics and best-selling fiction, and a large selection of Michelin guides.

Britain's largest private library is located at **Harrods** through which, for an annual subscription fee, customers can borrow newly published books, especially in the areas of biography, history, travel and fiction.

Non-book material: department store
Services: mail order   special order   library lending

Harvid Bookstore

(Sloane Square)

157 King's Road SW3
352-9841

M–Sat 9:30–7:00

architecture   art   biography   children's   cookery and food   DIY
fiction   film   gardening   history   literature   nature   occult   reference   religion   sciences   sports and games   theatre

Substituting a 'k' for the 't' in Boots's old red neon-sign the founding
joint managing director of Panther Books opened the first shop of his
group here in the middle of 1982. Athough it deals largely in
remainders, it is run as a proper bookshop with the staff knowledgeable and enthusiastic about the regularly changing stock. Both
paperbacks and hardbacks are carried, this branch being especially
aimed at the local mixture of literary and pop-music markets. Many
hardbacks are far cheaper than the current paperback edition.
Full-price books are also in stock, mostly in paperback with the
best-selling hardbacks.

Non-book material: cards   cassettes (at bargain prices)   maps
postcards   wrapping-paper
Services: special order

The Hill Bookshop

(Wimbledon)

87 High Street Wimbledon SW19
946-0198

M–T 9:30–5:30   W 9:30–1:00   Th–Sat 9:30–5:30

art   biography   child care and pregnancy   children's books   classics   cookery   fiction   gardening   health   history   humour   literature   military history   mysteries   naval history   poetry and verse
reference   religion   sports   travel guides

The Hill Bookshop is a general bookseller with a somewhat
up-market stock of current paperback and hardcover titles, much of
which is fiction, literature and art. At the rear of the shop is a
children's room with books including Asterix and Tintin titles, as well
as some BBC educational materials.

Services: mail order   special order

227

John Sandoe Books

10 Blacklands Terrace SW3
589-9473

M–Sat 9:30–5:30

ground floor:

antiques antiquities architecture art biography classics collecting cookery Eastern religions fiction furniture gardening history literature natural history pottery textiles travel guides

basement:

children's:
classics dance fairy tales fiction games and sport history music nursery rhymes story books verse

adult:
health psychology

first floor: paperbacks

classics drama drama criticism fiction history literature literary criticism philosophy poetry psychology religion sociology stage history Virago

John Sandoe is a complete general bookshop, set back from the King's Road in a lovely low-slung cottage. With three floors of books, the shop has a large children's section, an unusually wide range of hardcover books in all subjects and an excellent range of paperbacks. The friendly staff are highly knowledgeable.

Services: mail order special order
Catalogue: Christmas selections

H. Karnac (Books) Ltd

56–58 Gloucester Road SW7
584-3303

M–Sat 9:00–5:30

No. 58 ground floor

architecture art biography cookery crafts fiction furniture literature memoirs music natural history reference travel guides *basement*

group analysis   general Freudian and Jungian literature
psychoanalysis   psychotherapy

No. 56: paperback

anthropology architecture art biography child care children's
books cinema classics cookery Corgi, Everyman, Faber, Paladin,
Pan, Pelican, Penguin, Picador fiction film criticism history
language teaching linguistics literature music philosophy
photography plays poetry politics psychology reference science
fiction sciences sociology thrillers war fiction

Karnac is divided between a paperback shop and one that specializes
in psychoanalysis and psychotherapy while keeping some general
books on its ground floor. The general stock is concentrated on recent
fiction, art books and other non-fiction. (There is also a stock of
second-hand paperbacks at 25p each which often contains bargains
among the routine thrillers.) At No. 56 the stock is divided between
all the main paperback publishers, as well as some lesser-known ones,
with about equal amounts of fiction and non-fiction. (There are some
American publications as well.)

   Downstairs at No. 58 are books in the shop's speciality,
psychoanalysis and psychotherapy; all aspects of the subjects are
covered, making this the best-stocked shop of its sort in Europe.

Services: international mail order   special order
Catalogue: books on psychotherapy and psychoanalysis listed every
two years

Lamley & Co. (South Kensington)

1, 3, 5 Exhibition Road SW7
589-1276

M–F 9:00–5:30   Sat 9:30–1:00

architecture art biography biology business ceramics chemistry classics computer science cookery crafts design drama
ecology fiction games gardening geology history language
teaching literature mathematics music natural history photography physics poetry politics reference statistics technical
travel guides

Lamley carries a fairly large selection of academic text books and current popular fiction and non-fiction. For students, books in the sciences, technology and business are particularly prominent, while those taking a break from the nearby Victoria and Albert or Natural History Museums will find illustrated art and natural history titles, as well as contemporary fiction for the trip home.

Non-book material: artists' materials   cards   stationery   graphic design supplies
Services: mail order   special order

Oppenheim & Co. Ltd   (South Kensington)

7–9 Exhibition Road SW7
584-5641

M 8:30–6:00   T–F 7:30–7:00   Sat 9:00–6:00   Sun 10:00–6:00

antiques   architecture   art   British monuments and cathedrals Buddhism and Eastern religions   classics   cookery   crafts   decorative arts   economics   Everyman   fiction   film   gardening   history language teaching   literature   military   music   mysteries   natural history   philosophy   photography   poetry   politics   psychology reference   sex and pregnancy   sports   transport   travel guides

With a general selection of current paperback fiction and non-fiction, **Oppenheim** particularly concentrates on books in the field of art. Not only are full-price art books available, but the shop has two large tables full of reduced-price art books, some of which are remaindered, but many of which are the last few copies of current titles. A fine selection of contemporary paperback fiction is also on hand with writers such as Maxine Hong Kingston and Gunter Grass. There is always a good stock of Everyman titles at half-price or less. A section has been opened upstairs devoted to military and transport books.

Non-book material: calendars   prints
Services: mail order   special order (when possible)

The Pan Bookshop   (South Kensington)

158 Fulham Road SW10
373-4997

M–Sat 10:00am–10:00pm   Sun 2:30–6:30

art   art history & criticism   biography   children's books   cinema
classics   cookery   crime   drama   economics   feminism   fiction
gardening   health and sex   history   humour   literary criticism
literature   music   natural history   occult   philosophy   poetry
politics   psychology   reference   religion   science fiction   sociology
teach yourself

Owned by Pan Publishers and no doubt keeping longer hours than
their publishing parents, **Pan** is a general bookshop which stocks a
wide range of paperback literature and poetry, among other subjects.
In addition to these areas, however, are excellent selections of
hardcover and paperback books on the fine and visual arts.

Non-book material: cards   literary magazines
Services: mail order   special order

Paperback Centre   (Brixton)

10 Atlantic Road SW9
274-8342

M T Th Sat 8:00–5:30   W 8:00–1:30   F 8:00–6:00

Africa and Caribbean   biography   children's books   China   cookery   education   fiction   health   humour   labour history   Latin
America   Lenin   literary criticism   Marxism   philosophy   plays
poetry   politics   psychology   reference   science fiction   sciences
sexual politics   sociology   Soviet Union

As with the other two shops in this group the **Paperback Centre** has
an emphasis on left-wing and socialist literature, while this branch
has rather more stock of children's books and those about the
Caribbean and much of the stock is in paperback. The shop opens
early for the sale of a wide range of newspapers and magazines.

Non-book material: see above   maps   posters
Services: mail order   special order

The Penguin Bookshop

(Sloane Square)

157 King's Road SW3
351-1915

M–W 10:00–7:00   Th–S 10:00–8:00

ground floor:

children's books   crime   music   new titles

basement:

classics cookery drama education feminism health & medicine
history humour languages literature natural history philosophy poetry politics psychology recreation reference science
travel

Like its sister in Covent Garden, this shop stocks mainly paperbacks,
though not exclusively from the Penguin, Pelican and Puffin imprints,
most of the titles from which are on the shelves. Those that are not
can be ordered in up to two days.

Non-book material: greeting cards and postcards   wrapping-paper
Services: special order
Catalogue: Penguin monthly stocklist

Pulteney & Co.

(South Kensington)

22 Thurloe Street SW7
589-0522

M–F 9:30–5:30   Sat 9:30–2:00

antiques   applied art   art history   classics   collecting   cookery
crafts   decorative arts   drama   fiction   history   literature   music
natural history   philosophy and religion   poetry   psychology
sports   UK monuments and cathedrals

Pulteney carries new paperback fiction, as well as a large selection of
art books, in the fine and applied arts. An interesting frequently
changing number of remaindered books fills much of the shop.

Non-book material: cards   posters   prints
Services: special order

232

Response Community Bookshop

(West Brompton/
Earls Court)

300 Old Brompton Road SW5
370-4606

M 12:00–7:00   T–Sun 10:00–7:00

new:

around Earl's Court   art   biography   British history and politics
children's books   China   Earl's Court authors   education   feminism   fiction   food and booze   health   humour   Irish history and
politics   middle east   natural history   philosophy   photography
popular science   psychology   sexuality   sociology   supernatural
Third World   US history and politics   USSR

second-hand:

biography   cookery   history   hobbies   language teaching   literature   philosophy   poetry   religion   society   travel guides

Response is a small community bookshop with a welcoming,
living-room atmosphere created by sofas, a fireplace and midday
snacks served by the friendly staff. While the selection of books is
limited, the shop has acquired funds to expand the already well-
chosen stock of alternative and community oriented literature. In the
front room of the shop are current titles, including a nice range of
fiction with authors like Tom Sharpe and Muriel Spark. Non-fiction
is stocked with its usefulness to the neighbourhood in mind, so instead
of the Michelin guide to France, there is *The Hitchhiker's Guide to
Europe*. Second-hand books are in the rear of the shop, and include
some children's, as well as general fiction.

A printing workshop downstairs is available for community use, as
is the meeting room upstairs. A free community newspaper, *Response*,
is published by the shop and the back page of the paper is devoted to
news about books and the **Response** project. It is hoped to open a
darkroom.

Non-book material: badges   jewellery   postcards   painting
Services: special order
Publications: Response publish a community newspaper

233

Richard Worth Booksellers

(Putney Bridge)

9 Lower Richmond Road SW15
788-9006

M 12:00–6:00   T–Sat 10:00–6:00

ground floor:

animal and pets   business   child care   children's books   classics
drama   fiction   gardening   literary biography   literary criticism
literature   magic   music   natural history   reference   science fiction
Shakespeare   sports and games   transport   travel guides   war novels

basement:

art   biography   Buddhism   cookery   crafts   current affairs   dance
Eastern religions and philosophies   gardening   health   history
music   philosophy   plays   poetry   politics   psychology   reference
transport   travel guides

Richard Worth is a general bookshop specializing, in their words, in
'better books', all of which are new. The upstairs is devoted to fiction
and non-fiction, including a range of children's books and a few
illustrated titles on transport, animals, travel and natural history.
The basement holds a wide selection of books on fine, modern and
visual arts, Eastern religion, politics, poetry and biography, with
smaller sections in other areas.

Non-book material: stationery   greetings-cards   postcards
Services: mail order   special order

Sabarr Books

(Brixton)

378 Coldharbour Lane SW9
274-6785

M–T 10:00–6:00   W 10:00–2:00   Th–Sat 10:00–6:00

Africa: history, literature, politics   Americas: history, literature,
politics   art and media   biography   Caribbean: history, literature,
politics   children's books   civil liberties   classics   cookery   economics   education   fiction   health   history   literary criticism   literature   music   performing arts   philosophy   plays   poetry   politics
psychology   race relations   sociology   women

Sabarr is an excellent black community bookshop specializing in leftist literature in the areas of history, politics and fiction. Books within these fields on Africa, the Caribbean and North and South America are the main areas of concentration. About a third of the shop is devoted to multiracial children's books, many of which are imported from the USA and the Caribbean. Adult and child education is another field in which the shop specializes, carrying many titles of interest to students and post-graduates working in the areas of literacy, numeracy and education. Within the field of social science, books on civil liberties, economics and philosophy form the mainstay of the stock.

 Sabarr has opened another of the available floors in the building for discussion groups and art exhibitions. Debates on local issues (e.g., the Nationality Act) are already sponsored by the shop and a children's festival at the local community centre is also organized by the co-operative society which runs **Sabarr**.

Non-book material: cards   posters   prints   sculptures   postcards   artefacts   crafts
Services: mail order   special order when possible
Catalogue: complete list of titles

W. H. Smith   (Sloane Square)

36 Sloane Square SW1
730-0351

M–Sat 9:00–5:30

W. H. Smith   (Earl's Court)

266 Earl's Court Road SW5
370-3201

M–Sat 9:00–5:30

W. H. Smith   (East Putney)

111 High Stret SW15
788-2573

M–Sat 9:00–5:30

235

W. H. Smith

180 Streatham High Road SW16
677-3031

M–Sat 9:00–5:30

Tetric Bookshop

(Clapham Common)

116 Clapham High Street SW4
622-5344

M–F 10:00–6:00   Sat 9:30–6:00

anthropology art biography black studies child care children's books classics cookery crime DIY drama economics education electronics feminism fiction film games gardening humour literature mathematics medicine music natural history occult philosophy poetry politics psychology reference science short stories sociology sports transport travel guides US society war

To my mind this is the most interesting of the three **Tetric Bookshops**, perhaps because Clapham brings together such a variety of people and interests. Though it is a general bookshop, the shop specializes primarily in books on the social sciences, especially those on local and national political issues, black studies and sociology, as well as contemporary literature.

Non-book material: cards wrapping-paper
Services: special order

Tetric Bookshop

(Putney Bridge)

309 New King's Road SW6
731-2494

M–F 10:00–6:00   Sat 10:00–5:00

archaeology art biography black studies children's books cookery crafts drama economics education environment fiction

film   gardening   history   hobbies   humour   modern society   music
natural history   occult   philosophy   poetry   politics   psychology
reference   religion   sex   short stories   sociology   sports   travel
guides   young adults

This is one of three **Tetric Bookshops** owned and designed by an
architectural firm which has given a light and airy feeling to the
interior of each shop. The likenesses end, however, with the physical
similarities because each shop reflects the interests and needs of the
neighbourhood in which it exists.

The New King's Road shop is in the midst of a relatively properous
neighbourhood, with quite a few fathers who travel elsewhere to work
and many mothers who stay at home with children. As a result, the
shop has a large selection of children's classics, story books, picture
books and some non-fiction, and a separate young adults section.
Tetric also stocks hardcover and paperback fiction, and more
expensive 'coffee table' books suitable for gifts. More political or
alternative subject areas are adequately represented, but not as fully
as the other areas mentioned.

Non-book material: cards   stationery
Services: special order

Tetric Bookshop   (Tooting Broadway)

113 Mitcham Road SW17
767-0056

M–Sat 10:00–6:00

art   biography   business   child care   children's books   classics
cookery   drama   education   fiction   film   games   gardening   health
and medicine   history   humour   literature   music   natural history
occult   Penguin   poetry   politics   reference   religion   science
science fiction   sociology   study aids   travel guides   women

This is a general bookshop (one of three **Tetric** shops) with prominent sections of books on the arts, contemporary literature, women's
issues, blacks, politics and the social sciences, reflecting the literate,
working class and politically active profile of the area.

Non-book material: cards   magazines   journals
Services: special order

Truslove and Hanson   (Knightsbridge)

205 Sloane Square SW3
235-2128

M–T 9:00–5:30   W 10:00–7:00   Th–F 9:00–5:30   Sat 10:00–5:00

ground floor:

biography   British architecture and landscape   children's books
cookery   fiction   games   gardening   natural history   sports   travel
guides

basement:

antiques   architecture   art   biography   classics   crafts   crime and
mysteries   fiction   historical and romantic fiction   history   literature   philosophy   poetry   psychology   reference   science fiction

With an interior as neat and sparkling as the rest of Knightsbridge,
Truslove and Hanson, part of the W. H. Smith chain, stock current
titles which also reflect the tastes of their well-heeled 'neighbourhood'
clientele. Extensive sections of travel guides, children's books and
current fiction mark the general stock of this two-floor bookshop.

Non-book material: cards   records   stationery   wrapping-paper
Services: mail order   special order
Catalogue: Christmas, spring and autumn lists

Village Books   (Streatham/Streatham Common – British Rail)

17 Shrubbery Road SW16
677-2667

M–Sat 10:30–7:00 (often 7:30)

academic text books   art   business   child care and education
children's books   cinema   classics   cookery   crafts   DIY   fiction
gardening   health   history   humour   literature   local history and
authors   natural history   occult   philosophy   poetry   poetry criticism   politics   psychology   reference   religion   science fiction   sociology   sports and games   travel guides   war   women's studies

This small shop, a few yards from Streatham High Street, carries
mostly current titles; in its small space it contains a remarkably wide

stock owing to a system of keeping one copy of most titles and replacing them within a few days. More of the ground floor is being given to second-hand books of a general sort, while some of the rest of the stock has a distinct focus on 'alternative' literature and politics. However, as the owner of this friendly, enterprising shop remarks, he is willing to take any book, magazine, pamphlet, artwork etc. that looks interesting and, as a result, this shop draws customers from all over London. Certainly, it is a refreshing change from the bland chain-stores which fill much of the High Street.

Non-book material: cards   local artists' work   'freak' posters and comics   records   small corner of South American crafts
Services: mail order   special order   school & library supply

Waterstone's   (South Kensington)

99–101 Old Brompton Road SW7
581-8522

M–F 9:30am–10:30pm   Sat 9:30–7:00   Sun 12:00–7:00

art & antiques   biography & memoirs   children's books   cookery & diet   drama   gardening   health   history   literature   military   natural history   poetry   reference   religion & philosophy   travel & guides   twentieth-century fiction

This was the first **Waterstone's** to open, in 1982, and is still the smallest with about 25,000 titles. Each branch tries to cater to a particular market, and this one sees itself very much as a neighbourhood bookstore, taking a lot of special orders from local people.

Non-book material: maps   postcards   *London Review of Books, Books & Bookmen*
Services: mail order   search service and selective lists for account holders   **Waterstone's** credit card which can be used in all branches and by telephone

SOUTH WEST LONDON
Speciality Bookshops

ANTIQUES

Don Kelly
(Sloane Square)

Antiquarius Stand R8
135 King's Road SW3
352-8882

M–Sat 10:00–6:00

There are shelves of some 600 new books at this antique stand in King's Road, all of which deal with collecting and antiques (e.g., dolls, furniture, brass, pottery, watches, silver and porcelain).

Non-book material: antiques
Services: mail order   special order   search service

ART

ICA Bookshop
(Charing Cross)

Nash House
12 Carlton House Terrace SW1
930-0493

T–Sun 12:00–9:00

art artists biography cinema: biography, genres, theory ICA exhibition catalogues individual rights literature Marx philosophy photography politics sexual politics USSR women's issues and literature

The limited space available to the **ICA Bookshop** is unfortunate because in addition to having a good range of books on contemporary art and artists, the shop has the beginnings of an excellent selection of alternative literaure, modern classics, film theory and political philosophy. A unique section on children and art caught my eye, as did the wide range of arts, crafts, photography, film and political magazines from the UK, US and the Continent.

240

Non-book material: artists' cards   international selection of arts magazines (including back-issues)
Services: special order

Nigel Greenwood Inc.   (Sloane Square)

41 Sloane Gardens SW1
730-8824

M–F 10:00–6:00   Sat 10:30–1:30

Approaching this unassuming residence one would hardly expect the marvellous range of books on contemporary art to be found inside. **Nigel Greenwood** encourages browsers but not all the stock can be fitted on the shelves. It is primarily an art gallery, and its basic book business is mainly conducted by mail; still it is possible to see and buy books in person. They publish lists of titles on all aspects of contemporary art – the particular focus of the gallery – and recent lists have included titles on futurism, art and psychoanalysis, experimental theatre and performance texts, exhibition catalogues and reproductions of artists' notebooks. A particular interest of **Nigel Greenwood** is bookworks, or examples of artists using the book as an artistic medium. Their books come not only from the UK, but also the USA, France, Germany, Italy and the Netherlands. Their lists also feature a wide range of art journals and magazines.

   A regular perusal of **Nigel Greenwood**'s book list is enough to keep contemporary art enthusiasts up-to-date on the people and movements which are shaping modern art around the word.

Services: mail order   special order
Catalogue: regular comprehensive lists
Publications: Nigel Greenwood Inc. occasionally publishes material about the artists whose work is shown in the gallery

241

Pruskin

(Sloane Square)

Chenil Art Galleries
183 King's Road SW3
352-9095

M–Sat 10:00–6:00

Pruskin has a small selection of mainly second-hand books on fashion, textile design and the decorative arts during the period 1880 to 1930. The shop specializes in the work of Georges Barbier and Georges Le Pape, and the *Gazette du Bon Temps*, but is mainly concerned with objects.

Non-book material: art nouveau and deco objects
Services: mail order   wants lists accepted in field

St George's Gallery Books Ltd

(Piccadilly Circus)

8 Duke St/St James's SW1
930-0935

M–F 10:00–6:00   Sat 10:00–1:00

St George's is a compact shop which specializes in new and second-hand academic and scholarly books on fine art, antiques, architecture, glass, furniture, genres and related subjects. The range of the stock and the owner's knowledge make this an essential shop to visit for books on such subjects.

Services: mail order   special order
Catalogue: new titles lists

Tate Gallery Shop

(Pimlico)

Millbank SW1
834-5651

M–Sat 10:00–5:00   Sun 2:00–5:30

The **Tate Gallery Shop** has a selection of fine arts books in subject areas which relate, in some way, to the artists in the gallery and the

242

genres they represent. Also available are reference and exhibition catalogues from the gallery, and a selection of art related magazines.

Non-book material: calendars   cards   diaries   framing service   gifts   prints   slides   tote bags
Services: mail order   special order
Catalogue: Tate Gallery publications
Publications: The **Tate Gallery** publishes exhibition catalogues, studies of artists, cards, posters and prints

Victoria and Albert Museum Shop   (South Kensington)

Cromwell Road SW7
589-6371   ext. 244

M–Th 10:00–5:30   Sat 10:00–5:30   Sun 2:30–5:15

architecture   art history   art of the book   ceramics   children's books   conservation and restoration   design   engravings   furniture and woodwork   gallery guides   graphics   heraldry   illustrators   metal work   oriental art   paintings and water-colours   poster history   print collecting   psychology and art   sculpture   textiles   theatre   UK villages and gardens

The **V & A** bookshop carries new titles about aesthetic and technical aspects of all areas of art. An entire section is devoted to titles on the art of the book, another has a wide range of books about the conservation and restoration of antiques and art work, while all the titles, even in more traditional areas for a museum shop, seem to be chosen with great care. Adjoining the bookshop is an impressive gift and crafts shop.

Non-book material: cards   crafts   gifts   posters   prints   reproductions   slides
Services: mail order   special order (when possible)
Publications: The **V & A** publishes books through HMSO and with a variety of commercial publishers

BUSINESS

BEC Business Books

(Tooting Bec)

15 Trinity Road SW17
767-5356

M–Th 9:00–3:00 F 9:00–5:00 Sat (first in every month only) 9:00–5:00
Note. From September–November and January–February the shop is
open every weekday from 9:00–5:00

accountancy advertising banking commerce computers industry law marketing mathematics retailing secretarial statistics

The shop specializes in management and business studies, its books
being useful for both the student and the businessman.

Non-book material: stationery
Services: mail order telephone-ordering service special order
Catalogue: stocklist on request

CHILDREN'S BOOKS

Bookspread

(Tooting Bec)

58 Tooting Road SW17
767-6377

M 10:00–5:00 Th 10:00–9:00 F 10:00–5:00

birth death divorce fairy tales fiction films and TV history
literature marriage music myths natural history picture books
poetry reference story books

Current titles for and about children are the specialities of **Bookspread**. Located in one room of a building in a residential area of
Tooting Bec, the staff is concerned with making books and reading
fun. Titles are arranged according to age groups, so it is easy for
mothers, play group leaders, teachers and children to find the most
appropriate books. The shop which also carries books for adults
about children and child care, organizes storytellings, talks about
books, has visiting writers and runs an advisory service.

Non-book material: cassettes records
Services: mail order special order in any field boxes of books on

sale or return for schools and children's organizations
Catalogue: subject lists (e.g., birth and death)

The Children's Bookshop   (Wimbledon)

66 High Street SW19
947-2038

M–Sat 9:00–5:30

Sister to the Muswell Hill Children's Bookshop, this shop in Wimbledon village largely shares it stock, which caters for 0–14-year-olds. Adult bestsellers are on sale too, to catch the bigger children.

Non-book material: birthday cards   bookmarks   story tapes
wrapping-paper
Services: special order

The Mother's Union Bookshop   (Westminster)

Mary Summer House
24 Tufton Street SW1
222-5533

M–F 9:30–5:00

baptism   bible stories   bibles   children's books   crafts and hobbies
early learning   education   faith   family and children   history
literature   marriage   natural history   prayer   religion   religious
doctrine   social issues   travel guides and maps   worship   youth
clubs and school assemblies

The Mother's Union provides one rather chaotic room of new books on children, the family and religion. Within these subject areas little order can be discovered, but the largest and most useful section in the shop is of children's books.

Non-book material: cards   wrapping-paper
Services: mail order   special order
Catalogue: Mother's Union publications
Publications: The Mother's Union publishes books about the family and children

245

DESIGN

The Design Centre (Piccadilly Circus)

28 Haymarket SW1
839-8000

M–T 9:30–6:00   W–Th 9:30–8:00   F–Sat 9:30–6:00
Sun 1:00–6:00   Public holidays 2:30–6:00

architecture   art   automobiles   children's books   city and urban
design   cookery   crafts   design history   design theory   economics
engineering design   environmental design   futures   gardening
general paperbacks   graphics   home design   modern crafts
psychology

This bookshop is part of an unusual space developed by the Design
Council, which includes an exhibition area, a snack counter, a
gallery, and a gift shop featuring contemporary designs in housewares
and gift items. The bookshop itself is quite spacious (watch out for
steps, though) and specializes, naturally, in new books on all aspects
of home and commercial design from DIY to publications on
architecture for the professional designer. The general selection of
books includes imaginatively designed children's pop-up books.

Non-book material: see above
Services: mail order   special order
Catalogue: general book list, three to four times yearly
Publications: Design Council Publications produces titles on all
aspects of design; three magazines and a variety of design journals

DETECTIVE FICTION AND TRUE CRIME

Grey House Books (Sloane Square)

12a Lawrence Street SW3
352-7725

M–Sun 10:00–5:00 (telephone advisable first)

Camille Wolff has an excellent stock of books covering both true
crime and detective fiction. Who wrote it, as much as whodunit, is
certain to be known here. Hardback fiction, all of it in good condition
and frequently with dust-jackets, ranges from well-known authors
such as John Dickson Carr to the many lesser-known from all periods,
Mrs Wolff knowing many delightful books to be found amongst these.
(Detective fiction is becoming increasingly collected, one dealer
246

recently paying £2000 for a first edition of Ian Fleming's *Casino Royale* at an auction.) The true crime books range from the Notable British Trials series and the works of William Roughead to studies of forensic work and criminology.

Services: mail order
Catalogue: catalogue issued regularly

EASTERN EUROPE

Orbis Books (London) Ltd   (Earl's Court)

66 Kenway Road SW5
370-2210

M–F 9:30–5:30   Sat 9:30–4:30

Orbis specializes in new books, magazines and journals about, and from, Eastern Europe, with particular emphasis upon Poland, the Ukraine, the USSR and Czechoslovakia. Most of the books are in the languages of Eastern Europe, although the shop stocks books published in English which are relevant to the region. Politics, art, religion, women's issues, labour, language teaching and literature are just a few of the subjects covered, though they carry everything from children's books to specialized academic texts. **Orbis** has a small antiquarian section and are quite willing to attempt to track down out-of-print titles.

Non-book material: cassettes folk art records
Services: mail order special order
Catalogue: new titles list every four months
Publications: Orbis Books publishes books in Polish about Poland

EDUCATION

Ujamaa Centre   (Oval)

14 Brixton Road SW9
582-2068

M–F 10:00–6:00   Sat 10:00–5:00

Africa: fiction and non-fiction Asia: fiction and non-fiction Caribbean: fiction and non-fiction development education ecology economics employment, technology, industry energy family

247

health and food Latin America: fiction and non-fiction Middle
East politics population religion sociology women's issues

The **Ujamaa Centre** is one of over 30 organizations in the National
Association of Development Education Centres, each of which is
attempting to provide multi-ethnic education materials for teachers
and parents and to the general public, with more for adults than
previously. Issues touching the Third World, and global topics of
survival are most frequently confronted in the adult material, while
children's learning materials include books of myths, history, health
and basic political and economic issues. Not all the shop's material is
in book form, much appears in education packs, booklets, photo sets,
posters, games, records and slides.

Also housed at the centre is a reference library for use by **Ujamaa
Centre** members, and the South London Education department of
Oxfam.

Non-book material: see above
Catalogue: selected list of titles in stock, such as women's issues and
the Caribbean
Publications: Ujamaa Centre publishes posters, map sets and
various educational material

18th CENTURY AND OCCULT

Hollywood Road Bookshop

(Fulham Broadway/
Gloucester Road)

8 Hollywood Road SW10
352-4659

M–Sat 11:00–7:00

astrology Buddhism cricket diet eighteenth century fiction
literature medicine meditation mythology occult philosophy
poetry psychology reincarnation Sufism Taoism theosophy
Western mysticism

The name of this bookshop, recently opened in the increasingly lively
Fulham Road area, might give a momentary impression of the
cinema, but in fact contains a pleasingly idiosyncratic mixture of
books dealing with a general literature section, both new and
second-hand, and a substantial number of 18th-century books of
literature and poetry. The second-hand and antiquarian books are
reasonably priced, the **Hollywood Road Bookshop** making an
individual addition that will be increasing with the arrival of
American imports and more South American fiction.

248

Non-book material: astrological charts   candles   ephemera prints   Tarot cards
Services: mail order (world-wide)   special order   vigorous search service
Catalogue: astrology catalogue, and other lists in related fields

EQUESTRIAN

J. A. Allen & Co.   (Victoria)
The Horseman's Bookshop

1 Lower Grosvenor Place SW1
828-8855

M–F 9:00–5:30   Sat 9:00–1:00

anatomy   Arabians   betting   breeds and breeding   driving   equitation   events   fiction   general equestrian   hunting   nutrition   polo   racing   reference   stable management   training   veterinary medicine

J. A. Allen is London's leading bookshop for people interested in horses. New, second-hand and antiquarian books are available on all aspects of horse training, breeding, riding and racing.

Non-book material: anatomy charts   cards   calendars
Services: mail order   special order
Catalogue: new title lists   specialized lists   **J. A. Allen** publications catalogue
Publications: J. A. Allen & Co. publishes a wide range of books about horses

FRENCH LITERATURE AND CULTURE

Joanna Booth   (Sloane Square)

247 King's Road SW3
352-8998

M–Sat 10:00–6:00

18th-Century French literature and decorative antiquarian English books comprise part of the stock of this antique shop near the Chelsea Antique Market.

Non-book material: antiques   Old Master drawings
Services: mail order
Catalogue: selected list

Paperbooks

28 Bute Street SW7
584-2840

M–F 8:30–6:00   termtime (10:00–6:00 holidays)   Sat 10:30–5:00

Paperbooks is a friendly French bookshop with a cool, blue and white interior lined with current titles, imported from France, Larousse classics, Gallemard Folio fiction, poetry, literary criticism, thrillers and drama are all here, in French. Michelin guides, language texts, a shelf of cookery books and a large range of children's books – including Tintin and Asterix – are also featured. A small section is given over to English fiction, mainly OUP, Granada, Penguin and Pan.

For a helpful and well-informed staff on French literature and dictionaries, **Paperbooks** is the place to look.

Non-book material: cards   school satchels   wrapping-paper
Services: mail order   special order
Catalogue: specialized lists

Schola Books

7 Harrington Road SW7
589-5991

M–F 9:30–5:30   Sat 9:30–2:00

Schola Books specializes in new and second-hand French books, and books in English about France. Current Penguin classics, literature, reference books and titles in general subject areas are also available in English. French literature, classics, philosophy, history, travel guides, language teaching texts – among other subjects – are available in French. Publishers include Oxford University Press, Hugo, Didier, Harrap, Garnier-Flammarion and Longman. There is French literature in translation and a special children's book section in French.

Journals and newspapers from France are carried, and the shop gives a 10% discount to students. A few second-hand books, French and English are in boxes on the pavement.

Non-book material: cards   maps   posters   stationery   wrapping-paper   pen-repair service   photocopying
Services: mail order   special order

GEOLOGY

Geological Museum Bookshop   (South Kensington)

Exhibition Road SW7
589-3444   Ext. 298

M–Sat 10:00–5:00   Sun 2:30–6:00

fossils   geology   HMSO publications   land formation   minearology
minerals   palaeontology   petrology   rocks   UK regional geology
volcanos

All the books at the **Geological Museum Bookshop** are about geology and related subjects. Children's books, gift books, adult reading and museum catalogues are available, as well as a wide range of 'geological' gifts.

Non-book material: cards   geological charts   jewellery   maps
plaster casts of fossils   posters   prints   slides   stones
Services: mail order
Catalogue: complete list of stock annually
Publications: The Institute of Geological Services, of which the museum is a part, publishes in the field of geological sciences

GIRL GUIDES

Girl Guides Association Shop   (Victoria)

17–19 Buckingham Palace Road SW1
834-6242

M–F 9:00–5:30   Sat 9:00–1:00

badges   camping   charts   games   guiding books   handicrafts   knotting books   sporting

The book section is a small part of the **Girl Guides Association Shop**, containing new titles relevant to all aspects of guiding.

Non-book material: badges   camping equipment   uniforms
Services: mail order
Catalogue: complete list of Girl Guide Association publications annually
Publications: The Girl Guides Association publishes books and magazines about guiding

HERALDRY AND GENEALOGY

Heraldry Today   (Knightsbridge)

10 Beauchamp Place SW3
584-1656

M–W 9:30–5:00

academic dress and insignia   coins, orders and medals   decorations
family heraldry and history   flags and arms   French heraldry
genealogy   heraldic design   Italian heraldry   peerage   reference
royal heraldry   school arms   symbols   topography   UK heraldry

Located at the rear of the building at 10 Beauchamp Place, **Heraldry Today** specializes in new, second-hand and antiquarian books on genealogy and heraldry. Despite the small size of the shop (which is a branch of a much larger shop in Wiltshire) there is a comprehensive selection of titles about heraldry and related subjects in the UK and on the Continent. Burke's Peerage and Debretts publications are here as well as rare and more obscure books on, for example, Italian military insignia or English flags. The shop keeps current and back issues of relevant journals as well.

Services: mail order   special order in field   search service in field
Catalogue: selected list of second-hand and antiquarian books every four months   complete list of new titles every January
Publications: Heraldry Today has published original books and reprints in the field of heraldry

ILLUSTRATED BOOKS

Harrington Bros (Sloane Square)

Chelsea Antique Market
253 King's Road SW3
352-5689

M–Sat 10:00–6:00

Illustrated and decorated books on voyages, travel and natural history, bound literary sets, children's books, atlases and colour plate books are the speciality of this strictly antiquarian bookshop. Located on the ground and first floors of the Chelsea Antique Market, **Harrington** carries books that are as beautiful as they are interesting, most of which are from the 18th and 19th centuries.

Non-book material: decorative prints
Services: mail order   wants lists accepted

MARTIAL ARTS

Paul H. Crompton Ltd (Parsons Green)

638 Fulham Road SW6
736-2551

M–Sat 10:00–6:00

Most of this shop's business is wholesale, although the rather cramped quarters are open for retail customers. Their specialities are martial arts, Eastern religions and philosophies. The shop stocks new books and magazines from the UK, USA and East Asia, and the staff are friendly and helpful.

Non-book material: badges   posters
Services: mail order   special order in field
Catalogue: complete list
Publications: Paul H. Crompton publishes books on the martial arts and survival, with forty titles in print

MEDICAL AND SCIENTIFIC HISTORY

Michael Phelps   (Putney – British Rail)

19 Chelverton Road SW15
785-6766

M–F 10:00–5:00 (telephone first)

An excellent range of titles covering the history of medicine as well as of natural, pure and applied science can be found here, in all languages, and ranging from antiquarian to more recent titles. Topics such as baking and nutrition sometimes surface among the more specialized subjects. Runs of journals such as *Nature* can also be found here.

Services: mail order
Catalogue: a catalogue is issued of the more expensive titles, together with lists of cheaper ones on science and medicine as well as supplementary lists of various topics

MODERN FIRST EDITIONS AND ILLUSTRATED

Words Etcetera   (Gloucester Road/South Kensington)

327 Fulham Road SW10
351-2143

M–F 10:00–6:00

In recent years **Words Etcetera** has moved from Islington, via France, to Guildford, but has now found a permanent home opposite the Pan Bookshop in the increasingly interesting Fulham Road. Two booksellers, Julian Nangle and Peter Jolliffe, share the premises and their stock is very much aimed at the serious collector. The prices are not low, but all the books are in excellent condition, invariably with the original dust-jacket, and they frequently turn up much sought after titles. (There is also a section of the increasingly collected proof-copies and of presentation copies and autograph manuscripts.) The emphasis is on poetry and fiction, with some biography, as well as the illustrated books. Various runs of journals, such as *Horizon* and *Penguin New Writing*, are always in stock. **Words Etcetera** forms an enviable survey of the 20th century.

Non-book material: prints
Services: mail order   vigorous search service
Catalogue: various catalogues regularly issued

MUSIC

Kensington Music Shop   (South Kensington)

7 Harrington Road SW7
589-9054

M–F 9:00–5:45   Sat 9:00–2:00

biography   composers   harmony   instruments   music history
music teaching   orchestration   sight reading

In a portion of what is primarily an instrument shop, **Kensington
Music** has a limited section of hardcover and paperback titles about
composers, musicians and music theory and history.

Non-book material: instruments and accessories
Services: mail order   special order

NATURAL HISTORY

Il Libro   (Sloane Square)

Chenil Art Galleries C89
183 King's Road SW3
352-9041

M–F 10:00–6:00

botany   fine bindings   history   literature   natural history   ornithology   sport   theatre   travel

This lovely-looking market shop is owned by an elegant Italian whose
civilized tastes are evident upon browsing through the shop. Its
books, mainly 18th and 19th-century English titles on botany and
ornithology, are important documents in the development of natural
history, and their fine condition and lovely bindings make them
attractive aesthetic objects in themselves.

Non-book material: prints

Rowland Ward's of Knightsbridge   (Knightsbridge)

25B Lowndes Street SW1
235-4844/5641

M–F 9:30–5:30

Rowland Ward's specializes in modern natural history and illustrated books, as well as out-of-print and rare books on these subjects. Big game hunting, ornithology and Africa are particular areas of speciality in the stock. The shop is a gift shop, too, with rather exclusive items imported from all over the world.

Non-book material: gift items (catalogue available)
Services: mail order   special order   wants lists accepted
Catalogue: frequent selected listings of new, out-of-print and rare books
Publications: **Rowland Ward's** publishes books on big game hunting, natural history and sport

NUMISMATICS

Spink and Sons   (Green Park)

5–7 King Street SW1
930-7888

M–F 9:30–5:30

Spink and Son is a large, elegant Oriental and Islamic art dealer which has a relatively small book department on the third floor of the building on King Street. As part of the numismatic department at **Spink**, the book department specializes in new, second-hand and antiquarian books about coins and medals.

Non-book material: coins   decorations   English painting   Islamic art   medals   orders   Oriental art
Services: mail order   special order   search service
Catalogue: annual list   monthly numismatic circular with coins, medals, new and out-of-print books
Publications: Spink and Son Ltd London publishes books on numismatics

ORIENTAL

Books of Asia

(Parson's Green)

717 Fulham Road SW6

M–F 10:00–6:00   Sat 10:00–4:00

Han-Shan Tang Ltd
731-2447

John Randall
736-9424

In this huge, bright shop two firms combine to provide a comprehensive coverage of countries between Cairo and New Guinea: China, Tibet, India, Japan, Korea, South-East Asia, Indonesia and a developing Middle-East section. The emphasis is on scholarly and serious books, especially in the arts and cultures but technological subjects are covered as well, on all aspects of these countries, both in the original languages and in English and with a stock that ranges from antiquarian to second-hand and new. The Chinese section is particularly strong as the firm has a buyer there, and it is certain that the extremely efficient staff will be able to provide expert assistance on all matters relating to these countries. (A computerized reference system is in use.) Museum catalogues from around the world, together with a huge number of Chinese periodicals, add to the range of this splendid shop.

Non-book material: Chinese calligraphy and scrolls   periodicals photograph albums Japanese paper   prints
Services: mail order   special order
Catalogue: specialized catalogues, such as Japanese language and travel, regularly issued
Publications: Han-Shan Tang reprints rare works on Chinese art and carved jade as well as issuing an increasing number of its own books
Note: **Books of Asia** also has a small branch at Collectors' Corner in the Portobello Road on Saturdays from 8:30–4:00, as well as one in Hong Kong

POETRY

National Poetry Centre Bookshop (Earl's Court)

21 Earl's Court Square SW5
373-7861

M–F 10:00–5:00   during evening events   7:00p.m.–9:30p.m.

anthologies   children's poetry   classical poetry   collected works
criticism   individual poets

One nice retail characteristic of modern poetry is that the volumes are usually slim enough to require little shelf space so, although this shop is a small book room, there is much poetry on display. The majority of the work is by contemporary British poets, there are also small press publications and poetry from the USA, Canada and the Continent, as well as standard authors such as Sir Walter Scott and Shelley. It is run with knowledge and enthusiasm and makes a visit well worthwhile for books so often shunned even by the largest shops.

Non-book material: posters   poetry records   magazines
Services: mail order   special order
Catalogue: annual list
Publications: The **NPC** publishes a major poetry magazine, *Poetry Review*

PSYCHIC WORLDS

The Spiritualist Association of Great Britain (Hyde Park Corner)

33 Belgrave Square SW1
no telephone

M–F 10:00–6:00

Buddhism   cookery   inner knowledge   mediums   psychic worlds
spiritualism   vegetarianism   yoga

This is a small shop in the foyer of **The Spiritualist Association of Great Britain** building, selling new books, booklets, pamphlets, newspapers and magazines on the subjects of psychic and spiritualist interest (which here does not include magic and the occult).

Services: mail order   special order (only through publishers the shop stocks)

PUPPETRY

The Puppet Centre

(Clapham Junction – British Rail)

Battersea Arts Centre
Old Town Hall
Lavender Hill SW11
228-5335

M–F 2:00–6:00   (and also by appoointment)

Upstairs at Battersea Arts Centre is a thriving place for all aspects – practical and theoretical – of puppetry; it forms London's most specialized shop for books, new and second-hand, on the subject, together with an excellent reference library with many long out-of-print titles. **The Puppet Centre** acts very much as an information bureau, able, for example, to provide a directory of all the puppeteers around the country.

Non-book material: postcards (lists available)
Services: see above   mail order   special order   courses   exhibitions   school and eucational work, etc.
Catalogue: regular lists issued
Publications: many pamphlets (lists available) on all aspects of puppetry   a bi-monthly magazine, *Animations*, on world-wide puppetry

RELIGIOUS

The Abbey Bookshop

(Westminster)

21 Dean's Yard
Westminster Abbey SW1
222-5565

M–Sat 9:30–5:00

art   bibles   biography   children's books   cookery   history   London modern British literature   natural history   Penguin   plays   poetry psychology   religion   UK travel guides

About 50% of **The Abbey Bookshop**'s stock is bibles or books about religion. The rest of the books are stocked with the tourist in mind and include books (both paperback and hardcover) on the history and architecture of the abbey, the royal family, English history and classics of English literature.

259

Non-book material: calendars cards etchings gifts prints records of the Abbey Choir slides
Services: mail order special order (limited to publishers in stock)
Publications: The Abbey Bookshop has published a book about the abbey, *A House of Kings*

Catholic Truth Society   (Victoria)

Ashley Place SW1
834-1363

M–F 9:15–5:00   Sat 9:15–1:00

bibles biography children's books comparative religion death family marriage meditation Old and New Testaments prayers spiritual life Sunday readings travel guides

This shop sells new books relating exclusively to the Catholic faith, indeed only titles which carry the Imprimatur are in stock. Major Catholic newspapers and periodicals are sold as well.

Non-book material: cards crucifixes icons jigsaw puzzles rosaries
Services: mail order special order
Publications: The Catholic Truth Society publishes religious pamphlets and books

Church House Bookshop   (Westminster)

Great Smith Street SW1
222-9011

M–F 9:00–5:00

bibles biography children's books commentaries comparative religion doctrine ecumenism liturgy and worship moral theology pastoral work philosophy prayer religious education study aids vocations

This religion bookshop focuses on issues in Christianity, but also has a special section of books on Tolkien and C. S. Lewis. A variety of subject areas are covered, from daily religious life to church history, and the shop is the main outlet for publications of the General Synod.

Non-book material: calendars   church registers   posters   stationery
Services: mail order   special order
Catalogue: *Booklines* lists new titles three times yearly   Church Information Office publications catalogue
Publications: the shop is affiliated to the Church Information Office which publishes books and other materials on Christianity

Church Literature Association   (Westminster)

Faith House
7 Tufton Street SW1
222-6952

M–F 9:30–5:00

bible stories   bibles   biblical lands   children's books   Christian education   church history   church and politics   church and society commentaries   doctrine   ethics   faith   liturgy   Marx and Christ mysticism   poetry   prayer   religion   spirituality   theology   worship

This Christian bookshop is as quiet as the back streets of Westminster in which it is located. The shop's interior has the look and feel of a church and, indeed, the books here are about all aspects of Christianity and the Church.

The most recent books on the role of the church in society are available, as well as a selection of children's books.

Non-book material: cards   church stationery   devotional articles music and song books
Services: mail order   special order
Catalogue: CLA publications
Publications: The **Church Literature Association** publishes books about religion and related issues

Russian Orthodox Cathedral Bookshop

(South Kensington/ Knightsbridge)

67 Ennismore Gardens SW7
485-8102

Sat 5:00–5:30 7:15–7:45 Sun 10:00–10:30 12:15–1:00

Although it is only open for these short periods the Cathedral's bookshop is useful for being one of the few places to stock Orthodox books, prayer-books and Russian Bibles as well as American and English theology in English by Russian and Greek church authorities. Notable too is the section of Orthodox art books.

Non-book material: gramophone records and tapes of Orthodox church music   cards   Greek postcards
Services: mail order   special order
Catalogue: a book-list is available

United Society for the Propagation of the Gospel

(Westminster)

15 Tufton Street SW1
222-4222

M–F 9:30–5:30

Selling general religious books and more specialized titles aimed at overseas missions and their work, this very small shop covers a range of material from all religious denominations – Catholic, United Reformed Church, etc. The Church of England Missionary Society runs the shop with books and other educational materials in price ranges affordable for missionaries. The emphasis is on literature about, and from, the Third World and overseas centres, and there is a reference library as well.

Non-book material: film strips and slides with commentaries posters   prayer leaflets   study packs
Services: mail order   special order
Catalogue: general list of titles
Publications: The **USPG** publishes two magazines and a range of educational material (see above)

The Wall Bookshop

Elizabeth Street SW1
730-7303

M–F 10:00–6:00   Sat 10:00–2:00

bible stories and characters   bibles   children's books   Christianity
church history   death   family relations   healing   life and lifestyle
prayer   sickness   song books

This small Christian bookshop is on a mezzanine floor overlooking a
lovely new café, restaurant, giftshop complex. The shop has an
increasing stock and carries the most popular, new Christian titles in
subjects from church history to coping with death.

Services: mail order   special order

Westminster Cathedral Bookshop

Westminster Cathedral
Morpeth Terrace SW1
828-5582

M–Sat 9:30–5:00

bibles   breviaries   cathechisms   education   lives of saints   moral
theology   scriptures   spirituality   theology

This small bookshop concentrates on books of worship and literature
about the Catholic faith. In addition to the shop's main room of new
titles, there is a small room with second-hand and 'slow moving'
titles. A selection of Catholic newspapers is sold.

Non-book material: calendars   cards   cassettes   diaries   icons
records
Services: mail order   special order when possible
Catalogue: new titles list

Wimbledon Evangelical Book Centre (Wimbledon)

2 Queen's Road SW19
946-2634

M–T 10:00–5:00   W 10:00–1:00   Th–Sat 10:00–5:00

apologetics bible stories biography children's books Christian life Christian service Christology church history commentaries cults and deviations doctrine ethics evangelism healing last days missionary non-Christian religions persecution religion and science revival and renewal sermons and talks youth

With a speciality in the general area of Christian books, the **Wimbledon Evangelical Centre** concentrates particularly on titles relevant to evangelism in the modern world. Books approach the subject from a variety of practical, theoretical and academic perspectives. The shop also has a large section of educational and enjoyable children's books. Each August, the **Centre** organizes the Mustard Seed outreach programme on Wimbledon Common, in an effort to communicate with children in the area.

Non-book material: cards gift items posters records
Services: mail order special order

SCIENCE FICTION

At the Sign of the Dragon (Mortlake – British Rail)

131 Sheen Lane SW14
876-3855

M–T 10:00–6:00   W 10:00–1:30   Th–Sat 10:00–6:00

antiques children's books classics cookery fantasy fiction film gardening humour language teaching psychic world religion science fiction war novels

Although a portion of the stock is devoted to current fiction and non-fiction titles, this shop specializes in affordable children's books and current science fiction and fantasy titles. The owner has his own special interest in sicence fiction bibliographies and is, therefore, extremely knowledgeable in the field and very helpful. The commitment to children's books is realized in a range of fiction and non-fiction titles, mostly paperback, for all age levels (there is also a section of science fiction books for children).

A wonderfully chatty catalogue on science fiction titles is put out every three months, and the shop stocks a range of science fiction and fantasy magazines.

Non-book material: badges   cassettes   science fiction records   spoken word books   posters   fantasy games   T-shirts
Services: mail order   special order
Catalogue: science fiction and fantasy lists quarterly (includes books on science facts versus fiction)

TRAVEL AND TOPOGRAPHY

Vandaleur Antiquarian Books   (Mortlake – British Rail)
69 Sheen Lane SW14
878-6837   393-7752

M–Sat 11:00–6:00 (hours may vary; telephone advisable first)

This small shop close to Mortlake Station has a large stock, specializing in travel and topography from all periods, together with a general range of paperbacks and hardbacks and a number of illustrated books.

Non-book material: prints
Services: mail order
Catalogue: regular catalogues issued

TRAVEL AND TOURISM

British Tourist Authority   (Green Park)
64 St James's Street SW1
629-9191

Winter: M–F 9:15–5:30   Sat 9:15–12:30
Summer: M–F 9:00–6:00   Sat 9:00–2:30

Located in the large British Tourist Authority information centre, the bookshop carries guidebooks for all areas of Great Britain. They stock many local and regional tourist board publications as well as a large section of publications about London. The shop also carries illustrated books on the treasures and landmarks of Great Britain. The major travel guides are available in different languages and there are books for special interests and needs such as staying in castles and taking children on holidays.

Non-book material: maps posters T-shirts
Services: mail order
Publications: BTA publishes travel, hotel and restaurant guides, motorist and tourist maps

London Tourist Board Bookshop (Victoria)

26 Grosvenor Gardens SW1
(Victoria Station)
730-3450

M–F 9:15–5:30

The London Tourist Board runs a bookshop on the first floor of its Tourist Information Centre in Victoria Station which features books about, and guides to, London. Londoners as well as tourists are catered for, with books for visitors to London from overseas and the rest of Britain (e.g., accommodation and shopping guides, maps, picture books), and books for those taking day trips out of London. An exceedingly cordial staff make discovering our own city an enjoyable experience.

Non-book material: maps postcards posters prints slides
Services: mail order
Catalogue: book list
Publications: LTB publishes: *London for the Disabled Visitor, London is for Children, London is for Weekends*

UNIVERSITY BOOKSHOP AND TEXT BOOKS

Imperial College Bookshop (South Kensington)

223 Sherfield Building
Imperial College of Science and Technology
Exhibition Road SW7
589-5218

M–F 9:15–5:15

aeronautics art biology chemical engineering classics computing cookery fiction geology humanities life sciences literature

management   mechanical engineering   mining   Pelican, Penguin
physics   reference

In the short time since this college bookshop has been under new
management the proportion of academic textbooks to general titles
has shifted significantly in favour of the latter. Not to say that the **IC
Bookshop** is not still a source for a wide range of university level
textbooks, but about 40% of the titles are now general paperback
fiction and non-fiction. In the general subject areas, reference books
figure prominently, but there is also a selection of current fiction and
literary classics.

Non-book material: cards   drawing equipment   stationery
Services: mail order   special order

URBAN PLANNING

Planning Bookshop   (Charing Cross)

17 Carlton House Terrace SW1
930-8903/4/5

M–F 9:00–5:30

architecture   conservation   design   energy   environment   environmental education   general planning   history of planning   housing
impact assessment   land use: derelict and inner city   leisure   new
towns   planning in developing centres   planning in Europe   planning law and procedures   psychology   public participation   regional
planning   resources technology   rural planning   sociology   transport   urban and city planning

This is the bookshop of The Town and Country Planning Association
carrying only those new books related to city planning in the Greater
London area.

Services: mail order   special order
Catalogue: annual list updated quarterly
Publications: The Town and Country Planning Association pub-
lishes two magazines and an occasional book

SOUTH WEST LONDON
Second-hand Bookshops

Alpha Bookshop
(Streatham – British Rail)

193 Streatham High Street SW16
677-3740

M–Sat 10:00–6:30

biography crime detective fiction historical fiction humour
non-fiction romance science fiction technical thrillers war
westerns

Alpha carries general second-hand paperbacks and magazines (a few
of which are soft-core pornography), a selection of new Mills and
Boon romances, and a few hardcover non-fiction and fiction titles.
The shop offers to exchange books bought there for 50% credit
toward the next purchase and the owner is helpful and cordial both
buying and selling.

Non-book material: see above

Cobb and Webb Booksellers
(Putney Bridge)

21 Lacy Road SW15
789-8840

M–Sat 10:30–5:30

adventure fiction art bibles biography children's fiction classics drama espionage fiction film gardening history literary
criticism literature military history music mysticism natural
history Pelican performing arts philosophy poetry poetry criticism politics reference religion romance sports stage history
supernatural transport travel guides and accounts war novels

Cobb and Webb sells a general stock of second-hand books with a
particular concentration on the arts and literature. In the shop are
low-priced paperback romance and war novels side by side with an
excellent selection of out-of-print poetry and literary criticism. As one

moves toward the rear of the shop the titles are a bit more academic, but the shop has a range of books to please most people.

The Constant Reader   (Fulham Broadway)

627 Fulham Road SW6
731-0218

M–Sat 10:30–7:00

art archaeology children's books crime and detective fiction fiction film food and drink history humour illustrated journalism literature military and naval music natural history philosophy pocket edition poetry politics reference religion science fiction sport theatre topography travel

A recent addition to the Fulham Road is this excellent, general shop which has a certain emphasis on titles (in all categories) dealing with oriental topics. The stock here is considerably cheaper than in many shops (the reviser of this guide, for example, found a volume of Locke at less than a sixth of the list-price). A boon to the neighbourhood, **The Constant Reader** is well worth making a detour for.

Non-book material: ephemera   postcards
Services: mail order

Jennings Bookshop   (Streatham Common – British Rail)

556 Streatham High Road SW16
764-8135

Th–Sat 9:00–5:45

art biography cinema collecting cookery drama fiction history literature military history and equipment music natural history photography sports technical transport travel guides

Jennings carries new and second-hand books in a variety of subjects. Most of the titles (about 70%) are second-hand, including low-priced paperbacks and moderately-priced hardcover titles.

269

Non-book material: second-hand sheet music
Services: special order (limited to publishers in stock)

Richard Lally Ltd   (Putney – British Rail)

152 Upper Richmond Road SW15
788-9123

M–W 10:00–5:00   F–Sat 10:00–5:00

art   children's books   fiction   history   literature   travel

At the back of this antique shop is a room of books, all reasonably priced, which varies in stock from week to week. These paperbacks and hardbacks are well worth looking through. In the main part of the shop is a case of more valuable books in first editions and fine bindings.

Non-book material: antiques   furniture   prints   watercolours, etc.
Services: mail order

Take Five   (Wimbledon)

5 Prince of Wales Terrace
Hartfield Road SW19
947-4850

M–F 9:30–5:30   Sat 9:00–4:00

Africa   antiques   astronomy   aviation   biography   chemistry   children's books   cinema   classics   commerce   cookery   crafts   cricket   farming   fiction   fishing   French literature   gardening   Greek history   golf   judo   literature   maritime history   mathematics   military history   modern first editions   music   natural history   physics   poetry   psychology   radio and TV   royalty   Russia   Scotland   sociology   theatre   theology   travel guides and accounts

Take Five carries second-hand books in a range of subject areas and as the stock changes from week to week, the quality of the sections also varies. Most of the books are medium-sized hardcover titles and, when I stopped by, the selections of fiction, poetry and travel books were especially useful. An occasional review copy turns up on the shelvs as well.

SOUTH WEST LONDON
Antiquarian Bookshops

Cavendish Rare Books Ltd
(Piccadilly Circus)

2 Princes Arcade SW1
734-3840

M–F 10:00–6:00   Sat 9:30–1:30

Americas   Asia   English social history   exploration   Far East   fine bindings   foreign military campaigns   literature   maritime   merchant shipping   mountaineering   naval   North and South Poles   travel accounts

At the head of this newly restored Dickensian arcade is **Cavendish**, specializing in rare and antiquarian first-hand travel and exploration accounts (especially Polar exploration), maritime and naval history and English social history. The shop is small, but packed with fascinating (and expensive) rare accounts by world travellers.

Non-book material: ephemera   postcards
Services: mail order   search service in field
Catalogue: specialized lists, on travel, four times a year

Chelsea Rare Books
(Sloane Square)

313 King's Road SW3
351-0950

M–Sat 10:00–6:00

ground floor:

biography   children's books   drama   fiction   literary criticism   literature   London history and guides   natural history   poetry   topography   travel accounts and guides   UK guides

basement:

antiques   archaeology   architecture   biography   collecting   continental art   furniture   galleries and museums   interior design   music

271

Firmly rooted in the ambiance of Chelsea (and surviving when other bookshops in the area have closed their doors), this second-hand and antiquarian shop is particularly strong in the areas of literature (17th through 20th centuries), early travel accounts, art and children's books. Downstairs is a gallery with prints, engravings, watercolours and maps, as well as books on the arts.

Non-book material: see above
Services: mail order   search service
Catalogue: general catalogue two to three times annually   occasional specialized lists

John Faustus (Piccadilly Circus)

Lower Gallery
90 Jermyn Street SW1
930-1864

M–F 10:00–5:30

John Faustus specializes in 18th- and 19th-century antiquarian books, including Egyptian and Roman antiquities, poetry, religion, English literature, history and travel.

Non-book material: Rembrandt etchings   fine, general paintings

Pickering and Chatto (Piccadilly Circus)

17 Pall Mall SW1
930-2515

M–F 9:30–5:30

economics   English literature   history   medicine   music   social sciences   science and technology   travel

This excellent antiquarian shop was formerly part of the Dawson group of companies. It tends to receive more mentions in newspapers than many shops do, journalists being fascinated by the involvement of Sir William Rees-Mogg, a former editor of *The Times*. Working in this shop must certainly be more congenial than editing a national

newspaper: its stock, with considerable emphasis on English literature from 1660 to 1800, is the sort that could tempt customers to the
point of bankruptcy should they stay long. It has an interesting,
growing section of volumes of drama, and has sets of authors in
modern editions such as the Davis Swift and the Chapman Jane
Austen.

Non-book material: broadsides and song-sheets   autographs and
manuscripts
Services: mail order   search service
Catalogue: one annual catalogue with 20 supplements

Sanford Books   (Sloane Square)

Chelsea Antique Market
253 King's Road SW3
352-5581

M–Sat 10:00–6:00

architecture   art   ballet   bibliography   children's   cookery and
food   crime   fiction   furniture   history   illustrated   literature
modern firsts   natural history   poetry   theatre   travel

This addition to the King's Road, a little out of sight at the back of the
Antique Market, contains an excellent stock of some 5,000 books, all
in very good condition and their prices reasonable, whether antiquarian or modern. Modern fiction and poetry is especially strong and
there are sets, often in fine bindings, of standard authors such as the
Waverley novels. Notable, too, are the children's books, cookery, art
and architecture. Once known, this will not be a shop to pass by
without a look.

Non-book material: prints and watercolours
Services: mail order
Catalogue: none - the stock goes too quickly

Sims, Reed and Fogg

(Piccadilly Circus)

58 Jermyn Street SW1
493-5660/6952

M–F 10:00–6:00

Antiquarian and out-of-print on fine and applied arts are the speciality of **Sims, Reed and Fogg.** Most of their books are titles concerned with painting, architecture, jewellery, glass and silver, and considerably more stock is on display at these new premises.

Services: mail order   search service in field
Catalogue: catalogues on various subjects issued from six to eight times a year

SOUTH EAST LONDON
General Bookshops

The Arcade Bookshop

(Eltham Well Hall – British Rail)

3 The Arcade
Eltham High Street SE9
850-7803

M–W 9:00–5:30   Th 9:00–1:00   F–Sat 9:00–5:30

art   BBC publications   beauty   biography   biology   chemistry   children's books   cinema   classics   cookery   crafts   drawing and painting   English as a foreign language   fiction   gardening   health and child care   history   horror   literature   mathematics   paranormal   Pelican, Penguin   pet care   photography   plays   poetry   reference   science fiction   sports   travel guides

With bargain books overflowing on to the walk of the arcade, this bookshop carries both new and remaindered titles in general subject areas. **The Arcade Bookshop** has a wide range of children's books, paperback fiction and books in basic academic subjects (e.g., mathematics, early learning, English as a foreign language, study aids and BBC educational publications).

Services: mail order   special order

The Bookplace   (Peckham Rye – British Rail)

13 Peckham High Street SE15
701-1757

M–W 10:00–6:00   F–Sat 10:00–6:00

adult literacy   black studies and politics   children's books   China classics   cookery   **DIY**   economics   education   fiction   film and TV   gardening   health   heroes and villains   history   horror   indoor games   Ireland   literature   local history and culture   music mythology and paranormal   politics   pregnancy and parenthood psychology   science fiction   sociology   sports and hobbies   travel guides   women and sexual politics   young adult fiction

The Bookplace is an impressive community oriented general book-shop, admirably involved with the interests and needs of the neigh-bourhood. Of great concern to the staff of the shop are the areas of basic education – from infant to adult – including adult literacy and numeracy and multi-cultural children's learning materials. Books are available in these fields, and the shop tries to keep young adults involved with books, reading and learning by providing them with their own section of titles. A bit of whimsy creeps into the stock in their sections on heroes and villains and humour but another important dimension of the shop is provided by the books about black politics and 'people's' history – titles on Ireland, Africa, China and their very own Peckham – most with a multi-cultural perspective.

The shop functions as an informal counselling centre, with a staff who are almost always on call for help and advice. Publishing, education, writing and local business support groups each use the shop in the evenings for their meetings and every May **The Book-place** organizes a local book fair.

Non-book material: cards   photographs
Services: special order
Catalogue: shop bulletin   specialized lists (e.g., children's learning materials)
Publications: Peckham Publishing Project publishes books by local authors and about local history and culture

275

Books of Blackheath

(Blackheath – British Rail)

11 Tranquil Vale SE3
852-8185

M–Th 9:30–1:00 1:30–5:30   F 9:30–5:30   Sat 9:30–5:00

ground floor: new books

archaeology architecture art astronomy aviation bibles biography children's books classics cookery crafts drama education fiction gardening geography history language teaching linguistics London maritime history music mythology natural sciences philosophy photography poetry psychology reference religion sociology sports topography: foreign and British

first floor: remaindered books

anthropology archaeology architecture art aviation biography children's books cookery crafts education fiction gardening history industrial history literature maritime history music natural sciences philosophy photography poetry sociology sports topography: foreign and British

Nestled into a picturesque vale which borders the heath, **Books of Blackheath** offers two floors of new and remaindered books. The sections of history and philosophy are specially strong, although their stock of hardcover illustrated books, biographical works, literature and books about topography is also considerable. Generally, the shop has useful holdings in all the subjects listed above, with some interesting bargain books to be found upstairs.

Services: mail order   special order

Chener Books

(East Dulwich – British Rail)

52 Grove Vale SE22
299-0771

M–Sat 10:00–5:30

adventure stories art biography children's books classics crime dance history drama espionage fiction film gardening health history literary biography and criticism literature military history music natural history occult philosophy plays poetry politics science fiction topography transport travel guides

Chener Books is an orderly, and very appealing, general bookshop. Half of the one-room shop is lined with tightly packed shelves of current hardcover and paperback books of and about literature. The shop tries to stock the complete works of the authors they carry, so all of Eliot, Hardy, Hemingway or Plath, for instance, will be available.

The opposite side of the shop consists of second-hand books, which again are concentrated in the area of literature and literary criticism. Also featured are new books about local history and personalities and often the shop will have new and second-hand copies of the same book.

Services: search service for out-of-print (beginning with late 19th century)   special order   library supply

Deptford Booktraders   (Deptford – British Rail)
55 Deptford High Street SE8
691-8339

T–Wed 9:30–5:30   Th 9:30–1:30   F–Sat 9:30–5:30

Africa   art   astrology   biography   black fiction and studies   children's books   cookery/food   current affairs   drama   gardening   health   history   hobbies   language   literature   Latin America   Middle East   Poland   politics   psychology   reference   religion   science fiction   sociology   sport   travel

This wide-ranging shop with some emphasis on current events around the world is a part of the Deptford Literacy Centre, the enthusiastic staff especially keen on literacy among children and adults – regular classes are held, as well as story-reading sessions for children in the shop. The multi-cultural aspect of the shop is reflected throughout its stock which provides an extremely useful general bookshop for the area. Notable, too, is the stock of titles from various community publishing specialists such as Centerprise

Non-book material: badges   cards   guides   magazines   pamphlets   posters   wrapping-paper
Services: mail order   special order   (and see above)

Fagin's Hoard of Books   (Greenwich – British Rail)

26 Royal Hill SE10
no telephone

M–Sun 10:00–6:00

art biography children's books cookery fiction films gardening history mythology nostalgia philosophy photography politics

This small, full remainder shop may well have moved to another part
of Greenwich by this time, where with an increasing stock it should
continue to be well worth a visit when visiting the area's shops.
Notable among its wide-ranging stock is a section devoted to the
publications of the Village Press.

Non-book material: bookmarks cards film stills posters stationery
Services: mail order

Gallery Book Shop   (North Dulwich – British Rail)

1d Carlton Avenue SE21
693-2808

M–Th 9:30–5:30   F 9:30–8:00   Sat 9:30–5:30

ground floor:

art biography children's books cookery drama essays fiction
history humour language literature poetry reference sport
travel and guides

first floor:

antiquarian and second-hand

With a new owner the **Gallery Book Shop**, small but well-stocked,
has become a splendid local bookshop with an emphasis on the
humanities and an excellent children's section. More recent hardbacks, both fiction and non-fiction, are kept than is usual in such
shops and the service is highly knowledgeable and enthusiastic.
Upstairs, the owner's son, who also works at Maggs, has opened a
second-hand and antiquarian section which covers similar subjects;

this is open on each Friday and Saturday, or by appointment –
659-1640

Non-book material: cards   paintings   wrapping-paper
Services: mail order   special order   search service   valuation

The Greenwich Bookshop   (Greenwich – British Rail)

37 King William Walk SE10
858-5789

M–W 10:30–5:30   F–Sat 10:30–5:30

art   astronomy   biography   children's books   classics   cookery
crafts   DIY   education   fiction   gardening   health   history   letters
literature   London   natural history   poetry   politics   psychology
reference   religion   sociology   transport   women's presses and issues

On the corner of King William Walk and College Approach is the
Greenwich Bookshop, a general bookseller with current paperback
and hardcover books. Despite the proximity of another childrens'
bookshop (The Bookboat), **The Greenwich Bookshop** has a large
selection of titles for young readers. The shop is steadily expanding
the women's section, with literature from Virago and books on
feminist issues.

Non-book material: cards   diaries   gift   wrapping-paper   posters
Services: special order

Kirkdale Bookshop   (Sydenham – British Rail)

272 Kirkdale Sydenham SE26
778-4701

M–Sat 9:30–5:30

ground floor: new and remaindered books

anthropology   architecture   art   biography   children's books   classics   cookery   crafts   fiction   film   gardening   health and child
care   history   literature   local history   mathematics   natural his-

279

tory natural sciences Penguin photography poetry and verse
politics psychology reference science fiction sciences sports
travel guides women

basement: remaindered and second-handbooks

antiques archaeology architecture art astrology biography
British Isles cookery crafts economics fiction gardening history language teaching literary criticism literature memoirs
military history natural history occult Penguin performing arts
philosophy plays poetry politics science technology theology
transport travel and exploration

How nice to find that a large and comprehensive general bookshop
can be supported outside Central London. Two floors of new,
remaindered and second-hand books comprise the **Kirkdale Bookshop** where the second-hand section downstairs is expanding (and
where prices are quite reasonable). In each of the second-hand
categories listed above, they have a substantial number of books,
especially in second-hand literature, fiction, biography and philosophy. Current fiction and non-fiction, paperback and hardcover, are
on the ground floor, along with a selection of remaindered books
toward the rear of the shop.

Non-book material: cards posters prints
Services: mail order special order

Marcet Books (Greenwich – British Rail)

4a Nelson Road SE10
853-5408

M–Sun 10:00–6:00

architecture art biography children's books crime/detective
encyclopaedias Everyman's library fiction history literature
Penguin pocket editions poetry Reprint Society theatre World's
Classics

A welcome addition to the thriving Greenwich bookshops is this
general second-hand shop to be found along the alleyway at the side
of the Coach and Horses. The wide-ranging stock contains a number
of first editions, antiquarian titles as well as collections of out-of-print
Penguins and other well-known, useful imprints in pocket-sizes such
as Nelson's Library, together with sets of standard authors.

Non-book material: magazines pamphlets postcards
Services: mail order
Catalogue: in preparation

The Passage Bookshop   (Denmark Hill – British Rail)

Canning Cross
Grove Lane SE5
274-7607

M–T 10:00–6:00   W 10:00–2:00   Th–F 10:00–6:00   Sat 10:0–5:00

adventure fiction anthropology art children's books classics
cookery crime feminism fiction gardening health and child
care history literature magic medical texts music nursing
Pelican, Penguin philosophy poetry reference religion science
fiction sport and hobbies travel guides witchcraft

The Passage Bookshop, tucked away at the end of a quiet alley, has
the feel of a quiet English village shop. Here there is general fiction
and non-fiction, a special section of medical text books to fill the needs
of the students at the hospital nearby, and a third of the shop is
devoted to children's books, including picture books, fiction, sports
and classics.

Non-book material: Camberwell Society cards maps and prints
Services: special order

Roy Hayes (Booksellers) Ltd   (Eltham Well Hall – British Rail)

Chequers Parade
Passey Place SE9
850-4658

M–Sat 9:00–5:30

animals antiques and collecting architecture art children's
books classics cookery crafts fiction gardening health, pregnancy and child care horror literature local history music
natural history plays poetry science fiction topography transport travel

Roy Hayes is a general bookshop, with current paperback and hardcover titles in a variety of subjects and price ranges.

Services: mail order   special order

W. H. Smith   (Elephant and Castle)

Elephant and Castle Shopping Centre SE1
703-1825

M–Sat 9:00–5:30

W H. Smith   (Catford Bridge – British Rail)

The Catford Centre
23 Winslade Way SE6
690-1972

M–Sat 9:00–5:30

W. H. Smith   (Eltham Well Hall – British Rail)

92 Eltham High Street SE9
859-3019

M–Sat 9:00–5:30

W. H. Smith   (Lewisham – British Rail)

53 Riverside SE13
318-1316

M–Sat 9:00–5:30

W. H. Smith   (Woolwich Arsenal – British Rail)

68 Powis Street SE18
854-7108

M–Sat 9:00–5:30

South Bank Bookshop

(Elephant and Castle)

113 Borough Road SE1
928-4701

M 10:00–5:00   T–Th 10:00–6:00   F 10:00–5:00

accountancy bargains biography Black history and fiction business computers cookery drama economics education feminism fiction history law nursing poetry politics psychology and health reference sciences sociology

This recently-opened bookshop is close to the South Bank Polytechnic and its stock, mostly in paperback, caters very much for the needs of the students there, with some emphasis on politics, feminism and certain of the sciences as well as having a substantial stock of Black books such as the Heinemann African Writers series. Useful, too, is a section of books relating to Irish matters, and, as with many shops over the past couple of years, its computer section is growing rapidly; it has not yet, however, swamped a useful section of general titles here.

Non-book material: badges leaflets political magazines pamphlets postcards
Services: mail order special order

The Spread Eagle

(Greenwich – British Rail)

8 Nevada Street SE10
692-1618

M–Sat 10:00–5:30

art biography cinema cookery fiction gardening history illustrated children's books literature modern first editions music natural history poetry theatre topography travel

Opposite the Greenwich Theatre and the Rose and Crown is this shop on the site of the last coach-house on the route between Kent and London. A large number of books, antiquarian and second-hand, is kept among a general stock of antiques. The stock, which is especially strong on travel and topography, is regularly changing so that it is difficult to say exactly what will be found at any time; certainly it is reasonably priced and worth visiting along with the other Greenwich shops. Some of the rarer, large art books are kept in the shop's other branch next to Rogers Turner.

Non-book material: see above   general antiques   postcards ephemera   magazines
Services: mail order

SOUTH EAST LONDON
Speciality Bookshops

ART

Hayward Gallery Bookshop   (Waterloo)

South Bank SE1
928-3144

exhibition hours

This small foyer shop carries a selection of titles on contemporary art, art history, exhibition catalogues, books related to current exhibitions and Arts Council publications.

Non-book material: cards   prints   journals
Services: mail order   special order

BLACK STUDIES

Soma Books   (Kennington)

38 Kennington Lane SE11
735-2101

M–F 10:00–6:00   Sat 10:30–2:30

Africa   art   Buddhism   Caribbean   children's books   comparative literature   crafts   decorative arts   education   ethics   fiction   history   India   Islam   literature   meditation   mythology   philosophy poetry   politics   prayers and chants   reference   religion   sociology Sufism   women   yoga

Soma was initially a mail order business but has had a retail bookshop for the past few years. The shop's books are about India, Africa and the Caribbean, with an enormous variety of publications in English as well as Gujarati, Bengali, Hindi, Urdu and Punjabi. Titles on politics, art, history, literature, mythology and religion are stocked, but the shop's real speciality is in the area of children's learning materials. The Indian and West Indian staff are active in the field of multiracial education and are both knowledgeable and helpful. **Soma** is a black bookshop making a great effort to reach the white population of Britain.

Non-book material: cards   charts on mythology   hand-made stationery   miniatures
Services: mail order   special order
Catalogue: children's books and learning materials   subject lists

CHILDREN'S BOOKS

The Bookboat   (Greenwich – British Rail)

Cutty Sark Gardens
Greenwich Church Street SE10
853-4383

M–W 10:00–5:00   F–Sun 10:00–5:00

adventure stories   Asterix   boats, canals and ships   classics   colouring books   dictionaries   Dr Seuss   educational   Enid Blyton   fairy tales   fiction   films and TV   hobbies   Ladybird   Lion   mysteries   natural history   nursery rhymes   Paddington   picture books   poetry   Puffin   Richard Scarry   science fiction   song-books   storybooks   things to do   Topsy and Tim   Winnie the Pooh

Permanently moored alongside the Cutty Sark Gardens is London's only floating bookshop. A 60 foot Humber keel barge (built in Hull and once used to carry coal and steel) has been converted into one of London's few children's bookshops south of the Thames. A wide range of current titles is available for all ages and reading levels.

For kids who find themselves short of pocket money, the shop has a book club which children can join. Through the club, children can buy bookstamps which are redeemable for books at the shop, making a collecting adventure out of buying books. Children who have read a book from the shop and come and tell the staff about it receive a free stamp for their reporting.

Creativity has not stopped with **The Bookboat** either. A double-decker bus has been converted into a mobile children's educational bookshop and mini film theatre. Artists from Puffin and Collins publishers painted the outside of the vehicle.

Non-book material: badges   cards   talking books   stationery
Services: special order in any field

CINEMA

The Motion Picture Bookshop   (Waterloo)

National Film Theatre
South Bank SE1
928-3517

M–F 12:30–9:30   Sat Sun 2:30–9:30

BFI dossier series   biography   cartoons   criticism   documentary   early cinema   English cinema   genres   history   horror (films)   other media   science fiction (films)   screenplays   screenwriting   TV

As the bookshop of the NFT, **The Motion Picture Bookshop** specializes in new titles about film, TV and video. Many of the books concern the British cinema and film history, but they carry a range of titles often on foreign, international film, directors, stars and film theory. Technical aspects of the cinema, including the subject of writing for the screen, also feature in the shop's stock. Major cinema journals are available as well as the British Film Institute's publications. A small selection of second-hand books is available.

Non-book material: cards   posters   still photography   magazines   badges
Services: mail order   special order   search service
Catalogue: complete annual list   monthly updates

FEMINIST

Books Plus (New Cross)

23 Lewisham Way SE14
691-2833

M–F 11:00–6:00   Sat 10:00–5:00

anthropology   art and language   black studies   community and
social work   education   feminism   health care   history   individual
liberties   literature   Marxist studies   minorities   poetry   politics
psychology   religion   sociology   women's fiction   women's issues
women's studies

Book Plus is a feminist, socialist bookshop, selling new hardcover
and paperback books as well as a range of feminist and political
newspapers and magazines. Most of the books are concerned with
social, economic and political issues, but they carry a wide range of
women's fiction and literature. Women's issues and studies, black
studies and individual liberties are particularly interesting sections
here.

Non-book material: badges   cards   posters
Services: mail order   special order
Catalogue: complete list annually

MODERN LITERATURE

Stone Trough Books (Denmark Hill – British Rail)

59 Camberwell Grove SE5
708-0612

T–Sat 10:00–6:00

archaeology   art   biography   cathedrals and monuments   cookery
crime fiction   history   literary criticism   literature   medical books
modern first editions   opera   plays   poetry

Stone Trough is a newly opened second-hand bookshop specializing
in literature, art books and modern first editions. The shop is small,
uncluttered and very welcoming, with a stock which reflects the
personal interests of the owner. Only 25 authors' works are permitted
in the modern first editions section, including Evelyn Waugh, Aldous

Huxley, T. S. Eliot, Christopher Isherwood and Graham Greene. Prices are about one-third less than those for similar titles in Central London, and to make the trip even more worthwhile, there is a landmark tavern across the road which serves good pub fare.

Services: mail order   search service
Catalogue: modern first editions list twice yearly

POLITICAL

121 Bookshop (Brixton)

121 Railton Road SE24
733-2383

Th–F 2:00–6:00   Sat 12:00–6:00

The **121 Bookshop** is an anarchist and feminist shop oriented toward the needs of the Brixton community. Political issues take precedence among the subject areas, with books on race relations, civil liberties and international and revolutionary politics in stock. The feminist section includes titles about sexual politics, children, gay liberation and health. Most of the books are in the area of non-fiction (including self-help titles on, for instance, plumbing and printing), though a bit of anarchist fiction is available. Books on black studies and specific problems in the Third World are less plentiful at **121** because Sabarr Books, a black community bookshop, is just up the road.

121 also carries a range of political and community magazines and newspapers. The shop hopes to extend its hours and activities in the future by opening daily and sponsoring community meetings and discussion groups.

Non-book material: badges cards posters
Services: mail order special order in fields of anarchy and feminism
Catalogue: comprehensive list
Publications: a poetry and a political magazine are published by the shop

Labour Party Bookshop   (Elephant and Castle)

150 Walworth Road SE17
703-0833

M–F 9:00–5:00

biography   defence   economics   EEC   energy   fiction   history
industry   law   Marxism   philosophy   politics   reference   social
issues   socialism   Third World   trade unions   women

Located in the attractive new Labour Party headquarters, the
Labour Party Bookshop specializes in books on political, social and
economic issues. Pamphlets, booklets, reports and leaflets are in
abundance, on topics from socialism to sexism.

Non-book material: badges   balloons   beer mats   posters
scarves   ties
Services: mail order   special order
Catalogue: monthly lists planned
Publications: The Labour Party publishes campaign handbooks,
discussion documents, reports and a party newspaper

PRINTING AND DESIGN

Francis Marsen Books for Printers   (Elephant and Castle)

London College of Printing
(St George's Road)
Elephant and Castle SE1
735-8484

M–F 10:15–6:15

bookbinding   cinema   colour printing   composing   design   design
history   economics   graphic reproduction   graphics   gravure printing   journalism   law   lithographic, screen and flexographic printing
management   photography   print finishing   printing   science
typography

This is a bookstall, just above the foyer in the London College of
Printing, which carries new titles related to the printing and design
courses given at the college.

Non-book material: artists' and printing material
Services: mail order   special order

RELIGIOUS

The Christian Bookshop   (East Dulwich – British Rail)

17 Lordship Lane SE22
693-7969

M W F–Sat 9:00–5:30

apologetics Banner of Truth bible stories bible study bibles
children's books Christian life church history concordances
devotion dictionaries evangelism home and marriage major
religious authors missions music poetry prayer religion
teaching aids testimony youth

The Christian Bookshop specializes in books on evangelism and
evangelistic education. The scope of their titles is, however, interdenominational, with a good selection of books on bible and gospel
commentary.

Non-book material: cards posters records
Services: mail order special order

Daybreak Books   (Lee – British Rail)

68 Baring Road SE12
857-1188

M–Sat 9:00–1:00 2:00–5:30

bibles biography children's books Christianity church history
commentaries cookery daily life education faith fiction gardening literature poetry and verse prayer reference religion spirituality

Daybreak Books carries a very limited selection of current general
titles in addition to their speciality in Christian books. There are two
floors of books on all aspects of Christanity from scholarly bible
commentaries to accounts of daily Christian life, and the staff are
quite willing to help with anything you don't find on their shelves.

Non-book material: cards cassettes posters records stationery.
Services: mail order special order
Catalogue: selected lists quarterly

Publications: Daybreak Publications has published two books on Christianity

The Mustard Tree   (Forest Hill – British Rail)

37 Brockley Rise SE23
699-4500

M–Sat 9:30–5:00

bibles   children's books   daily Christian life   ethics   faith   health
spirituality   teenagers' books

The Mustard Tree is a very small shop, run by members of the Ichthus Christian Fellowship, which carries a limited selection of new and second-hand books about Christian faith and practice.

Non-book material: cards   crafts   gifts
Services: special order

SCIENCE FICTION

Phantasmagoria   (North Dulwich – British Rail)

8 Colwell Road SE22
693-1938

M–F 9:30–4:30

In this small shop in Dulwich is an impressive collection of pre-Second World War science fiction and fantasy books, 19th century magazines on all subjects, 20th-century science fiction magazines (including *Amazing Stories, Weird Tales* and *Astounding Science Fiction*) and American pulp magazines – all of which are in very good condition. Victorian and Edwardian science fiction writers – Verne, Wells, etc. – are the special interests of the owner, and his prices are quite reasonable.

Non-book material: see above
Services: mail order   wants lists accepted
Catalogue: selected lists of books and magazines six to eight times annually

291

THEATRE AND DANCE

National Theatre Bookshop (Waterloo/Embankment)

National Theatre
South Bank SE1
928-2033   ext. 600

M–Sat 10:00am–11:00pm

autobiography   biography   children's books   contemporary plays
and play-texts   criticism   film   humour   memoirs   photography
play-texts   Shakespeare   stage-history

The **National Theatre** contains three bookshops, the main one being
set in the foyer of the Lyttelton theatre: its free-standing bookcases
contain a surprisingly large cross-section of play-texts (including
those at present being staged by the National Theatre), drama
criticism and stage-history, together with some arts-related titles; the
one in Olivier foyer, which is open from six in the evening and all day
on Saturdays, contains stock along similar lines, the titles themselves
different; the rather smaller one at the Cottesloe has some play-texts
for sale, and is open at performance-times.

Non-book material: T-shirts   shoulder-bags   posters   records
cassettes   maps   newspapers   magazines

UNIVERSITY BOOKSHOPS AND TEXT BOOKS

Goldsmith's College Book (New Cross)
& Stationery Shop

Lewisham Way SE14
692-7171

M–F 9:00–7:30 during term   M–F 9:00–5:00 vacation

art   biology   chemistry   design   education   fiction   French (language)   geography   German (language)   health   history   linguistics   literature   mathematics   music   Open University   philosophy
physics   plays   poetry   politics   psychology   reference
Shakespeare   sociology   technology

Most of the books here are current paperback titles related to the
courses given at the college. Each subject area is represented by a
good range of titles, and the shop is well labelled and organized.

Non-book material: artists' materials   stationery
Services: mail order   special order
Publications: stock selected publications from the college

Mercury Bookshop   (Woolwich Arsenal – British Rail)

Thames Polytechnic
Wellington Street SE18
854-2030

M–T Th 8:45–11:15   11:30–2:15   3:15–5:25   W 3:15–5:00

architecture   art   economics   education   engineering: civil, electrical, mechanical   fiction   history   literature   Penguin   plays   poetry
politics   psychology   sociology   surveying

This is a fairly small college bookshop in the foyer of the Thames
Polytechnic. All the books are new and the shop caters to the student
interests and courses at the polytechnic though there is a general
selection of Penguin paperbacks.

Services: mail order (infrequently)   special order

SOUTH EAST LONDON
Second-hand Bookshops

Bookshop Crystal Palace   (Crystal Palace – British Rail)

89 Church Road SE19
(South Norwood)
771-9719

M–Sat 9:30–6:00

art   astronomy   biography   cookery   education   fiction   geology
history   humour   language teaching   literature   local history   mari-

time history mathematics military history music natural history
ornithology palaeontology poetry romance sciences sports
travel and exploration travel guides

With substantial holdings of books in the sciences, this general
bookshop carries second-hand, remaindered and new books. Natural
history, geology, ornithology, palaeontology and education theory are
particularly large sections here, but second-hand Pelicans, cookery
books, sporting guides and titles on European, African and Asian
history are also available, as well as books on other general subjects.

Services: mail order by request only

The Greenwich Book-Place & Paperback Centre

(Greenwich – British Rail)

258 Creek Road SE10
no phone

M–F 10:00–6:00   Sat Sun & Bank Hols 1:00–6:00

ground floor: second-hand

Africa archaeology astronomy Australia biography Britain
building construction business child care children's books classics communications detective fiction drama economics education essays fiction foreign literature French non-fiction German
non-fiction historical biography history humour language
teaching law literature London maritime history medicine
Middle East military history music mysticism mythology New
Zealand North America occult philosophy plays poetry politics population psychology racial issues religion royal family
sex in society Shakespeare sociology sports stamp collecting
textbooks theatre thrillers transport travel zoology

basement: new & second-hand paperbacks

adventure fiction biography children's books classics detective
fiction drama economics education fiction history literature
medicine modern first editions naval history poetry politics
psychology science fiction Shakespeare sociology supernatural
thrillers westerns

The Greenwich Book-Place is a huge shop selling primarily
second-hand hardcover and paperback books, though the basement

of the shop has just been opened to provide space for new paperback fiction and non-fiction. With books piled high and shelves crammed into the dwindling space on the ground floor, some people will have a difficult time just getting in the door – but the effort is worth the trouble. Something like 20,000 books are available and if you take the time to browse through this rabbit warren, not minding the noise from the cars and lorries whizzing by on Creek Road, then the chances are good that you'll find a book to catch your fancy. The humanities are the strong points of the shop (the owner is also a philosopher and likes to concentrate his book buying in this and related areas), and the recent acquisitions come in so quickly that many of them are not even shelved yet.

From the chaos of the ground floor, you can descend into a world of order in the whitewashed basement, where the shelves are helpfully labelled to distinguish between new and second-hand paperbacks. A special feature of the stock in the basement is the selection of poetry pamphlets. When I visited, the basement had just opened and the stock was still being put on the shelves, but from what I saw of the number of books the shelves will be packed soon enough. To make space for the deluge of recent purchases, the shop has a yearly sale with discounts of 20% on weekends and 30% during the week.

Non-book material: cards   maps
Services: informal wants lists service

Greenwich Market

(Greenwich – British Rail)

Greenwich High Road SE10

Sat 9:00–4:00

Several, varying and various second-hand stalls are to be found among the traders here on a Saturday.

Swan's Bookstall

(New Cross)

29 Deptford Market SE8
691-3705

T–W F–Sat 9:30–3:30

espionage fiction horror romance science fiction thrillers war
westerns

Swan's is a second-hand paperback bookstall with mostly science
fiction and western adventure novels, though they also carry a
substantial number of Mills and Boon romance titles.

Note: **Swan's** Bookstall has another branch at: 5 Tooting Market
SW17   672-4980
M–T 9:00–5:00   Th–Sat 9:00–5:00   F 9:00–6:00

Hillyers

(Lower Sydenham – British Rail)

301 Sydenham Road SE26
778-6361

M–T Th–Sat 8:30–4:30

Opening early and not closing for lunch, Mr. Hillyer keeps a small
general stock of books among his antiques and furniture. The books
are not necessarily related to these but depend very much upon what
happens to arrive from week to week.

Non-book material: see above
Services: mail order

Jane Gibberd

(Waterloo)

20 Lower Marsh SE1
633-9562

W–F 11:00–7:00

In the Cut Market close to Waterloo station and to the Old Vic is this
shop which although it has a medium-sized stock, has a high

turnover, about a quarter of its stock each week. Its stock of remainders and second-hand books is general, always of a good quality and with both the hardbacks and paperbacks confined to the humanities.

Services: mail order

SOUTH EAST LONDON
Antiquarian Bookshops

The Bookshop   (Blackheath – British Rail)

74 Tranquil Vale SE3
852-4786

M–W 9:00–5:00   F–Sat 9:00–5:00

animal biology architecture art history artists Asia biography British topography chemistry children's books classics collecting commercial art cookery essays Europe fiction: 19th and 20th centuries gardening health history literature London and local history maritime history mathematics military history modern first editions natural history plays poetry sports theatre translations travel

The Bookshop which faces the edge of Blackheath is a meticulously organized second-hand and antiquarian shop. Every inch of space in the shop is used, with children's books, first editions, modern and 19th-century fiction and titles on natural history standing out as particularly strong sections. A few new and remaindered titles creep on to the shelves but the majority of the stock is second-hand books.

Non-book material: prints of local topography
Services: mail order   search service
Publications: The Bookshop Blackheath Ltd publishes books about local history

Rogers Turner Books Ltd   (Greenwich – British Rail)

22 Nelson Road SE10
853-5271

M–W 10:00–6:00   Th 10:00–2:00   F–Sun 10:00–6:00

art biography geography history horology language literature
natural history   naval and military   philosophy   religion   science
travel

This shop contains an excellent range of antiquarian, old and
out-of-print books, with some emphasis on academic works. All
languages are covered (an office is kept in Paris which makes the
European service especially good), the prices are reasonable, service
friendly and highly knowledgeable, all making this recent addition to
Greenwich well worth a visit alone.

Non-book material: ephemera   a few pamphlets   magazines
Services: mail order   special order for books throughout Europe
and the world   commissions for all major auctions in Europe   appraisal   search service
Catalogue: eight issued a year on history, history of science, horology, linguistics, etc.

Index   Bookshops by Speciality

Accounting

Chapman's Professional Bookshop
(WC2) 22
Parks Bookshop (WC1) 23–24

Acupuncture

East Asia Company (NW1) 136–7
Genesis Books (EC1) 83–4

Africa

Africa Book Centre (WC2) 13
Charles Sawyer (W1) 213
Grassroots Storefront (W10) 177–8
New Beacon Bookshop (N4) 111
New Era Bookshop (N4) 119–20
Operation Headstart Books and Crafts
(N15) 112
Rowland Ward's of Knightsbridge
(SW1) 256
Sabarr Books (SW9) 234–5
Seal Books (W5) 209
Soma Books (SE11) 284–5
Walter Rodney Bookshop (W13) 178

Albania

The Albanian Shop (WC2) 13

Alternative Bookshops

Balham Food & Book Co-op (SW12)
220–1
Bookmarks (N4) 104–5
The Bookplace (SE15) 275
Centerprise (E2) 92–3
Compendium (NW1) 126–7
The Kilburn Bookshop (NW6) 129
Response Community Bookshop (SW5)
233
Sabarr Books (SW9) 234–5
Sisterwrite (N1) 114
THAP Community Bookshop (E1)
96–7

Village Books (SW16) 238–9
Walter Rodney Bookshop (W13) 178
The Whole Thing (E15) 97

American Literature

Bertram Rota Ltd (WC2) 72
Compendium (NW1) 126–7
English Continental Book Market Ltd
(NW4) 127–8
Gay's The Word (WC1) 40
Skoob Books Ltd (WC1) 69–70

Angling

Anglebooks Ltd (WC2) 59–60

Antiquarian

Alan Brett (WC2) 63
J.A. Allen & Co. The Horseman's
Bookshop (SW1) 249
Al Saqi Books (W2) 189
Andrew Block (WC1) 71
Andrew Edmunds (W1) 211
Archive Bookstores (NW1) 155
Arthur Page Books (WC1) 71–2
J. Ash (EC2) 91
M. Ayres Rare Books (WC1) 17
Bernard Quaritch Ltd (W1) 211–12
Bertram Rota Ltd (WC2) 72
Bibliopola (NW8) 156
Bondy Books (WC1) 73
The Bookshop (SE3) 297
Brian Bailey (W11) 212
Caissa Books (W1) 213
Camden Passage Antique Market (N1)
123
Cavendish Rare Books Ltd (SW1) 271
Chancery Lane Bookshop (WC2) 66
Charles Sawyer (W1) 213
Chelsea Rare Books (SW3) 271–2
Christopher Mendez (W1) 214

The Clarke-Hall Bookshop (EC4) 89–90
The Corner Bookshop (NW1) 148
Demetzy Books (W11) 214
Dillons Bookshop (WC1) 3–4
Fine Books Oriental Limited (WC1) 50–1
Fisher & Sperr (N6) 123–4
H.M. Fletcher (WC2) 73
Foyles (WC1) 5–6
Francis Edwards (WC2) 69
Frognal Rare Books (WC2) 38
Gabriel Byrne (W11) 204
Game Advice (NW5) 135–6
Green Knight Bookshop (WC2) 74
Harold Storey (WC2) 74
Harriet Truscott Books (W11) 196
Harrington Bros (SW3) 253
Hatchards (W1) 163–4
Henry Sotheran Ltd (W1) 214–15
G. Heywood Hill Ltd (W1) 164
Hollywood Road Bookshop (SW10) 248–9
Il Libro (SW3) 255
Joanna Booth (SW3) 249–50
John Faustus (SW1) 272
E. Joseph (W1) 215–16
Levrant Rare Books (W11) 216
Maggs Bros Ltd (W1) 216–17
The Marchmont Bookshop (WC1) 67–8
Marlborough Rare Books Ltd (W1) 217
Mellor & Baxter (W1) 218
Michael Phelps (SW15) 254
The Museum Bookshop (WC1) 14
Peter Eaton (Booksellers) Ltd (W11) 218–19
Pickering and Chatto (SW1) 272–3
Primrose Hill Books (NW1) 130
Provincial Booksellers Fairs Association (WC1) 68
Quevedo (WC2) 74
Remington (WC2) 63
Rogers Turner Books Ltd (SE10) 298
Sanford Books (SW3) 273
Sims, Reed and Fogg (SW1) 274
The Spread Eagle (SE10) 283–4
Stanley Crowe (WC1) 75
Stanley Smith and Keith Fawkes (NW3) 153
Timothy Shaw (W9) 219
The Village Bookshop (NW3) 153–4

G.W. Walford (N1) 125
The Woburn Bookshop (WC1) 75
Wyvern Bookshop (W4) 210–11

Antiques & Collecting

The Angel Bookshop (N1) 103–4
Don Kelly (SW3) 240
G. Heywood Hill Ltd (W1) 164
St George's Gallery Books Ltd (SW1) 242
Victoria and Albert Museum Shop (SW7) 243
Waterstone's (W8) 171–2

Archaeology

The Museum Bookshop (WC1) 14

Architecture

Bondy Books (WC1) 73
The Design Centre (SW1) 246
G. Heywood Hill Ltd (W1) 164
London Art Bookshop Ltd (W8) 173
Marlborough Rare Books Ltd (W1) 217
Royal Institute of British Architects Bookshop (W1) 174
St George's Gallery Books Ltd (SW1) 242
(Ian) Shipley (Books) Ltd (WC2) 19
Triangle Bookshop (WC1) 14–15
A. Zwemmer (WC2) 19–20

Art: Decorative

Andrew Edmunds (W1) 211
Books and Things (W11) 175
G. Heywood Hill Ltd (W1) 164
Paperchase (WC1) 18–19
Peter Stockham at Images (WC2) 24
Pruskin (SW3) 242
St George's Gallery Books Ltd (SW1) 242

Art: Fine and Applied

Academy Bookshop (W8) 174–5
The Art Book Company (WC2) 15
Arts Bibliographic-Modern Arts Bookshop (WC1) 15–16
The Arts Council Bookshop (WC2) 16–17
M. Ayres Rare Books (WC1) 17
Bernard Quaritch Ltd (W1) 211–12
Bernard Shaw Bookshop (British

Museum (WC1) 17–18
Bondy Books (WC1) 73
Books and Things (W11) 175
Canonbury Bookshop (N1) 105–6
Chelsea Rare Books (SW3) 271–2
Dillons Bookshop (WC1) 3–4
Eric & Joan Stevens Booksellers (NW6) 148–9
The Flask Bookshop (NW3) 149–50
Foyles (WC1) 5–6
Green Knight Bookshop (WC2) 74
Harrods (SW3) 226
Hatchards (W1) 163–4
Hayward Gallery Bookshop (SE1) 284
G. Heywood Hill Ltd (W1) 164
Holborn Books (WC2) 66–7
Hosains Books (W2) 189–90
ICA Bookshop (SW1) 240–1
John Sandoe Books (SW3) 228
Maggs Bros Ltd (W1) 216–17
Marlborough Rare Books Ltd (W1) 217
National Portrait Gallery Bookshop (WC2) 18
Nigel Greenwood Inc. (SW1) 241
Notting Hill Books (W8) 208
Oppenheim & Co. Ltd (SW7) 230
Paperchase (WC1) 18–19
Peter Stockham at Images (WC2) 24
Pulteney & Co. (SW7) 232
Richard Worth Booksellers (SW15) 234
Royal Academy of Arts (W1) 176
St George's Gallery Books Ltd (SW1) 242
(Ian) Shipley (Books) Ltd (WC2) 19
Sims, Reed and Fogg (SW1) 274
Stone Trough Books (SE5) 287–8
Tate Gallery Shop (SW1) 242–3
Victoria and Albert Museum Shop (SW7) 243
Waterstone's (WC2) 11–12
A. Zwemmer (WC2) 19–20

Australia

Australian Gift Shop (WC2) 20
Caissa Books (W1) 213

Automobiles

Connoisseur Carbooks (W4) 176

Aviation History

The Aviation Bookshop (N19) 110

W.E. Hersant Ltd (The Chomley Bookshop) (N6) 110–11
The History Bookshop (N11) 114–15
Motor Books (WC2) 58
Solosy (WC2) 47

BBC Publications

BBC Bookshop (W1) 177

Bibles

The Abbey Bookshop (SW1) 259–60
The Bible Society Bookshop (EC4) 87
Henry Sotheran Ltd (W1) 214–15

Biography

Books of Blackheath (SE3) 276
Kirkdale Bookshop (SE26) 279–80
World of Books (W1) 210

Black Studies

The Bookplace (SE15) 275
Books Plus (SE14) 287
Centerprise (E2) 92–93
Grassroots Storefront (W10) 177–8
New Beacon Bookshop (N4) 111
Operation Headstart Books & Crafts (N15) 112
Sabarr Books (SW9) 234–5
Soma Books (SE11) 284–5
South Bank Bookshop (SE1) 283
Walter Rodney Bookshop (W13) 178
The Whole Thing (E15) 97

Bookworks & Book Design

Nigel Greenwood Inc. (SW1) 241

Botany

Il Libro (SW3) 255

Buddhism

Luzac & Co. Ltd (WC1) 46

Building & Construction

Building Bookshop Ltd (WC1) 20–1
Royal Institute of British Architects Bookshop (W1) 174

Business & Management

Barbican Business Book Centre (EC2) 82
BEC Business Books (SW17) 244

British Institute of Management (WC2) 21

The Business Bookshop (NW1) 135

Chapman's Professional Bookshop (WC2) 22

Dillons Bookshop (WC1) 3–4

Economists Bookshop (WC2) 22

Economists' Second-hand (WC2) 23

Jones & Evans Bookshop Ltd (EC4) 82

Parks Bookshop (WC1) 23–4

Witherby & Co. Ltd (EC4 & SE1) 83

Caribbean

Grassroots Storefront (W10) 177–8

New Beacon Bookshop 111

Operation Headstart Books and Crafts (N15) 112

Paperbacks Centre (SW9) 231

Sabarr Books (SW9) 234–5

Soma Books (SE11) 284–5

Walter Rodney Bookshop (W13) 178

Cartography

Jonathan Potter Ltd (W1) 178–9

Chess

Caissa Books (W1) 213

Game Advice (NW5) 135–6

Children's Books

At The Sign Of The Dragon (SW14) 264–5

Barker and Howard Limited (E1) 91–2

Battersea Arts Centre Bookshop (SW11) 221–2

Bernard Stone/Turret Book Shop (WC2) 53

Bondy Books (WC1) 73

Book Bargains (for the Spastics Association) (NW1) 147–8

The Bookboat (SE10) 285–6

The Bookshop (SE3) 297

Bookspread (SW17) 244–5

Canonbury Bookshop (N1) 105–6

Chelsea Rare Books (SW3) 271–2

Children's Bookshop (N10) 112

Children's Bookshop (SW19) 245

Dillons Bookshop (WC1) 3–4

Elgin Books (W11) 162

Fanfare Bookcentre (E17) 93

Foyles (WC1) 5–6

Foyles Educational Bookshop (W1) 181

Game Advice (NW5) 135–6

M. & R. Glendale (W1) 180

The Greenwich Bookshop (SE10) 279

Hammicks (WC2) 6

Hampstead Book Corner (NW8) 136

Harrington Bros (SW3) 253

Harrods (SW3) 226

Hatchards (W1) 163–4

G. Heywood Hill Ltd (W1) 164

High Hill Bookshops Ltd (NW3) 128

The Hill Bookshop (SW19) 227

John Sandoe Books (SW3) 228

The Mothers' Union Book Shop (SW1) 245

New Beacon Bookshop (N4) 111

Newham Parent's Centre (E13) 98

Owl Bookshop (NW5) 129–30

Paperbacks Centre (SW9) 231

Paperbooks (SW7) 250

Paperchase (WC1) 18–19

The Passage Bookshop (SE5) 281

Peter Stockham at Images (WC2) 24

Pleasure of Past Times (WC2) 24–5

Sabarr Books (SW9) 234–5

Soma Books (SE11) 284–5

Tetric Bookshop (SW6) 236–7

THAP Community Bookshop (E1) 96–7

Ujamaa Centre (SW9) 247–8

The Village Bookshop (NW3) 153–4

Waterstone's (WC2) 11–12

Waterstone's (W8) 171–2

Writers and Readers Bookshop (NW1) 133–4

Writer's Cramp (NW3) 134

Young World (Children's Book Centre Ltd) (W8) 179

China

Books of Asia (SW6) 257

Collet's Chinese Gallery and Bookshop (WC1) 25–6

Fine Books Oriental Limited (WC1) 50–1

Guanghua (WC2) 26

New Era Books (N4) 119–20

Churchill, Winston

Charles Sawyer (W1) 213

The History Bookshop (N11) 114–15

Cinema & Film History

The Cinema Bookshop (WC1) 26–7
ICA Bookshop (SW1) 240–1
The Motion Picture Bookshop (SE1) 286
Vermillion Books (WC1) 10

Community Bookshops

The Bookplace (SE15) 275
Centerprise (E2) 92–3
Grassroots Storefront (W10) 177–8
121 Bookshop (SE24) 288
Response Community Bookshop (SW5) 233
Sabarr Books (SW9) 234–5
Sun Power (N4) 113
THAP Community Bookstore (E1) 96–7
The Whole Thing (E15) 97

Cookery

Books for Cooks (W11) 180
Game Advice (NW5) 135–6
Writers and Readers Bookshop (NW1) 133–4
Writer's Cramp (NW3) 134

Crafts

The Craftsmen Pottery Shop (W1) 199

Crime, Romance, Thrillers

Alpha Bookshop (SW16) 268
Books Etc. (SW1) 224
Sky Books (W6) 209
Swan's Bookstall (SE8 & SW17) 296–7
Walm Lane Bookmart (NW10) 154–5

Design & Graphics

The Art Book Co. (WC2) 15
The Design Centre (SW1) 246
Francis Marsden Books for Printers (SE1) 289
Marlborough Rare Books Ltd (W1) 217
(Ian) Shipley (Books) Ltd (WC2) 19
A. Zwemmer (WC2) 19–20

Detective Fiction

Bell, Book & Radmall Ltd (WC2) 54
Grey House Books (SW3) 246–7
Kings Cross Bookshop (N1) 155

Early Printed Books & Manuscripts

Bernard Quaritch Ltd (W1) 211–12
Francis Edwards (WC2) 69
Henry Sotheran Ltd (W1) 214–15
Maggs Bros Ltd (W1) 217
Marlborough Rare Books Ltd (W1) 217

Eastern Europe

Central Books (WC1) 28
Collet's International Bookshop (WC2) 28–9
Orbis Books (London) Ltd (SW5) 247

Eastern Religions & Philosophies

Balham Food and Book Co-op (SW12) 220–1
Fine Books Oriental Limited (WC1) 50–1
Genesis Books (EC1) 83–4
Luzac & Co. Ltd (WC1) 46
Paul H. Crompton Ltd (SW6) 253
Richard Worth Booksellers (SW15) 234
The Theosophical Bookshop & Publishing House (WC1) 50
Watkins Books Ltd (WC2) 32–3

Economics

The Alternative Bookshop (WC2) 54
Economists Bookshop (WC2) 22
Economists' Second-hand (WC2) 23
Frognal Rare Books (WC2) 38
The History Bookshop (N11) 114–15
Parks Bookshop (WC1) 23–4

Education

The Bookplace (SE15) 275
Bookshop Crystal Palace (SE19) 293–4
Deptford Booktraders (SE8) 277
Foyles Educational Bookshop (W1) 181
New Beacon Bookshop (N4) 111
Newham Parents' Centre (E13) 98
Sabarr Books (SW9) 234–5
Soma Books (SE11) 284–5
Ujamaa Centre (SW9) 247–8

Electronics

The Modern Book Co. (W2) 182

English as a Foreign Language

Keltic (W8) 187

LCL Benedict Ltd (NW1) 141
Tutor Tape Co. Ltd (WC1) 37

Equestrian

J.A. Allen & Co. — The Horseman's
Bookshop (SW1) 249

Esperanto

The British Esperanto Association Inc.
(W11) 182–3

Family

The Catholic Marriage Advisory
Council Bookroom (W11) 183
The Mothers' Union Book Shop (SW1)
245

Family Planning

Family Planning Association Book
Centre (W1) 183–4

Far East

Arthur Probsthain (WC1) 44–5
Books of Asia (SW6) 257
East Asia Company (NW1) 136–7
Fine Books Oriental Limited (WC1)
50–1
Luzac & Co. Ltd (WC1) 46

Fashion and Textile Design

Academy Bookshop (W8) 174–5
Pruskin (SW3) 299–300
(Ian) Shipley (Books) Ltd (WC2) 19

Feminist

Books Plus (SE14) 287
Compendium (NW1) 126–7
Elgin Books (W11) 162
Eric & Joan Stevens Booksellers (NW6)
148–9
Gay's the Word (WC1) 40
The Greenwich Bookshop (SE10) 279
Housmans Bookshop (N1) 118–19
121 Bookshop (SE24) 288
Silver Moon (WC2) 29
Sisterwrite (N1) 114

Fine Bindings

Green Knight Bookshop (WC2) 74
Il Libro (SW3) 255
Maggs Bros Ltd (W1) 217

Wade Galleries (N1) 113

Folk Traditions

The Folk Shop (NW1) 137

Foreign Language Texts

Al Hoda (WC2) 44
All Things New (E7) 101
Al Saqi Books (W2) 189
Books of Asia (SW6) 257
Collet's International Bookshop (WC2)
28–9
East Asia Company (NW1) 136–7
Foyles (WC1) 5–6
Frognal Rare Books (WC2) 38
Grant & Cutler Ltd (WC2) 136–7
Guanghua (WC2) 26
Hachette Bookshop (W1) 184
The Hellenic Book Service (WC2) 30–1
Japanese Publications Centre (W1) 186
The Muslim Bookshop (N4) 115–16
OCS Bookshop (NW1) 139
Orbis Books (London) Ltd (SW5) 247
Paperbooks (SW7) 250
Publications India (W1) 186
Rogers Turner Books Ltd (SE10) 298
Schola Books (SW7) 250–1
B.A. Seaby Ltd (W1) 197
(Ian) Shipley (Books) Ltd (WC2) 19
Soma Books (SE11) 284–5
Zeno (WC2) 31

French Fiction & Non-fiction

Grant & Cutler Ltd (WC2) 36–7
Hachette Bookshop (W1) 184
Joanna Booth (SW3) 249–50
Paperbooks (SW7) 250
Schola Books (SW7) 250–1

Gay Issues

Gay's The Word (WC1) 40

General

The Angel Bookshop (N1) 103–4
The Arcade Bookshop (SE9) 274–5
Army & Navy (SW1) 220
Athena (W1) 156–7
At the Sign of the Dragon (SW14)
264–5
The Baker Street Bookshop (W1) 157

Balham Food and Book Co-op (SW12) 220–1

Barbican Bookshop (EC1) 76

Barker and Howard Limited (E1) 91–2

Barkers of Kensington (W8) 157–8

Battersea Arts Centre Bookshop (SW11) 221–2

Belgravia Books (SW1) 222

Belsize Bookshop (NW3) 125–6

Berger & Tims (SW1) 222

The Bloomsbury Bookplace (WC1) 65–6

Bolingbroke Bookshop (SW11) 223

Book Inn (WC2) 1

The Bookcase (EC4) 76–7

Bookmarks (N4) 104–5

The Bookplace (DE15) 275

Books Etc. (WC2) 1

Books Etc. (EC4) 77

Books Etc. (SW3) 223

Books Etc. (SW1) 224

Bookshop Crystal Palace (SE19) 293–4

The Booksmith (Charing Cross, WC2) 2

The Booksmith (Maiden Lane, WC2) 2

The Booksmith (EC3) 77–8

The Booksmith (W8) 158

Books of Blackheath (SE3) 275

Buckinghams (W1) 158–9

Bush Books (W12) 159

C. & L. Booksellers (NW4) 126

Canonbury Bookshop (N1) 105–6

Central Books (WC1) 28

Centerprise (E2) 92–3

Chain Libraries Ltd (EC2) 78

Chener Books (SE22) 276–7

Christopher Foss (W1) 159–60

City Booksellers Ltd (EC2) 78

City Booksellers Ltd (EC3) 79

Claude Gill Books (WC2) 2–3

Claude Gill Books (James St, W1) 160

Claude Gill Books (Oxford St, W1) 160–1

Claude Gill (Piccadilly, W1) 161

Collet's International Bookshop (WC2) 28–9

Collet's Penguin Bookshop (WC2) 56

Compendium (NW1) 126–7

Crouch End Bookshop (N8) 106

Dennys Booksellers Ltd (EC1) 79–80

Deptford Booktraders (SE8) 277

Dillons Bookshop (WC1) 3–4

Ealing Books (W5) 161–2

Elgin Books (W11) 162

English Continental Book Market (NW4) 127–8

Essex Hall Bookshop (WC2) 4–5

Faculty Books (N3) 107

Fagin's Bookshop (N14) 107–8

Fanfare Bookcentre (E17) 93

Fielders (SW19) 225

Foyles (WC1) 5–6

Foyles Educational Bookshop (W1) 181

Gabriels Bookshop (NW10) 150

Gallery Bookshop (SE21) 278–9

Gallery Book Store (E5) 94

The Gloucester Road Bookshop (SW7) 225–6

The Greenwich Bookshop (SE10) 279

Hammicks (WC2) 6

Hammicks Bookshop Ltd (W6) 163

Hammick Sweet & Maxwell (WC2) 38–9

Harrods (SW3) 226

Harvid Bookstore (EC4) 80

Harvid Bookstore (EC3) 80

Harvid Bookstore (SW3) 227

Hatchards (W1) 163–4

Henry Sotheran Ltd (W1) 214–15

G. Heywood Hill Ltd (W1) 164

Highgate Bookshop (N6) 108

High Hill Bookshops Ltd (NW3) 128

The Hill Bookshop (SW19) 227

Housmans Bookshop (N1) 118–19

Imperial College Bookshop (SW7) 266–7

Jennings Bookshop (SW16) 269–70

John Sandoe Books (SW3) 228

Jones & Evans Bookshop Ltd (EC4) 82

H. Karnac (Books) Ltd (SW7) 228–9

The Kensington Bookshop Ltd (W8) 165

The Kilburn Bookshop (NW6) 129

Kings Bookshop (WC1) 7

Kirkdale Bookshop (SE26) 279–80

Lamley & Co (SW7) 229–30

Liberty & Co (W1) 165

Mandarin Books (W11) 166

Marcet Books (SE10) 280–1

The Modern Book Co. (W2) 182

A.N. Mowbray & Co. Ltd (W1) 201

The Museum Bookshop (WC1) 14

Muswell Hill Bookshop (N10) 108–9
New Era Books (N4) 119–20
Newham Parents' Centre (E13) 98
Oppenheim & Co. Ltd (SW7) 230
Owl Bookshop (NW5) 129–30
The Pan Bookshop (SW10) 231
Paperbacks Centre (E17) 94–95
Paperbacks Centre (W1) 166–7
Paperbacks Centre (SW9) 231
The Passage Bookshop (SE5) 281
Peter Eaton (Booksellers) Ltd (W11)
    218–19
Primrose Hill Books (NW1) 130
Pulteney & Co. (SW7) 232
Quartet Bookshop (W1) 167
Regent Bookshop (NW1) 130–1
Richard Worth Booksellers (SW15) 234
Riverside Studies Bookshop (W6) 168
Roy Hayes (Booksellers) Ltd (SE9)
    281–2
St Martin's Lane Bookshop (WC2) 7
Selfridges (W1) 168–9
L. Simmonds (EC4) 81
W. H. Smith (General note) 7–8
W.H. Smith (WC2) 8
W.H. Smith (EC1) 81
W.H. Smith (London Wall, EC2) 81
W.H. Smith (Cheapside, EC2) 81
W.H. Smith (N8) 109
W.H. Smith (N12) 109
W.H. Smith (N13) 109
W.H. Smith (N22) 109
W.H. Smith (NW2) 131
W.H. Smith (NW3) 131
W.H. Smith (Hendon Way, NW4) 131
W.H. Smith (Brent Cross, NW4) 131
W.H. Smith (NW6) 132
W.H. Smith (NW7) 132
W.H. Smith (NW11) 132
W.H. Smith (W4) 169
W.H. Smith (W5) 169
W.H. Smith (W6) 169
W.H. Smith (W8) 169
W.H. Smith (W11) 169
W.H. Smith (W13) 170
W.H. Smith (SW1) 235
W.H. Smith (SW5) 235
W.H. Smith (SW15) 235
W.H. Smith (SW16) 236
W.H. Smith (SE1) 282
W.H. Smith (SE6) 282
W.H. Smith (SE9) 282

W.H. Smith (SE13) 282
W.H. Smith (SE18) 282
South Bank Bookshop (SE1) 283
Souvenir Press Ltd (WC1) 8
The Spread Eagle (SE10) 283–4
Strathmore Book Shop (NW8) 132
Swiss Cottage Books Ltd (NW3) 133
Templar Books (Chancery Lane, WC2)
    9
Templar Books (High Holborn, WC2)
    9
Tetric Bookshop (SW4) 236
Tetric Bookshop (SW6) 236–7
Tetric Bookshop (SW17) 237
THAP Community Bookshop (E1)
    96–7
Truslove and Hanson (SW3) 238
Vanessa Williams-Ellis (W9) 170
Vermillion Books (WC1) 10
Village Books (SW16) 238–9
Waterstone and Davies (WC1) 10–11
Waterstone's (WC2) 11–12
Waterstone's (W1) 171
Waterstone's (W8) 171–2
Waterstone's (SW7) 239
Writers and Readers Bookshop (NW1)
    133–4
Writer's Cramp (NW3) 134

Geology

Bookshop Crystal Palace (SE19) 293–4
Geological Museum Bookshop (SW7)
    251

Germany

The German Book Centre Ltd (W1) 185
The Village Bookshop (NW3) 153–4

Girl Guides

Girl Guides Association Shop (SW1)
    251–2

Golfing

Golfiana Miscellanea Ltd (WC2) 30

Greece

The Hellenic Book Service (WC2) 30–1
Kimon Bookshop (NW1) 138
Zeno (WC2) 31

Guns & Weapons

Willen Limited (E11) 101

HMSO Publications

HMSO Bookshop (WC2) 64

Hairdressing

Willen Limited (E11) 101

Health & Nutrition

Balham Food and Book Co-op (SW12) 220–1
Genesis Books (EC1) 83–4
Robert Chris Bookseller (WC2) 32
Wholefood of Baker Street (W1) 185
Writer's Cramp (NW3) 134

Heraldry & Genealogy

Heraldry Today (SW3) 252

History

Archive Bookstores (NW1) 155
Bertram Rota Ltd (WC2) 72
Books of Blackheath (SE3) 276
Dillons Bookshop (WC1) 3–4
Frognal Rare Books (WC2) 38
The History Bookshop (N11) 114–15
Maggs Bros Ltd (W1) 216–17
Quevedo (WC2) 74
World of Books (W1) 210

Holistic Subjects

Changes Bookshop (NW6) 141–2
Watkins Books Ltd (WC2) 32–3

Horse Racing

Turf Newspapers Ltd (W1) 202–3

Horticulture

Grower Books (WC1) 33
Wholefood of Baker Street (W1) 185

Housing & Urban Planning

The Design Centre (SW1) 246
Housing Centre Trust Bookshop (WC1) 34
Planning Bookshop (SW1) 267

Hunting

Rowland Ward's of Knightsbridge (SW1) 256

Illustrated Books

Archive Bookstores (NW1) 155
The Art Book Co (WC2) 15
M. Ayres Rare Books (WC1) 17
Basilisk Press and Bookshop (NW3) 143
Bernard Quaritch Ltd (W1) 211–12
Bernard Shapero (W1) 204
Bernard Stone/Turret Book Shop (WC2) 53
Bibliopola (NW8) 156
Brian Bailey (W11) 212
Chancery Lane Bookshop (WC2) 82–3
Charlotte Robinson Bookshop (W1) 191
Christopher Mendez (W1) 214
The Clarke-Hall Bookshop (EC4) 89–90
Demetzy Books (W11) 214
Francis Edwards (WC2) 69
M. and R. Glendale (W1) 180
Green Knight Bookshop (WC2) 74
Harold Storey (WC2) 74
Harrington Bros (SW3) 253
Henry Sotheran Ltd (W1) 214–15
Hosains Books (W2) 189–90
Joanna Booth (SW3) 249–50
Marlborough Rare Books Ltd (W1) 217
Mellor & Baxter (W1) 218
Peter Stockham at Images (WC2) 24
Rowland Ward's of Knightbridge (SW1) 256
The Village Bookshop (NW3) 153–4

India

Books of Asia (SW6) 257
Books From India (UK) Ltd/Hindi Book Centre (WC1) 34–5
Knightsbridge Books (WC1) 45
Publications India (W1) 186
Soma Books (SE11) 284–5

Industrial History

A.A. Miles (NW1) 151–2
Wyvern Bookshop (W4) 210–11

Insurance

Witherby & Co. Ltd (EC4 & SE1) 83

Ireland

Chancery Lane Bookshop (WC2) 66

307

The Kilburn Bookshop (NW6) 129
New Era Books (N4) 119–20

Islam

Al Hoda (WC2) 44
Hosains Books (W2) 189–90
Islamic Book Centre (NW1) 138
The Muslim Bookshop (N4) 115–16
Soma Books (SE11) 284–5

Italian Literature

Bibliopola (NW8) 156
Grant & Cutler Ltd (WC2) 136–7

Japan

Fine Books Oriental Limited (WC1)
  50–1
Japanese Publications Centre (W1) 186
OCS Bookshop (NW1) 139

Jazz

Collet's Record Shop (WC2) 47–8

Judaica & Hebraica

J. Aisenthal (NW1) 139
R. Golub & Son Ltd (E1) 98–99
Hebrew Book & Gift Centre (N16) 116
Jerusalem The Golden (NW11) 140
Jewish Chronicle Bookshop (EC4) 84
Jewish Memorial Council Bookshop
  (WC1) 35
Menorah Print & Gift Centre/Hebrew
  Booksellers (NW11) 140

Labour Relations & Trade Unions

Bookmarks (N4) 104–5
Central Books (WC1) 28
Paperbacks Centre (E17) 94–95

Language Teaching

East Asia Company (NW1) 136–7
Dillons Bookshop (WC1) 3–4
European Bookshop (WC1) 36
Foyles (WC1) 5–6
Grant & Cutler Ltd (WC2) 36–7
Guanghua (WC2) 26
Keltic (W8) 187
LCL Benedict Ltd (NW1) 141
Linguaphone (W1) 187
Publications India (W1) 186
L. Simmonds (EC4) 81

Tutor Tape Co. Ltd (WC1) 37

Law

Butterworth's Legal Bookshop (WC2)
  37–8
Frognal Rare Books (WC2) 38
Hammick Sweet & Maxwell (WC2)
  38–9
Law Notes Lending Library (WC2) 39
Parks Bookshop (WC1) 23–4
Wildy and Sons Ltd (WC2) 39–40

Literature & Literary Criticism

Andrew Block (WC1) 71
Any Amount of Books (W6) 206
Arthur Page Books (WC1) 71–2
Arts Bibliographic-Modern Arts
  Bookshop (WC1) 15–16
J. Ash (EC2) 91
Bell, Book & Radmall Ltd (WC2) 47
Bernard Quaritch Ltd (W1) 211–12
Bernard Stone/Turret Book Shop
  (WC2) 53
Bertram Rota Ltd (WC2) 72
The Bookshop (SE3) 297
Chelsea Rare Books (SW3) 271–2
Chener Books (SE22) 276–7
Cobb & Webb Booksellers (SW15)
  268–9
Compendium (NW1) 126–7
Demetzy Books (W11) 214
Dillons Bookshop (WC1) 3–4
Edna Whiteson (N11) 117
Elgin Books (W11) 162
Eric & Joan Stevens Booksellers (NW6)
  148–9
Fisher & Sperr (N6) 123–4
The Flask Bookshop (NW3) 149–50
Foyles (WC1) 5–6
Green Knight Bookshop (WC2) 74
The Greenwich Book-Place &
  Paperback Centre (SE10) 294–5
Hammicks (WC2) 6
Harrods (SW3) 226
Henry Sotheran Ltd (W1) 214–15
G. Heywood Hill Ltd (W1) 164
High Hill Bookshop Ltd (NW3) 128
Hollywood Road Bookshop (SW10)
  248–9
ICA Bookshop (SW1) 240–1
John Sandoe Books (SW3) 228

Kirkdale Bookshop (SE26) 279–80
Maggs Bros Ltd (W1) 216–17
Notting Hill Books (W8) 208
Owl Bookshop (NW5) 29–30
Pickering and Chatto (SW1) 272–3
Quartet Bookshop (W1) 167
Quevedo (WC2) 74
Skoob Books (WC1) 69–70
Stanley Smith and Keith Fawkes
  (NW3) 153
Stone Trough Books (SE5) 287–8
Vermillion Books (WC1) 10
The Village Bookshop (NW3) 153–4
Walden Books (NW1) 154
Waterstone's (WC2) 11–12
Waterstone's (W1) 171
Waterstone's (W8) 171–2
Waterstone's (SW7) 239
Words Etcetera (SW10) 254–5
Writer's Cramp (NW3) 134

Local History

Anglebooks Ltd (WC2) 59–60
The Bookplace (SE15) 275
Canonbury Bookshop (N1) 105–6
Centerprise (E2) 92–3
Chener Books (SE22) 276–7
The History Bookshop (N11) 114–15
The Museum of London Bookshop
  (EC2) 85
Stanley Crowe (WC1) 75
THAP Community Bookshop (E1)
  96–7
Waterstone and Davies (WC1) 10–11
World of Books (W1) 210

Magic, Occult & Witchcraft

Atlantis (WC1) 49
Compendium (NW1) 126–7
Genesis Books (EC1) 83–4
Hollywood Road Bookshop (SW10)
  248–9

Maritime History

Anthony J. Simmonds Books (N6) 117
Cavendish Rare Books Ltd (SW1) 271
Maggs Bros Ltd (W1) 216–17
Paul Minet's Bookshop (E1) 103
Remington (WC2) 63

Martial Arts

Atoz Martial Arts Centre (WC2) 41
Paul H. Crompton Ltd (SW6) 253

Medicine & Science

Arthur Page (WC1) 71–2
Bernard Quaritch Ltd (W1) 211–12
Bookshop Crystal Palace (SE19) 293–4
Dennys Booksellers Ltd (EC1) 79–80
Dillons Bookshop (WC1) 3–4
Foyles (WC1) 5–6
Graham Weiner (W1) 210
Jenner Medical History Bookshop
  (WC1) 42
Kimpton's Medical Bookshop (W1) 188
H.K. Lewis & Co. Ltd (WC1) 42–3
Maggs Bros Ltd (W1) 216–17
Mellor & Baxter (W1) 218
Michael Phelps (SW15) 254
The Passage Bookshop (SE5) 281
L. Simmonds (EC4) 81
West End Books (WC1) 43

Mental Handicap

MENCAP Bookshop (EC1) 85

Middle East

Al Hoda (WC2) 44
Al Saqi Books (W2) 189
Arthur Probsthain (WC1) 44–5
Books of Asia (SW6) 257
Hosains Books (W2) 189–90
Knightsbridge Books (WC1) 45
Luzac & Co. Ltd (WC1) 46

Militaria

W.E. Hersant Ltd (The Chomley Book
  Shop) (N6) 110–11
Francis Edwards (WC2) 69
The History Bookshop (N11) 114–15
Ken Trotman (NW3) 142
Maggs Bros Ltd (W1) 217
Motor Books (WC2) 58
B.A. Seaby Ltd (W1) 197
Solosy (WC2) 46–7
Tradition (W1) 190
Under Two Flags (W1) 190–1
Vermillion Books (WC1) 10

Miniature Books

Bondy Books (WC1) 73

Modern First Editions

Bell, Book & Radmall Ltd (WC2) 47
Bertram Rota Ltd (WC2) 72
Charlotte Robinson Bookshop (W1) 191
Edna Whiteson (N11) 117
Foyles (WC1) 5–6
G. Heywood Hill Ltd (W1) 164
Maggs Bros Ltd (W1) 217
Seal Books (W5) 209
Stone Trough Books (SE5) 287–8
The Village Bookshop (NW3) 153–4
Words Etcetera (SW10) 254–5

Museum Bookshops

Bernard Shaw Bookshop (British Museum) (WC1) 17–18
Geological Museum Bookshop (SW7) 251
Hayward Gallery Bookshop (SE1) 284
The Museum of London Bookshop (EC2) 85
National Portrait Gallery Bookshop (WC2) 18
Tate Gallery Shop (SW1) 242–3
Victoria and Albert Museum Shop (SW7) 243

Music

Archive Bookstores (NW1) 155
Arthur Page Books (WC1) 71–2
Boosey & Hawkes Music (W1) 192
Brian Jordan Music Books (W5) 192
Chappell (W1) 193
The Chimes Music Shop (W1) 193
Collet's Record Shop (WC2) 47–8
J.B. Cramer & Co. Ltd (WC2) 48
Foyles (WC1) 5–6
The Gramophone Exchange (WC2) 48–9
Kensington Music Shop (SW7) 255
Music Book Centre (W1) 194
Music Boutique (W1) 194
Peters Music Shop (W1) 195
Schott & Co. Ltd (W1) 195
Travis & Emery (WC2) 49
Waterstone's (WC2) 11–12

Natural History

Basilisk Press and Bookshop (NW3) 143
Bernard Quaritch Ltd (W1) 211–12
The Bookshop (SE3) 297
Bookshop Crystal Palace (SE19) 293–4
Harriet Truscott Books (W11) 196
Il Libro (SW3) 255
Maggs Bros Ltd (W1) 216–17
Rowland Ward's of Knightsbridge (SW1) 256

Nautical & Shipping

Brown & Perring Ltd (EC3) 86
Edward Stanford Ltd (WC2) 60
Kelvin Hughes Charts and Maritime Supplies (E1) 99
London Yacht Centre Ltd (E1) 100
J.D. Potter (EC3) 86–7
Witherby & Co. Ltd (EC4 & SE1) 83

Naval History

Cavendish Rare Books Ltd (SW1) 271
W.E. Hersant Ltd (The Chomley Book Shop) (N6) 110–11
Francis Edwards (WC2) 69
The History Bookshop (N11) 114–15
Motor Books (WC2) 58
B.A. Seaby Ltd (W1) 197
Solosy (WC2) 47

New Zealand

Whitcoulls Ltd New Zealand (W1) 196

Numismatics

Mayfair Coin Co. (W1) 197
B.A. Seaby Ltd (W1) 197
Spink & Sons (SW1) 256

Ornithology

Bookshop Crystal Palace (SE19) 293–4
Il Libro (SW3) 255
Roland Ward's of Knightsbridge (SW1) 256
Vermillion Books (WC1) 10

Outdoor Activities & Sports

Edward Stanford Ltd (WC2) 60
YHA Bookshop (WC2) 61

Performing Arts & Stage History

Arts Bibliographic-Modern Arts
  Bookshop (WC1) 15–16
The Arts Council Bookshop (WC2)
  16–17
Dance Books Ltd (WC2) 27
Divertissement (EC1) 87
Foyles (WC1) 5–6
French's Theatre Bookshop (WC2) 203
Gallery Book Store (E5) 94
National Theatre Bookshop (SE1) 292
Offstage Theatre Shop and Gallery
  (NW1) 147
Pickering and Chatto (SW1) 272–3
Pleasures of Past Times (WC2) 24–5
RSC Bookshop (WC2) 62
Reads (WC2) 69
Riverside Studies Bookshop (W6) 168
Vermillion Books (WC1) 10

Philatelic History & Collecting

Harris Publications Ltd (WC2) 51
Stanley Gibbons (WC2) 51–52

Philosophy

Bernard Quaritch Ltd (W1) 211–12
The Bloomsbury Bookplace (WC1)
  65–6
Books of Blackheath (SE3) 276
Compendium (NW1) 126–7
Dillons Bookshop (WC1) 3–4
Foyles (WC1) 5–6
The Greenwich Book-Place &
  Paperback Centre (SE10) 294–5
Kirkdale Bookshop (SE26) 279–80
Rudolph Steiner Bookshop (WC1) 58–9
Rudolph Steiner Bookshop (NW1)
  146–7
The Theosophical Bookshop &
  Publishing House (WC1) 50
Waterstone's (WC2) 11–12

Photography

Academy Bookshop (W8) 174–5
Creative Camera (WC1) 52
The Photographer's Gallery (WC2)
  52–3

Poetry

Any Amount of Books (W6) 206

Bernard Stone/Turret Book Shop
  (WC2) 53
Bertram Rota Ltd (WC2) 72
Compendium (NW1) 126–7
Dillons Bookshop (WC1) 3–4
Eric & Joan Stevens Booksellers (NW6)
  148–9
Foyles (WC1) 5–6
Gallery Book Store (E5) 94
The Greenwich Book-Place &
  Paperback Centre (SE10) 294–5
National Poetry Centre Bookshop
  (SW5) 258
Sanford Books (SW3) 273
Words Etcetera (SW10) 254–5

Poland

Orbis Books (London) Ltd (SW5) 247
Polonez (W12) 198

Polar Exploration

Cavendish Rare Books Ltd (SW1) 271
Maggs Bros Ltd (W1) 217

Political

The Alterntive Bookshop (WC2) 54
Balham Food and Book Co-op (SW12)
  220–1
Bellman Bookshop (NW5) 142–3
The Bloomsbury Bookplace (WC1)
  65–6
Bookmarks (N4) 104–5
Books Plus (SE14) 287
Centreprise (E2) 92–3
CND Bookshop (N4) 118
Collet's London Bookshop (WC2) 54–5
Compendium (NW1) 126–7
The Corner House Bookshop (WC2) 55
Dillons Bookshop (WC1) 3–4
Freedom Bookshop (E1) 100
Gay's the Word (WC1) 40
Housmans Bookshop (N1) 118–19
The Kilburn Bookshop (NW6) 129
Labour Party Bookshop (SE17) 289
New Era Books (N4) 119–20
121 Bookshop (SE24) 288
The Other Bookshop (N1) 120
Paperbacks Centre (E17) 94–95
Paperbacks Centre (W1) 166–7
Paperbacks Centre (SW9) 231

The Poland Street Book Centre (W1) 198–9
Quartet Bookshop (W1) 167
Sabarr Books (SW9) 234–5
Tetric Bookshop (SW4) 236
Tetric Bookshop (SW17) 237
THAP Community Bookshop (E1) 96–7
Walter Rodney Bookshop (W13) 178
The Whole Thing (E15) 97

Printing & Typography

Francis Marsden Books For Printers (SE1) 289

Private Press Publications

Basilisk Press and Bookshop (NW3) 143
Bernard Quaritch Ltd (W1) 211–12
Bertram Rota Ltd (WC2) 72

Psychic Worlds

Atlantis (WC1) 49
Psychic News Bookshop (WC2) 55–6
The Spiritualist Association of Great Britain (SW1) 258
Watkins Books Ltd (WC2) 32–3

Psychology

Changes Bookshop (NW6) 141–2
Dillons Bookshop (WC1) 3–4
Foyles (WC1) 5–6
H. Karnac (Books) Ltd (SW7) 228–9
Swiss Cottage Books Ltd (NW3) 133

Publishers's Bookshops

Collet's Penguin Bookshop (WC2) 56
The Golden Cockerel Bookshop (WC2) 12–13
The Literary Guild Bookshop (W1) 200
Penguin Bookshop (WC2) 56–7
Penguin Bookshop (SW3) 232
Reader's Digest (W1) 200
Souvenir Press Ltd (WC1) 8
Writers and Readers Bookshop (NW1) 133–4
Zwemmer's Oxford University Press Bookshop (WC2) 57

Puppetry

The Puppet Centre (SW11) 259

Religious

The Abbey Bookshop (SW1) 259–60
All Things New (E7) 101
The Bible Society Bookshop (EC4) 87
Catholic Truth Society (SW1) 260
The Christian Bookshop (SE22) 290
Christian Literature Crusade (EC4) 88
Church House Bookshop (SW1) 260–1
Church Literature Association (SW1) 261
Daybreak Books (SE12) 290–1
Essex Hall Bookshop (WC2) 4–5
Friends Book Centre (NW1) 144
Methodist Church Overseas Division Bookshop (NW1) 144–5
The Mothers' Union Book Shop (SW1) 245
A.R. Mowbray & Co. Ltd (W1) 201
Mustard Seed (NW1) 145
The Mustard Tree (SE23) 291
Protestant Truth Society (EC4) 88–9
Russian Orthodox Cathedral Bookshop (SW7) 262
SCM Bookroom (N1) 121
SPCK Church Bookshop (NW1) 145–6
Scripture Union Bookshop (W1) 202
United Society for the Propagation of the Gospel (SW1) 262
The Wall Bookshop (SW1) 263
Westminster Cathedral Bookshop (SW1) 263
Wimbledon Evangelical Book Centre (SW19) 264

Remaindered Books/Book Bargains

The Arcade Bookshop (SE9) 274–5
Book Bargains (for the Spastics Association) (NW1) 147–8
Book Inn (WC2) 1
The Bookcase (EC4) 76–7
Books Etc. (WC2) 1
Books Etc. (EC4) 77
Bookshop Crystal Palace (SE19) 293–4
Books of Blackheath (SE3) 276
The Booksmith (Charing Cross, WC2) 2
The Booksmith (Maiden Lane, WC2) 2
The Booksmith (EC3) 77–8
The Booksmith (W8) 158
C. & L. Booksellers (NW4) 126

Claude Gill Books (James St, W1) 160
Claude Gill Books (Oxford St, W1) 160–1
Claude Gill Books (Piccadilly, W1) 161
Collet's London Bookshop (WC2) 54–5
Dillons Bookshop (WC1) 3–4
Gallery Book Store (E5) 94
Harvid Bookstore (SW3) 227
Henry Sotheran Ltd (W1) 214–15
James Smith (WC1) 67
Kirkdale Bookshop (SE26) 279–80
Leather Lane Book Centre (EC1) 90
Notting Hill Books (W8) 208
Oppenheim & Co. Ltd (SW7) 230
Henry Pordes (WC2) 68
St Martin's Lane Bookshop (WC2) 7
Templar Books (Chancery Lane, WC2) 70
Templar Books (High Holborn, WC2) 9
A. Zwemmer (WC2) 19–20

Sailing

Edward Stanford Ltd (WC2) 60
Kelvin Hughes Charts and Maritime Supplies (E1) 99
London Yacht Centre Ltd (E1) 100
J.D. Potter (EC3) 86–7

Samuel Johnson

The Clarke-Hall Bookshop (EC4) 89–90

Science Fiction & Fantasy

At the Sign of the Dragon (SW 14) 264–5
Book Inn (WC2) 1
Fantasy Centre (N1) 121
Ferret Fantasy (W1) 210
Forbidden Planet (WC2) 59
Phantasmagoria (SE22) 291
Sky Books (W6) 209
Swan's Bookstall (SE8 & SW17) 296–7

Second-Hand

Alan Brett (WC2) 63
J.A. Allen Co. — The Horseman's Bookshop (SW1) 249
Al Saqi Books (W2) 189
Alpha Bookshop (SW16) 268
Any Amount of Books (W6) 206

Archive Bookstores (NW1) 155
Arthur Page Books (WC1) 71–2
J. Ash (EC2) 91
The Bloomsbury Bookplace (WC1) 65–6
Bonaventure (N6) 122
Bondy Books (WC1) 73
The Book Gallery (W1) 206–7
Bookmarks (N4) 104–5
Books and Things (W11) 175
The Bookshop (SE3) 297
Bookshop Crystal Palace (SE19) 293–4
Brian Bailey (W11) 212
Caissa Books (W1) 213
Camden Passage Antique Market (N1) 123
Chancery Lane Bookshop (WC2) 66
Chelsea Rare Books (SW3) 271–2
Chener Books (SE22) 276–7
The Clarke-Hall Bookshop (EC4) 89–90
Cobb & Webb Booksellers (SW 15) 268–9
Collet's London Bookshop (WC2) 54–5
The Constant Reader (SW6) 269
The Corner Bookshop (NW1) 148
Crouch End Bookshop (N8) 106
Demetzy Books (W11) 214
Dillons Bookshop (WC1) 3–4
Economists' Second-hand (WC2) 23
Edna Whiteson (N11) 117
Eric & Joan Stevens Booksellers (NW6) 148–9
Fisher & Sperr (N6) 123–4
The Flask Bookshop (NW3) 149–50
H.M. Fletcher (WC2) 73
W.A. Foster (W4) 207
Foyles (WC1) 5–6
Gabriels Bookshop (NW10) 150
Gaby Goldscheider and Helga Wellingham (W11) 208
Gallery Bookshop (SE21) 278–9
Gallery Book Store (E5) 94
Game Advice (NW5) 135–6
George Greer Books (NW1) 150–1
The Gramophone Exchange (WC2) 48–9
The Greenwich Book-Place & Paperback Centre (SE10) 294–5
Greenwich Market (SE10) 295
Harriet Truscott Books (W11) 196

Hatchards (W1) 163–4
Henry Sotheran Ltd (W1) 214–15
G. Heywood Hill Ltd (W1) 164
Hillyers (SE26) 296
The History Bookshop (N11) 114–15
Holborn Books (WC2) 66–7
Jane Gibberd (SE1) 296–7
Jenner Medical History Bookshop
   (WC1) 42
Jennings Bookshop (SW16) 269–70
E. Joseph (W1) 215–16
Kirkdale Bookshop (SE26) 279–80
Lionel Halter (NW7) 151
Marcet Books (SE10) 280–1
The Marchmont Bookshop (WC1) 67–8
A.A. Miles (NW1) 151–2
Norman Lord (E17) 102
Paul Minet's Bookshop (E1) 103
Peter Eaton (Booksellers) Ltd (W11)
   218–19
Phase One Books (NW3) 152
Primrose Hill Books (NW1) 130
Provincial Booksellers Fairs
   Association (WC1) 68
Reads (WC2) 69
Remington (WC2) 63
Response Community Bookshop (SW5)
   233
Richard Law Booksellers (NW2) 152
Richard Lally Ltd (SW15) 270
Robert Chris Bookseller (WC2) 32
Seal Books (W5) 209
Skoob Books (WC1) 69
Sky Books (W6) 209
The Spread Eagle (SE10) 283–4
Stanley Smith and Keith Fawkes
   (NW3) 153
Stone Trough Books (SE5) 287–8
Swan's Bookstall (SE8 & SW17) 296–7
Take Five (SW19) 270
The Village Bookshop (NW3) 153–4
Walden Books (NW1) 154
Walm Lane Bookmart (NW10) 154–5
Whetstone Books (N20) 124
The Woburn Bookshop (WC1) 75
World of Books (W1) 210
Wyvern Bookshop (W4) 210–11

Social Sciences

The Bloomsbury Bookplace (WC1)
   65–6

Compendium (NW1) 126–7
Dillons Bookshop (WC1) 3–4
Economists Bookshop (WC2) 22
Economists' Second-hand (WC2) 23
Foyles (WC1) 5–6
Muswell Hill Bookshop (N10) 108–9
Swiss Cottage Books Ltd (NW3) 133
Tetric Book Shop (SW4) 236
Waterstone's (WC2) 11–12
Waterstone's (W8) 171–2
The Whole Thing (E15) 97

Soviet Union

Central Books (WC1) 28
Collet's International Bookshop (WC2)
   28–9
Orbis Books (London) Ltd (SW5) 247
Russian Orthodox Cathedral Bookshop
   (SW7) 262

Technology & Energy

Intermediate Technology Bookshop
   (WC2) 61–2
Sun Power (N4) 113

Theology

Christian Literature Crusade (EC4) 88
Dillons Bookshop (WC1) 3–4
Maggs Bros Ltd (W1) 216–17
A.R. Mowbray and Co. Ltd (W1) 201
SCM Bookroom (WC1) 121
SPCK Church Bookshop (NW1) 145–6
Waterstone's (WC2) 11–12

Topography

Alan Brett (WC2) 63
Bertram Rota Ltd (WC2) 72
Bondy Books (WC1) 73
Gabriel Byrne (W11) 204
The Spread Eagle (SE10) 283–4
Stanley Crowe (WC1) 75
Vandaleur Antiquarian Books (SW14)
   265

Tourist

The Abbey Bookshop (SW1) 259–60
British Tourist Authority (SW1) 265–6
Foyles (WC1) 5–6
Harvid Bookstore (EC3) 80
London Tourist Board Bookshop
   (SW1) 266

Transport

The Baker Street Bookshop (W1) 157
Hambling (Models) Ltd (WC2) 57–8
Model Railway (Manufacturing) Co.
  Ltd (N1) 120–1
Motor Books (WC2) 58
Willen Limited (E11) 101
Wyvern Bookshop (W4) 210–11

Travel Accounts & Guides

Bernard Quaritch Ltd (W1) 211–12
Bernard Shapero (W1) 204
Bertram Rota Ltd (WC2) 72
British Tourist Authority (SW1) 271
Chelsea Rare Books (SW3) 271–2
Edward Stanford Ltd (WC2) 60
Foyles (WC1) 5–6
Gabriel Byrne (W11) 204
Geographia (EC4) 89
Green Knight Bookshop (WC2) 74
Harold Storey (WC2) 74
Harriet Truscott Books (W11) 196
Harrods (SW3) 226
The History Bookshop (N11) 114–15
London Tourist Board Bookshop
  (SW1) 266
McCarta Ltd (WC1) 41
Maggs Bros Ltd (W1) 216–17
Mellor & Baxter (W1) 218
Quevedo (WC2) 74
Remington (WC2) 63
The Spread Eagle (SE10) 283–4
Stanley Smith and Keith Fawkes
  (NW3) 153

The Travel Bookshop Ltd (W8) 205
Vandaleur Antiquarian Books (SW14)
  265
Waterstone's (WC2) 11–12
Waterstone's (W8) 171–2
World of Books (W1) 210
YHA Bookshop (WC2) 61

**University Bookshops & General
  Textbooks**

Acton Book Centre (W3) 205
Austin Parish Ltd (N6) 122
City Lit Bookshop (WC1) 64–5
Dillons at Queen Mary College (E1) 102
Dillons Bookshop (WC1) 3–4
Faculty Books (N3, NW4 &
  Tottenham) 107
Fanfare Bookcentre (E17) 93
Foyles (WC1) 5–6
Foyles Educational Bookshop (W1) 181
Goldsmith's College Book & Stationery
  Shop (SE14) 292–3
Imperial College Bookshop (SW7)
  266–7
Lamley & Co. (SW7) 229–30
Mercury Bookshop (SE18) 292–3
L. Simmonds (EC4) 81
Skoob Books (WC1) 69–70
South Bank Bookshop (SE1) 283

Wodehouse, P.G.

The Flask Bookshop (NW3) 149–50

Index   Alphabetical

The Abbey Bookshop (SW1) 259–60
Academy Bookshop (W8) 174–5
Action Book Centre (W3) 205
Africa Book Centre (WC2) 13
J. Aisenthal (NW1) 139
Alan Brett (WC2) 63
The Albanian Shop (WC2) 13
All Hoda (WC2) 44

All Things New (E7) 101
J.A. Allen & Co. — The Horseman's
  Bookshop (SW1) 249
Alpha Bookshop (SW16) 268
Al Saqi Books (W2) 189
The Alternative Bookshop (WC2) 54
Andrew Block (WC1) 71
Andrew Edmunds (W1) 211

The Angel Bookshop (N1) 103–4
Anglebooks Ltd (WC2) 59–60
Anthony J. Simmonds Books (N6) 117
Any Amount of Books (W6) 206
The Arcade Bookshop (SE9) 274–5
Archive Bookstores (NW1) 155
Army & Navy (SW1) 220
The Art Book Company (WC2) 15
Arthur Page Books (WC1) 71–2
Arthur Probsthain (WC1) 44–5
Arts Bibliographic-Modern Arts
    Bookshop (WC1) 15–16
The Arts Council Bookshop (WC2)
    16–17
J. Ash (EC2) 91
Athena (W1) 156–7
Atlantis (WC1) 49
Atoz Martial Arts Centre (WC2) 41
At the Sign of the Dragon (SW14)
    264–5
Austin Parish Ltd (N6) 122
Australian Gift Shop (WC2) 20
The Aviation Bookshop (N19) 110
M. Ayres Rare Books (WC1) 17

BBC Bookshop (W1) 177
The Baker Street Bookshop (W1) 157
Balham Food and Book Co-op (SW12)
    220–1
Barbican Bookshop (EC1) 76
Barbican Business Book Centre (EC2)
    82
Barker and Howard Limited (E1) 91–2
Barker's of Kensington (W8) 157–8
Basilisk Press and Bookshop (NW3)
    143
Battersea Arts Centre Bookshop
    (SW11) 221–2
BEC Business Books (SW17) 244
Belgravia Books (SW1) 222
Bell, Book & Radmall Ltd (WC2) 47
Bellman Bookshop (NW5) 142–3
Belsize Bookshop (NW3) 125–6
Berger & Tims (SW1) 222
Bernard Quaritch Ltd (W1) 211–12
Bernard Shapero (W1) 204
Bernard Shaw Bookshop (WC1) 17–18
Bernard Stone/Turret Book Shop
    (WC2) 53
Bertram Rota Ltd (WC2) 72
The Bible Society Bookshop (EC4) 87

Bibliopola (NW8) 156
The Bloomsbury Bookplace (WC1)
    65–6
Bolingbroke Bookshop (SW11) 223
Bonaventure (N6) 122
Bondy Books (WC1) 73
Book Bargains (for the Spastics
    Association) (NW1) 147–8
The Bookboat (SE10) 285–6
The Bookcase (EC4) 76–7
The Book Gallery (W1) 206–7
Book Inn (WC2) 1
Bookmarks (N4) 104–5
The Bookplace (SE15) 275
Books and Things (W11) 175
Books Etc (WC2) 1
Books Etc (EC4) 77
Books Etc (SW3) 223
Books Etc (SW1) 224
Books for Cooks (W11) 180
Books from India (UK) Ltd/Hindi
    Book Centre (WC1) 34–5
Books of Asia (SW6) 257
Books of Blackheath (SE3) 276
The Bookshop (SE3) 297
Bookshop Crystal Palace (SE19) 293–4
The Booksmith (Charing Cross Road,
    WC2) 2
The Booksmith (Maiden Lane, WC2) 2
The Booksmith (EC3) 77–8
The Booksmith (W8) 158
Books Plus (SE14) 287
Bookspread (SW17) 244–5
Boosey and Hawkes Music (W1) 192
Brian Bailey (W11) 212
Brian Jordan Music Books (W5) 192
The British Esperanto Association Inc.
    (W11) 182–3
British Institute of Management (WC2)
    21
British Tourist Authority (SW1) 265–6
Broadway Books (SW6) 224
Brown & Perring Ltd (EC3) 86
Buckinghams (W1) 158–9
Building Bookshop Ltd (WC1) 20–21
Bush Books (W12) 159
The Business Bookshop (NW1) 135
Butterworth's Legal Bookshop (WC2)
    37–8

C. & L. Booksellers (NW4) 126

Caissa Books (W1) 213
Camden Passage Antique Market (N1) 123
Canonbury Bookshop (N1) 105–6
The Catholic Marriage Advisory Council Bookroom (W11) 183
Catholic Truth Society (SW1) 260
Cavendish Rare Books Ltd (SW1) 271
Central Books (WC1) 28
Centerprise (E2) 92–3
Chain Libraries Ltd (EC2) 78
Chancery Lane Bookshop (WC2) 66
Changes Bookshop (NW6) 141–2
Chapman's Professional Bookshop (WC2) 22
Chappell (W1) 193
Charles Sawyer (W1) 213
Charlotte Robinson Bookshop (W1) 191
Chelsea Rare Books (SW3) 271–2
Chener Books (SE22) 276–7
Children's Bookshop (N10) 112
Children's Bookshop (SW19) 245
The Chimes Music Shop (W1) 193
The Chomley Bookshop *see* W.E. Hersant Ltd
The Christian Bookshop (SE22) 290
Christian Literature Crusade (EC4) 88
Christopher Foss (W1) 159–60
Christopher Mendez (W1) 214
Church House Bookshop (SW1) 260–1
Church Literature Association (SW1) 261
The Cinema Bookshop (WC1) 26–7
City Booksellers Ltd (EC2) 78
City Booksellers Ltd (EC3) 79
City Lit Bookshop (WC2) 64–5
The Clarke-Hall Bookshop (EC4) 89–90
Claude Gill Books (WC2) 2–3
Claude Gill Books (James Street W1) 160
Claude Gill Books (Oxford Street W1) 160–1
Claude Gill Books (Piccadilly W1) 161
CND Bookshop (N4) 118
Cobb and Webb Booksellers (SW15) 268–9
Collet's Chinese Gallery and Bookshop (WC1) 25–6
Collet's International Bookshop (WC2) 28–9

Collet's London Bookshop (WC2) 54–5
Collet's Penguin Bookshop (WC2) 56
Collet's Record Shop (WC2) 47–8
Compendium (NW1) 126–7
Connoisseur Carbooks (W4) 176
The Constant Reader (SW6) 269
The Corner Bookshop (NW1) 148
The Corner House Bookshop (WC2) 55
The Craftsmen Pottery Shop (W1) 199
J.B. Cramer & Co. Ltd (WC2) 48
Creative Camera (WC1) 52
Crouch End Bookshop (N8) 106

Dance Books Ltd (WC2) 27
Daybreak Books (SE12) 290–1
Demetzy Books (W11) 214
Dennys Booksellers Ltd (EC1) 79–80
Deptford Booktraders (SE8) 277
The Design Centre (SW1) 246
Dillons at Queen Mary College (E1) 102
Dillons Bookshop (WC1) 3–4
Divertissement (EC1) 87
Don Kelly (SW3) 240

Ealing Books (W5) 161–2
East Asia Company (NW1) 136–7
Economists Bookshop (WC2) 22
Economists' Second-hand (WC2) 23
Edna Whiteson (N11) 117
Edward Stanford Ltd (WC2) 60
Elgin Books (W11) 162
English Continental Book Market Ltd (NW4) 127–8
Eric & Joan Stevens Booksellers (NW6) 148–9
Essex Hall Bookshop (WC2) 4–5
European Bookshop (WC1) 36

Faculty Books (N3) 107
Fagin's Bookshop (N14) 107–8
Fagin's Hoard of Books (SE10) 278
Family Planning Association Book Centre (W1) 183–4
Fanfare Bookcentre (E17) 93
Fantasy Centre (N1) 121
Ferret Fantasy (W1) 210
Fielders (SW19) 225
Fine Books Oriental Limited (WC1) 50–1
Fisher & Sperr (N6) 123–4
The Flask Bookshop (NW3) 149–50
H.M. Fletcher (WC2) 73

The Folk Shop (NW1) 137
Forbidden Planet (WC2) 59
W.A. Foster (W4) 207
Foyles (WC1) 5–6
Foyles Educational Bookshop (W1) 181
Francis Edwards (WC2) 69
Francis Marsden Books for Printers
  (SE1) 289
Freedom Bookshop (E1) 100
French's Theatre Bookshop (WC2) 203
Friends Book Centre (NW1) 144
Frognal Rare Books (WC2) 38

Gabriel Byrne (W11) 204
Gabriels Bookshop (NW10) 150
Gaby Goldscheider and Helga
  Wellingham (W11) 208
The Gallery Bookshop (SE21) 278–9
Gallery Book Store (E5) 94
Game Advice (NW5) 135–6
Gay's the Word (WC1) 40
Genesis Books (EC1) 83–4
Geographia (EC4) 89
Geological Museum Bookshop (SW7)
  251
George Greer Books (NW1) 150–1
The German Book Centre Ltd (W1) 185
Girl Guides Association Shop (SW1)
  251–2
M. and R. Glendale (W1) 180
The Gloucester Road Bookshop (SW7)
  225–6
The Golden Cockerel Bookshop (WC2)
  12–13
Goldsmith's College Book & Stationery
  Shop (SE14) 292–3
Golfiana Miscellanea Ltd (WC2) 30
R. Golub & Son Ltd (E1) 98–99
Graham Weiner (W1) 210
The Gramophone Exchange (WC2)
  48–9
Grant & Cutler Ltd (WC2) 136–7
Grassroots Storefront (W10) 177–8
Green Knight Bookshop (WC2) 74
The Greenwich Book-Place &
  Paperback Centre (SE10) 294–5
The Greenwich Bookshop (SE10) 279
Greenwich Market (SE10) 295
Grey House Books (SW3) 246–7
Grower Books (WC1) 33
Guanghua (WC2) 26

HMSO Bookshop (WC2) 64
Hachette Bookshop (W1) 184
Hambling (Models) Ltd (WC2) 57–8
Hammicks (WC2) 6
Hammicks Bookshop Ltd (W6) 163
Hammick Sweet & Maxwell (WC2)
  38–9
Hampstead Book Corner (NW8) 136
Harold Storey (WC2) 74
Harriet Truscott Books (W1) 196
Harrington Bros (SW3) 253
Harris Publications Ltd (WC2) 51
Harrods Book Department (SW3) 226
Harvid Bookstore (EC4) 80
Harvid Bookstore (EC3) 80
Harvid Bookstore (SW3) 227
Hatchards (W1) 163–4
Hayward Gallery Bookshop (SE1) 284
Hebrew Book & Gift Centre (N16) 116
The Hellenic Book Service (WC2) 30–1
Henry Sotheran Ltd (W1) 214–15
Heraldry Today (SW3) 252
Her Majesty's Stationery Office
  Bookshop *see* HMSO
W.E. Hersant Ltd (The Chomley
  Bookshop) (N6) 110–11
G. Heywood Hill Ltd (W1) 164
Highgate Bookshop (N6) 108
High Hill Bookshops Ltd (NW3) 128
The Hill Bookshop (SW19) 227
Hillyers (SE26) 296
The History Bookshop (N11) 114–15
Holborn Books (WC2) 66–67
Hollywood Road Bookshop (SW10)
  248–9
Hosains Books (W2) 189–90
Housing Centre Trust Bookshop
  (WC2) 34
Housmans Bookshop (N1) 118–19

ICA Bookshop (SW1) 240–1
Il Libro (SW3) 255
Images *see* Peter Stockham at Images
Imperial College Bookshop (SW7)
  266–7
Intermediate Technology Bookshop
  (WC2) 61–2
Islamic Book Centre (NW1) 138

James Smith (WC1) 67
Jane Gibberd (SE1) 296

Japanese Publications Centre (W1) 186
Jenner Medical History Bookshop
  (WC1) 42
Jennings Bookshop (SW16) 269–70
Jerusalem The Golden (NW11) 140
Jewish Chronicle Bookshop (EC4) 84
Jewish Memorial Council Bookshop
  (WC1) 35
Joanna Booth (SW3) 249–50
John Faustus (SW1) 272
John Sandoe Books (SW3) 228
Jonathan Potter Ltd (W8) 178–9
Jones & Evans Bookshop Ltd (EC4) 82
E. Joseph (W1) 215–16

H. Karnac (Books) Ltd (SW7) 228–9
Keltic (W8) 187
Kelvin Hughes Charts and Maritime
  Supplies (E1) 99
The Kensington Bookshop Ltd (W8)
  164–5
Kensington Music Shop (SW7) 255
Ken Trotman (NW3) 142
The Kilburn Bookshop (NW6) 129
Kimon Bookshop (NW1) 138
Kimpton's Medical Bookshop (W1)
  188–9
Kings Bookshop (WC1) 7
Kirkdale Bookshop (SE26) 279–80
Knightsbridge Books (WC1) 45

LCL Benedict Ltd (NW1) 141
Labour Party Bookshop (SE17) 289
Lamley & Co. (SW7) 229–30
Law Notes Lending Library (WC2) 39
Leather Lane Book Centre (EC1) 90
Levrant Rare Books (W11) 216
H.K. Lewis & Co Ltd (WC1) 42–3
Liberty & Co. (W1) 165
Linguaphone (W1) 187
Lionel Halter (NW7) 151
The Literary Guild Bookshop (W1) 200
London Art Bookshop Ltd (W8) 173
London Tourist Board Bookshop
  (SW1) 266
London Yacht Centre Ltd (E1) 100
Luzac & Co Ltd (WC1) 46
McCarta Ltd (WC1) 41
Maggs Bros Ltd (W1) 217
Mandarin Books (W11) 166
Marcet Books (SE10) 280–1

The Marchmont Bookshop (WC1) 67–8
Marlborough Rare Books Ltd (W1) 217
Mayfair Coin Co. (W1) 197
Mellor & Baxter (W1) 218
MENCAP Bookshop (EC1) 85
Menorah Print & Gift Centre/ Hebrew
  Booksellers (NW11) 140
Mercury Bookshop (SE18) 293
Methodist Church Overseas Division
  Bookshop (NW1) 144–5
Michael Phelps (SW15) 254
A.A. Miles (NW1) 151–2
Model Railway (Manufacturing) Co.
  Ltd (N1) 120–1
The Modern Book Co. (W2) 182
The Mothers' Union Book Shop (SW1)
  245
The Motion Picture Bookshop (SE1)
  286
Motor Books (WC2) 58
A.R. Mowbray & Co. Ltd (W1) 201
The Museum Bookshop (WC1) 14
The Museum of London Bookshop
  (EC2) 85
Music Book Centre (W1) 194
Music Boutique (W1) 194
The Muslim Bookshop (N4) 115–16
Mustard Seed (NW1) 145
The Mustard Tree (SE23) 291–2
Muswell Hill Bookshop (N10) 108–9

National Poetry Centre Bookshop
  (SW5) 258
National Portrait Gallery Bookshop
  (WC2) 18
National Theatre Bookshop (SE1) 292
New Beacon Bookshop (N4) 111
New Era Books (N4) 119–20
Newham Parents' Centre (E13) 98
Nigel Greenwood Inc. (SW1) 241
Notting Hill Books (W8) 208

OCS Bookshop (NW1) 139
Offstage Theatre Shop and Gallery
  (NW1) 146
121 Bookshop (SE24) 288
Operation Headstart Books and Crafts
  (N15) 112
Oppenheim & Co. Ltd (SW7) 230
Orbis Books (London) Ltd (SW5) 247
The Other Bookshop (N1) 120

Owl Bookshop (NW5) 129–30

The Pan Bookshop (SW10) 231
Paperbacks Centre (E17) 94–95
Paperbacks Centre (W1) 166–7
Paperbacks Centre (SW9) 231
Paperbooks (SW7) 250
Paperchase (WC1) 18–19
Parks Bookshop (WC1) 23–4
The Passage Bookshop (SE5) 281
Paul H. Crompton Ltd (SW6) 253
Paul Minet's Bookshop (E1) 103
Penguin Bookshop (WC2) 56–7
Penguin Bookshop (SW3) 232
Peter Eaton (Booksellers) Ltd (W11) 218–19
Peters Music Shop (W1) 195
Peter Stockham at Images (WC2) 24
Phantasmagoria (SE22) 291
Phase One Books (NW3) 152
The Photographer's Gallery (WC2) 52–3
Pickering & Chatto (SW1) 272–3
Planning Bookshop (SW1) 267
Pleasures of Past Times (WC2) 24–5
The Poland Street Book Centre (W1) 198–9
Polonez (W12) 198
Henry Pordes (WC2) 68
J.D. Potter (EC3) 86–7
Primrose Hill Books (NW1) 130
Protestant Truth Society (EC4) 88–9
Provincial Booksellers Fairs Association (WC1) 68
Pruskin (SW3) 242
Psychic News Bookshop (WC2) 55–6
Publications India (W1) 186
Pulteney & Co. (SW7) 232
The Puppet Centre (SW11) 259

Quartet Bookshop (W1) 167
Quevedo (WC2) 74

RSC Bookshop (WC2) 62
Reader's Digest (W1) 200
Reads (WC2) 69
Regent Bookshop (NW1) 130–1
Remington (WC2) 63
Response Community Bookshop (SW5) 233
Richard Lally Ltd (SW15) 270

Richard Law Booksellers (NW2) 152
Richard Worth Booksellers (SW15) 234
Riverside Studios Bookshop (W6) 168
Robert Chris Booksellers (WC2) 32
Rogers Turner Books Ltd (SE10) 298
Rowland Ward's of Knightsbridge (SW1) 256
Royal Academy of Arts (W1) 176
Royal Institute of British Architects Bookshop (W1) 174
Roy Hayes (Booksellers) Ltd (SE9) 281–2
Rudolph Steiner Bookshop (WC1) 58–9
Rudolph Steiner Bookshop (NW1) 146–7
Russian Orthodox Cathedral Bookshop (SW7) 262

SCM Bookroom (N1) 121
SPCK Church Bookshop (NW1) 145–6
Sabarr Books (SW9) 234–5
St George's Gallery Books Ltd (SW1) 242
St Martin's Lane Bookshop (WC2) 7
Sanford Books (SW3) 273
Schola Books (SW7) 250–1
Schott & Co. Ltd (W1) 195
Scripture Union Bookshop (W1) 202
B.A. Seaby Ltd (W1) 197
Seal Books (W5) 209
Selfridges (W1) 168–9
(Ian) Shipley (Books) Ltd (WC2) 19
Silver Moon (WC2) 29
L. Simmonds (EC4) 81
Sims, Reed and Fogg (SW1) 274
Sisterwrite (N1) 114
Skoob Books Ltd (WC1) 69–70
Sky Books (W6) 209
W. H. Smith (General note) 7–8
W.H. Smith (WC2) 8
W.H. Smith (EC1) 81
W.H. Smith (London Wall, EC2) 81
W.H. Smith (Cheapside, EC2) 81
W.H. Smith (N8) 109
W.H. Smith (N12) 109
W.H. Smith (N13) 109
W.H. Smith (N22) 109
W.H. Smith (NW2) 131
W.H. Smith (NW3) 131
W.H. Smith (Hendon Way, NW4) 131
W.H. Smith (Brent Cross, NW4) 131

W.H. Smith (NW6) 132
W.H. Smith (NW7) 132
W.H. Smith (NW11) 132
W.H. Smith (W4) 169
W.H. Smith (W5) 169
W.H. Smith (W6) 169
W.H. Smith (W8) 169
W.H. Smith (W11) 169
W.H. Smith (W13) 170
W.H. Smith (SW1) 235
W.H. Smith (SW5) 235
W.H. Smith (SW15) 235
W.H. Smith (SW16) 236
W.H. Smith (SE1) 282
W.H. Smith (SE6) 282
W.H. Smith (SE9) 282
W.H. Smith (SE13) 282
W.H. Smith (SE18) 282
Solosy (WC2) 47
Soma Books (SE11) 284–5
South Bank Bookshop (SE1) 283
Souvenir Press Ltd (WC1) 8
Spink and Sons (SW1) 256
The Spiritualist Association of Great
    Britian (SW1) 258
The Spread Eagle (SE10) 283–4
Stanley Crowe (WC1) 75
Stanley Gibbons (WC2) 51–2
Stanley Smith and Keith Fawkes
    (NW3) 153
Stone Trough Books (SE5) 287–8
Strathmore Book Shop (NW8) 132
Sun Power (N4) 113
Swan's Bookstall (SE8 & SW17) 296–7
Swiss Cottage Books Ltd (NW3) 133

Take Five (SW19) 270
Tate Gallery Shop (SW1) 242–3
Templar Books (Chancery Lane, WC2)
    9
Templar Books (Chancery Lane, WC2)
    70
Templar Books (High Holborn, WC2)
    9
Tetric Bookshop (SW4) 236
Tetric Bookshop (SW6) 236–7
Tetric Bookshop (SW17) 237
THAP Community Bookshop (E1)
    96–7
The Theosophical Bookshop &
    Publishing House (WC1) 50

Timothy Shaw (W9) 219
Tower Hamlets Arts Project
    Community Bookshop *see* THAP
    Community Bookshop
Tradition (W1) 190
The Travel Bookshop Ltd (W8) 205
Travis & Emery (WC2) 49
Triangle Bookshop (WC1) 14–15
Truslove and Hanson (SW3) 238
Turf Newspapers Ltd (W1) 202–3
Tutor Tape Co. Ltd (WC1) 37

Ujamaa Centre (SW9) 247–8
Under Two Flags (W1) 190–1
United Society for the Propagation of
    the Gospel (SW1) 262

Vandaleur Antiquarian Books (SW14)
    265
Vanessa Williams-Ellis (W9) 170
Vermillion Books (WC1) 10
Victoria and Albert Museum Shop
    (SW7) 243
Village Books (SW16) 238–9
The Village Bookshop (NW3) 153–4

Wade Galleries (N1) 113
Walden Books (NW1) 154
G. W. Walford (N1) 125
The Wall Bookshop (SW1) 263
Walm Lane Bookmart (NW10) 154–5
Walter Rodney Bookshop (W13) 178
Waterstone and Davies (WC1) 10–11
Waterstone's (WC2) 11–12
Waterstone's (W1) 171
Waterstone's (W8) 171–2
Waterstone's (SW7) 239
Watkins Books Ltd (WC2) 32–3
West End Books (WC1) 43–4
Westminster Cathedral Bookshop
    (SW1) 263
Whetstone Books (N20) 124
Whitcoulls Ltd New Zealand (W1) 196
Wholefood of Baker Street (W1) 185
The Whole Thing (E15) 97
Wildy & Sons Ltd (WC2) 39–40
Willen Limited (E11) 101
Wimbledon Evangelical Book Centre
    (SW19) 264
Witherby & Co. Ltd (EC4 & SE1) 83
The Woburn Bookshop (WC1) 75

Words Etcetera (SW10) 254–5
World of Books (W1) 210
Writers and Readers Bookshop (NW1)
133–4
Writer's Cramp (NW3) 134
Wyvern Bookshop (W4) 210–11

YHA Bookshop (WC2) 61

Young World (Children's Book Centre
Ltd) (W8) 179

Zeno (WC2) 31
A. Zwemmer (WC2) 19–20
Zwemmer's Oxford University Press
Bookshop (WC2) 57